Analysing Socia

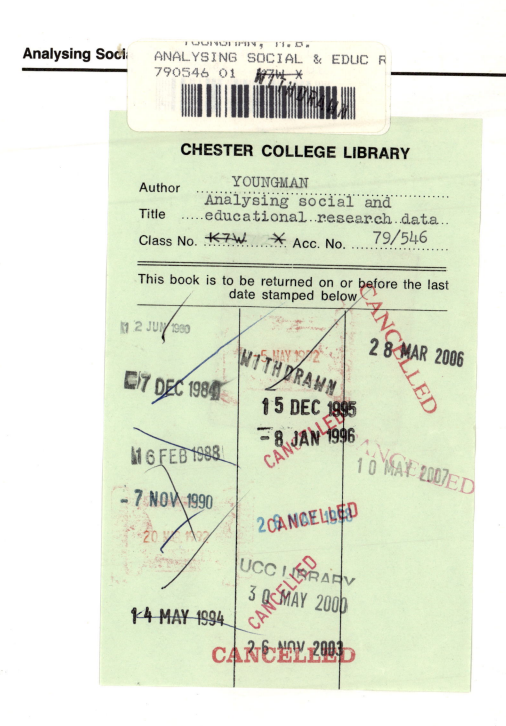

Analysing Social and Educational Research Data

Michael B. Youngman
School of Education
University of Nottingham

McGraw-Hill Book Company (UK) Limited

London · New York · St Louis · San Francisco · Auckland
Bogotá · Guatemala · Hamburg · Johannesburg · Lisbon
Madrid · Mexico · Montreal · New Delhi · Panama · Paris
San Juan · São Paulo · Singapore · Sydney · Tokyo · Toronto

Published by

McGraw-Hill Book Company (UK) Limited

Maidenhead · Berkshire · England

British Library Cataloguing in Publication Data

Youngman, Michael Brendon
Analysing social & educational research data.
1. Social sciences—Statistical methods
I. Title
300′.7′2   HA29   78-41065

ISBN 0-07-084089-X

1 2 3 4 5 WC & S 81079

PRINTED AND BOUND IN GREAT BRITAIN

Contents

Preface   ix

Part 1   PREPARATION   1

CHAPTER 1   Preliminary Considerations   3
        1.1   An outline of a research programme   3
        1.2   The relationship between hypotheses, data, and analysis   4
        1.3   Characterizations of data   7
        1.4   Analytical strategies   9
        1.5   Practical considerations   13
        1.6   A guide to statistical texts   14

CHAPTER 2   Preparation of Data   16
        2.1   Data recording and coding   16
        2.2   Treatment of missing data   21
        2.3   Modifications to data   21
        2.4   Preparing data for the computer   22
        2.5   Data checking   23

CHAPTER 3   Computer Usage   26
        3.1   Programs and packages available   26
        3.2   General procedures   27
        3.3   Data format specification in FORTRAN   29
        3.4   Analysis specifications   33
        3.5   Special considerations in computer usage   39
        3.6   A guide to program availability   41

CHAPTER 4   The Demonstration Dataset   43
        4.1   The research problem   43
        4.2   Sample   43
        4.3   Data   44

Part 2   ANALYTICAL PROCEDURES   51

CHAPTER 5   Initial Descriptions of the Data   53
        5.1   Frequency tables and charts   53
        5.2   Measures of tendency   57
        5.3   Measures of spread and shape   58

CHAPTER 6   Relationships Between Pairs of Measures   62
   6.1   Scatter plots   62
   6.2   Cross-tabulations   65
   6.3   Measures of association   69

CHAPTER 7   The Analysis of Groups   78
   7.1   The definition of subgroups   78
   7.2   Confirming variation between subgroups   80
   7.3   Locating differences between groups   83
   7.4   Multiple classifications   90
   7.5   Further considerations in subgroup analysis   93

CHAPTER 8   Relationships Between More Than Two Measures   95
   8.1   Using multivariate methods   95
   8.2   The application of factor analysis   97
   8.3   Multiple regression analysis and its uses   111
   8.4   Other multivariate relationships   121

CHAPTER 9   Classification and Discrimination Within Data   125
   9.1   Applying cluster analysis: a comparative demonstration 125
   9.2   Multiple discrimination between groups   139
   9.3   The allocation of individuals to groups   146
   9.4   Further developments in multiple discrimination   147

Part 3   SPECIALIZED TECHNIQUES   151

CHAPTER 10   The Analysis of Questionnaires   153
   10.1   The importance of planning   153
   10.2   Questionnaire coding   153
   10.3   Tabulating the raw data   154
   10.4   Recoding variables prior to main analysis   156
   10.5   Obtaining cross-tabulations and statistics   156
   10.6   Forming scales from sets of related questions   157
   10.7   Recoding into binary form for multivariate analysis   161
   10.8   Cluster analysis of attribute data   165
   10.9   Further analysis of questionnaires   168

CHAPTER 11 The Construction of Scales and Tests   175
   11.1   Item analysis   176
   11.2   Assessing the reliability and validity of tests   179
   11.3   Alternative approaches to test construction   183
   11.4   Sources of tests and scales   186

CHAPTER 12 The Measurement of Change   189
   12.1   The nature of change   189
   12.2   Difference and residualized change scores   190
   12.3   Covariates in determining change   193
   12.4   The interpretation of change measures   195

APPENDICES   199

APPENDIX 1 PMMD: Programmed Methods for Multivariate Data   201
      A1.1 Outline   201
      A1.2 Documentation   201
      A1.3 Structure   201
      A1.4 Program facilities   203
      A1.5 Program statistics   208
      A1.6 Availability   208

APPENDIX 2 The Demonstration Data File   210

APPENDIX 3 Two Classification Techniques   221

INDEX   231

Preface

Social research provides a stimulating yet tantalizing ordeal for many students. Its problems and possible explanations offer the challenge expected of a chosen field of study. But eventually there comes the need to tackle the analytical procedures used in developing a theoretical structure. Although the research methods seldom present any lasting difficulty the same cannot be said of the statistical techniques employed. Nevertheless they cannot be ignored. The validity of research findings is heavily dependent on the statistics used to produce them.

This book does more than just accept the role of statistics in social research. It is written on the necessary assumption that analytical approaches go a long way towards determining the eventual conclusions. Such a strong bias towards the application of statistics requires a different approach from that usually followed in statistics texts. Instead of presenting detailed derivations of computational formulae, it is accepted that the bulk of modern statistical analysis is carried out on the computer. It therefore becomes more important to discuss the choice of methods, their assumptions and their interpretation. To that end a specific research problem is studied in depth. The author's own statistical package, PMMD, is used to demonstrate the various techniques but this does not imply a restricted appeal. The methods are standard and are available on many widely distributed statistical packages.

The first part of the book deals with the preliminary stages in research analysis, specifically the overall strategy, the preparation of data, and the basics of computer usage. Following that, the main central section covers most of the univariate and multivariate statistical methods used in social sciences. These include the relatively novel techniques of cluster analysis and discriminant function analysis as well as better known procedures such as subgroup analysis, factor analysis, and multiple regression. The final section of the book is more specialized. It considers three topics, the analysis of questionnaires, scale construction, and the measurement of change. Throughout the book the treatment is essentially descriptive. Occasionally formulae are supplied either for explanation or to enable certain simple operations to be performed. Generally, however, it is assumed that the reader will have access to a traditional statistics text for computational details. There is no shortage of suitable texts of this kind. Appropriate computing documentation may also be needed.

Without doubt this text is more a manual than a reader. By studying the discussions and examples anyone with a grounding in statistics should be able to achieve sufficient understanding of the methods to try them himself. The demonstration dataset is listed for just this purpose, although the reader may prefer to use his own data. Either way this practice stage is essential to a proper appreciation of the methods. No one would expect to learn to drive a car by reading books on motoring. This book, then, is suitable as a guide for the individual research student, for use as a teaching text at postgraduate level, or as a reference text on particular topics.

Rooted as it is in the practical problems of data analysis, this book owes everything to the many friends, colleagues, teachers, and students who have influenced me over the years. It would be unfair to single out individuals and impossible to list everyone. However, I can and should identify two major determinants of my standpoint on social research analysis. The first is Professor Donald J. Veldman whose book *FORTRAN Programming for the Behavioral Sciences* was in 1967, and still is ten years later, the basic text in this area. My other stimulus came from Professor John Heywood, of Trinity College, Dublin. It was he who first provided the opportunity and the encouragement to come to grips with the joint problems of research, statistics, and computing. I can only hope that by passing on the experience gained from all of these sources my gratitude is fully expressed.

Part 1
Preparation

1. Preliminary Considerations

There is a striking similarity between the roles of the data analyst and the family doctor. More often than not, researchers consult a data analyst because of some numerical illness. The symptoms are presented, usually in the form of tables or lists of figures, and the analyst is expected to produce a diagnosis, and then to offer a suitable cure. This cure is required to be quick, easy, and unequivocal, and to demand the minimum of effort from the patient. Although extreme, this picture is not uncommon. But it is unreasonable. Most people would accept that anyone's physical health is at least as much his own responsibility as his doctor's. The same obligation applies to the social researcher. Even though statistical analysis might be hard work, it cannot be ignored.

1.1 An outline of a research programme

The first rule for simplifying research analysis is to plan ahead, paying as much attention to the statistical strategies as to the research itself. Figure 1.1 summarizes the various steps within a research project. The progression from formulating the problem to writing up the results is essentially chronological, but the double-pronged nature of the plan is often ignored. Analysis is not an afterthought, chosen to make the most of acquired results. It is an integral feature of a research design. The working hypotheses determine the range of analytical methods suitable to test them. The finer details of sample, measurements, and procedures reduce the choice even further. Indeed there is an interactive effect since statistical methods may themselves influence certain aspects of research design. For example, the decision to use factor analysis to identify patterns within a range of measures forces the need for larger samples than a comparison of two or three measures would entail.

Another common misjudgement concerns the time needed to achieve a particular analysis. The use of computers does generally enable a calculation to be done more quickly. But that assumes that all the groundwork involved in acquiring suitable programs and learning how to use them has already been done. Rather than leave everything until the last minute, these administrative details should be tackled early in any research project. So the initial planning can be summarized as the need to consider the precise relationship between the hypotheses, the data, and the analyses, and then to produce a realistic strategy to represent this relationship. Once this is done it is surprising how often many of the subsequent problems disappear through being automatic components of the overall design.

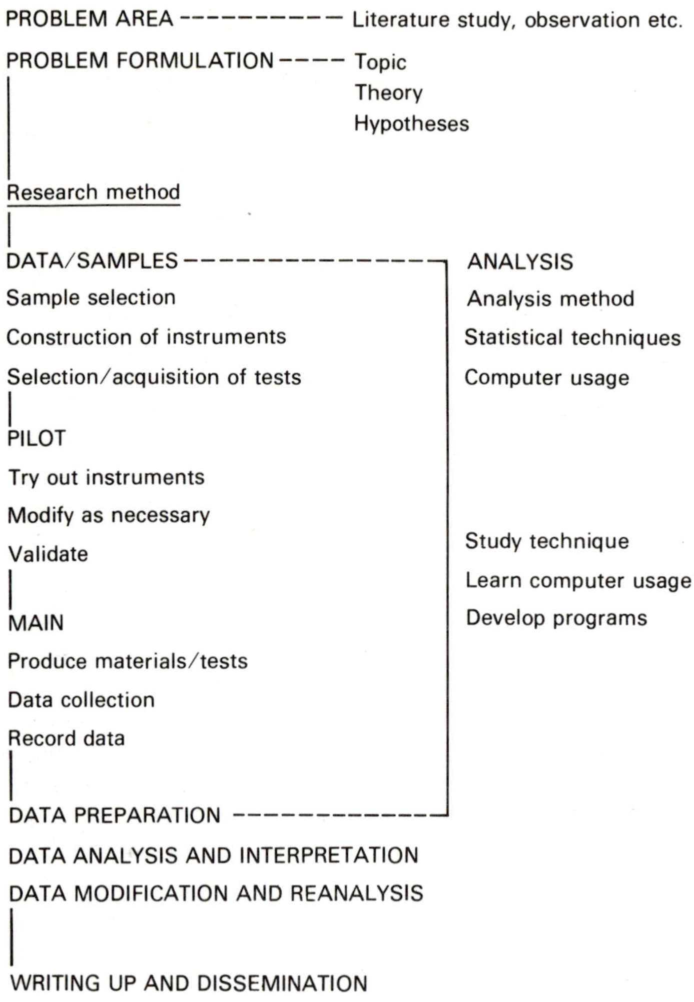

PROBLEM AREA ————————— Literature study, observation etc.

PROBLEM FORMULATION ———— Topic
                                                   Theory
                                                   Hypotheses

Research method

DATA/SAMPLES —————————————┐   ANALYSIS

Sample selection   Analysis method

Construction of instruments   Statistical techniques

Selection/acquisition of tests   Computer usage

PILOT

Try out instruments

Modify as necessary

Validate   Study technique

                                                               Learn computer usage

MAIN   Develop programs

Produce materials/tests

Data collection

Record data

DATA PREPARATION —————————————┘

DATA ANALYSIS AND INTERPRETATION

DATA MODIFICATION AND REANALYSIS

WRITING UP AND DISSEMINATION

Fig. 1.1 *A research outline.*

1.2   The relationship between hypotheses, data, and analysis

The salient feature of the outline given in Fig. 1.1 is the interrelatedness of the three main components of a research design. A first attempt at defining a working hypothesis will tend to be rather loose, more an observation than a theoretical construct. In specifying the samples and measures appropriate to test the hypothesis it usually becomes clear that extra precision is needed. This in turn draws attention to the analytical techniques required, and so the relationship is completed.

As an example consider the problem of transferring from primary to secondary school. Anyone teaching secondary school entrants might feel that the move causes distress in children. In this form the hypothesis is too vague to be testable. What is meant by distress? How do we know that the transfer has caused it? To answer these two questions requires some measure of distress, or its converse adjustment, and a means of isolating the effect of moving schools. The latter is not easy to achieve since in Britain most children are subject to this transition. In seeking a solution to this dilemma one is naturally directed towards the problem of analysis. One possibility might be to measure levels of adjustment at various times on either side of the transfer, and to examine these results for any indication of deterioration. But again, even a marked drop could arise from the measure of adjustment being inappropriate to older children. Once more the analytical considerations hold further implications for the data, and consequently for the hypotheses. In this instance it is clear that a comparable sample not suffering transfer is needed to test whether the transition or some other feature affects adjustment. And this in turn necessitates a slight change in the hypothesis; it now suggests that children experiencing transfer will show inferior adjustment on entering secondary school than comparable children not experiencing transfer. To test this further data are needed, and the subsequent analysis must incorporate a comparison of the two samples. The whole process is one of continual refinement, all three components being considered in turn. Eventually, a satisfactory design is reached and the details can be finalized.

The bulk of this book deals with the various details that need to be considered in evaluating the research design. Although many of these points can be treated individually, it is necessary to bear in mind the overall research implications. Missing data, for example, may appear to be no more than a clerical inconvenience, but with certain research topics they could constitute an important phenomenon in themselves. In educational research, particularly, missing data usually imply absence from school, truantism in its extreme form. If the research is examining adjustment to school then to ignore these cases is to exclude one clear instance of poor adjustment. There are no simple rules to guarantee relevance throughout research analysis, and this makes it all the more important for the researcher to be forever aware.

One further principle is even more fundamental, but fortunately more clearly defined. It concerns *the concept of statistical significance*. The natural variability within social research data forces the researcher to summarize results using a variety of statistics. The hypotheses are tested by comparing obtained statistics with each other, or against some external value. The principle of statistical significance enables the researcher to assess these findings within the context of his research. Whether or not social significance or importance can also be assumed is a completely separate matter. In statistical terms, significance is simply the degree to which a value could not have occurred by chance. This is usually expressed in the form of a probability or a percentage. So the .01 or 1 per cent level of significance indicates a probability of one chance in a hundred, a highly unlikely result. A significance level of .05 implies five chances in a hundred, one in twenty. Since this is a *less unlikely* result, it is therefore less significant statistically. It is vital that this slightly confusing relationship be understood. The numerical value .05 is larger than .01, but its statistical significance is lower. More likely by chance means less significant. As a simple demonstration consider the familiar distribution of intellectual ability scores, the normal or Gaussian distribution. For intelligence tests this typically has a mean, M, of 100 and a standard deviation of about 15 points. Yet from these two pieces of information it is possible to say a lot about the scores one would expect to find. For example, any normal distribution will include 45 per cent of its recorded scores within 1.645 standard deviations of the mean. Since the mean is at the 50 per cent point, it follows that 95 per cent of intelligence test scores are less than:

$$100 + 15 \times 1.645 = 124.7$$

Therefore only one in twenty of the population represented by Fig. 1.2 will record scores above this value. In statistical terms one could say that anyone in this category records significantly high intelligence at the 5 per cent level. Points B and C correspond to the $2\frac{1}{2}$ per cent and 1 per cent levels respectively. Any score *below* the specified value is deemed non-significant, no matter where it falls. Our 5 per cent level only defines *highness*. But what if we do want to call a score significant if it is very high or very low? Assuming that the definition of one chance in twenty is maintained, the 5 per cent level, then we need two cut-off points that encompass 95 per cent between them. Given that the normal distribution is symmetric about its mean, this effectively requires points with $2\frac{1}{2}$ per cent below and above them, that is Y and B. Any score falling *outside* that range can now be called significant. Although the qualification 'high' is not applied, we can instead identify any significantly *extreme* score no matter whether it is high or low. The cost is that the deviation from the mean, x, has to be larger before it becomes significant.

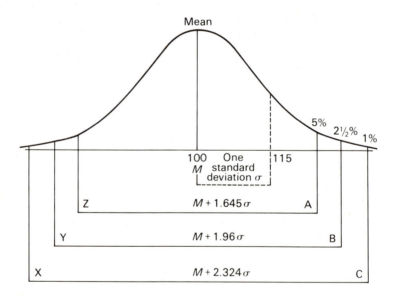

Fig. 1.2 *The distribution of intellectual ability scores. The points A, B, and C correspond to the upper 5%, $2\frac{1}{2}$%, and 1% cut-offs for the normal distribution. They would be used for one-tailed significance testing. However, if either extreme is to be considered a two-tailed test is needed. At the 5% level this would imply the range Y to B.*

Direction is particularly important when statistical tests are applied to hypotheses. If we are only required to show that some value is significantly high, then we can apply the test so that only the upper tail of the distribution is considered, hence the name *one-tailed test*. In doing so significance is reached for a value equivalent to A. But no matter how low a score is, it can only be interpreted as non-significant. More often research is interested in values which might be significantly high or significantly low. In that case a *two-tailed test* is needed, and in consequence a larger deviation, B or Y, is required for significance at the same level. Most statistical programs operate two-tailed tests and therefore all results can be interpreted. If the research specifically hypothesizes a direction, and anything else is to be ignored, then output significance values (probabilities) can be halved. The general principle of significance testing is little different from this example. Most statistics have known distributions and their significance can be evaluated in a comparable manner.

1.3 Characterizations of data

Initially data are simply research observations recorded in a variety of forms including ticks, timings, scores, question responses or ratings. Before any statistical analysis can be performed some modification is usually needed. The objective is to produce a system that enables comparisons to be made. The degree of refinement required will depend on the particular type of comparison envisaged. If the only information sought is the relative incidence of a range of occurrences, then all that is needed is a set of category labels. These could be letters, symbols, number codes or even names. As the complexity of the comparison increases, so does the precision of the coding system.

The most widely used characterization of data distinguishes four *levels of measurement* for data. These are *nominal, ordinal, interval,* and *ratio*.

NOMINAL DATA

Here observations are differentiated only by *type*. Nominal implies that each type is named, but clearly this could include a numbered system of identification as well as letters or labels. Obvious examples are eye colour, occupation, school, sex or political affiliation. The important feature of nominal data is that there is no implicit relationship between the different categories. Even if numbers are used, they are allocated arbitrarily and the traditional relationships between numbers (size, ordering or arithmetic accessibility, for example) do not apply.

ORDINAL DATA

At a slightly higher level of measurement one might accept an *ordered* relationship between data categories. For clarity these would normally be coded numerically but literal codes are used. Where objects are rated in order of importance or size, then the obtained data are ordinal. Attitude scales frequently employ gradations of agreement, coded in a variety of ways including:

STRONGLY AGREE	AGREE	NEUTRAL	DISAGREE	STRONGLY DISAGREE
SA	A	N	D	SD
1	2	3	4	5
5	4	3	2	1

Elsewhere different descriptions are used:

DEFINITELY YES	PROBABLY YES	POSSIBLY YES	POSSIBLY NO	PROBABLY NO	DEFINITELY NO

These methods are generally assumed to produce ordinal data although the acceptability of systems with an intermediate category such as NEUTRAL depends on the precise nature of this middle response. If the ordering relationship can be guaranteed there is no problem. However, if the middle category includes multiple responses such as NOT APPLICABLE, NO OPINION or worse, both AGREE and DISAGREE depending on context, then the ordered pattern is broken. Ideally these interfering responses should be catered for in a separate category which can be excluded from subsequent analysis if necessary.

INTERVAL DATA

The extra qualification for interval data is that the categories are equally spaced as well as being ordered. Referring to the examples given for ordinal data, it is clear that this additional condition is not automatically met. There is no obvious way of assessing the size of the intervals between STRONGLY AGREE and AGREE, or between PROBABLY and POSSIBLY. What is needed is some way of defining quantity in social characteristics since that determines the equivalence of gaps. With physical data there is less difficulty, a temperature rise of 4° at 30°C is considered equivalent to the same rise at 130°C. But this presupposes a definition of temperature in terms of calories. If, instead, we are interested in the ease of achieving such a rise then comparability is less certain. Increasing the temperature of water at 30°C by 4° is considerably easier than doing so at 130°C. It is this difficulty that exists in social research. The principle is beyond the scope of this introduction. On the pragmatic level, the usual assumption is that most scaled social data can be treated as interval unless the limitations already discussed obviously apply. However, many social statisticians would take the opposing stand, that data must be considered ordinal unless the interval condition can be proven. In practice the argument is not particularly productive or relevant since many other considerations must also be taken into account before any analysis can be accepted as valid.

RATIO DATA

The final level of measurement is rarely achieved in social research. It requires that rational equivalence should be satisfied as well as the conditions already demanded for interval data. This means that proportions hold at all points of a scale. A score of 6 should imply twice as much of the characteristic as a score of 3; to score 40 requires four times as much as to score 10. While attributes such as height, salary or age might be acceptable at this level, what about the similar measures of size, wealth or experience? Is someone measuring six feet tall only twice as big as a three-footer? Does a salary of £10 000 carry twice the wealth of one of £5000? The same dilemma exists with age and experience. The argument returns to the comparability problem already discussed in relation to interval data. In social terms what might appear to be ratio data need not operate at that level, and it is this operational effect that matters.

In reality the characterization of data by level of measurement may not be particularly useful. It can be important to differentiate between nominal and non-nominal data and this is not difficult to do. Similarly, the interval qualification is needed if concepts are to be added. There is no point in adding scale items to produce a total score if roughly comparable increments do not result. The techniques used to construct scales do implicitly achieve this objective.

An alternative classification of data which is both realistic and simple can be produced by developing the above discussion. Nominal or *categoric* data are easily identified, as are ordered data. The term *continuous* can be used to describe any data usually called interval or ratio. It can also include ordinal data where the variations between categories are not gross. Consequently, a simple classification into categoric or continuous results. There is also a useful hybrid category for dichotomous or *binary* data. Any measure with two response categories—YES/NO, MALE/FEMALE, RICH/POOR, ABSENCE/PRESENCE—fits this description. The virtue of including this possibility is that variables so defined can be treated as categoric or continuous to suit the statistical occasion, bearing in mind any limitations on binary data implicit in the statistical method used.

1.4 Analytical strategies

It is unduly optimistic to assume that there is a simple correspondence between research designs and statistical strategies. The discussion of the previous section should have convinced the reader that the hypotheses determine the statistical analysis needed as much as the design or data do. Fortunately, by considering various research designs together with expectations of them, it is possible to generate a reasonably efficient analytical framework. Table 1.1 classifies research objectives into seven areas:

    I.   Data description and modification.
    II.   Comparing two measures.
    III. Comparing three measures.
    IV. Comparing many measures.
    V.   Differentiating two groups only.
    VI. Differentiating many groups.
    VII. Generating groups.

These are not necessarily exclusive; they are intended to simplify the otherwise confusing problem of selecting a suitable statistical method. Consequently, what might seem artificial separations (particularly V and VI) do have important statistical implications. Where more than one statistical method is suggested for a particular

Table 1.1 A guide to statistical strategies
The left hand section of the table lists statistical methods suitable for the specified research objectives. The right hand section comprises the key to the abbreviations used. Most of the methods listed are described in the chapters indicated. Occasionally only a reference is offered.

Research objective		Statistical strategy		
I. DATA DESCRIPTION AND MODIFICATION		**CHAPTER 5**		other chapters
data listing and checking	abh	a	frequency charts	
data tendencies	cfgh	b	frequency tabulation	
data variations	degh	c	mean, median, mode	
pictorial representations of data	agh	d	standard deviation	
data recoding	PQR	e	skewness, kurtosis	
scale construction	FST	f	percentages	10, 6
scale refinement	STUVW	g	histograms	
scale scoring	S			
data reduction	FI	**CHAPTER 6**		
change measurement	pDHXYZ	h	scatter plots	
missing data treatments	cDL	i	cross-tabulation	10
		j	chi-square test	7
II. COMPARING TWO MEASURES		k	Fisher exact test	
visual comparison	h	l	Kendall's S-method	
compiling tables	i	m	contingency coefficient	
significance of table patterns	j	n	Kendall's tau	
significance of 2×2 tables	k	o	Spearman's rho	
significance of ordered tables	lno	p	McNemar test	
comparing tables	m	q	Cochran's Q	
comparing related dichotomies	p	r	product moment correlation	
comparing related measures	q	s	phi coefficient	
comparing dichotomies	rs			
comparing ordered measures	no	**CHAPTER 7**		
comparing continuous measures	r	t	t-test	
		u	Mann–Whitney U test	
III. COMPARING THREE MEASURES		v	one-way analysis of variance	
visual comparison	h	w	Tukey test	
compiling three-way tables	i	x	Scheffé test	
compare two / other fixed	C	y	subgroup extraction	
predict one from the others	D	z	linear trend test	
relate all three	E	A	multi-way analysis of variance	
		B	sign test	
IV. COMPARING MANY MEASURES				
identifying patterns	F	**CHAPTER 8**		
predict one from many	D	C	partial correlation	
determine causal patterns	G	D	multiple correlation	12
determine causes of change	DH	E	Kendall's W	
		F	factor analysis	10
V. DIFFERENTIATING TWO GROUPS ONLY		G	causal path analysis	
unrelated groups/nominal measure	j	H	analysis of covariance	12
unrelated groups/binary measure	jkm			
unrelated groups/ordered measure	u	**CHAPTER 9**		
unrelated groups/continuous measure	jtvwxD	I	discriminant function	
related groups/nominal measure	p	J	multivariate analysis of variance	
related groups/binary measure	p	K	Ward's clustering method	
related groups/ordered measure	B	L	relocation clustering method	
related groups/continuous measure	tDH	M	multidimensional scaling	
controlling certain measures	DH	N	percentage agreements	
differentiating on many measures	DI	O	kappa	

Table 1.1 (continued)

Research objective		Statistical strategy	
VI. DIFFERENTIATING MANY GROUPS		CHAPTER 10	other chapters
one way/one measure	Dvj	P combining response categories	
one way/many measures	IJ	Q partitioning measures	
many ways/one measure	AD	R binary coding	
many ways/many measures	J	S factor analysis of scales	
nominal groups/one measure	jq	T Guttman scalogram analysis	
ordered groups/one measure	lz		
differentiate one group from rest	wx	CHAPTER 11	
differentiate pairs of groups	jwx	U item analysis	10
control certain measures	H	V reliability estimation	10
		W validity estimation	
VII. GENERATING GROUPS			
extracting subgroups	y	CHAPTER 12	
classifying small samples	K	X difference scores	
classifying large samples	L	Y specific residuals	
identifying similarity patterns	M	Z extended residuals	
characterizing groups	vwxI		
allocating cases to groups	ILMD		
comparing classifications	NO		
identifying questionnaire patterns	RL		
refining classifications	L		
validating classifications	MNOV		

research need, it is likely that a more detailed specification of what is wanted will restrict the choice to one or two only. For example, in differentiating two unrelated groups on continuous measures six methods are suggested ranging from chi-square analysis to multiple correlation. In fact, some of the methods are equivalent for two groups, specifically one-way analysis of variance, the t-test, and Scheffé's method. Also the application of multiple correlation techniques to this problem would produce the same results. Its use would be largely expedient. To assist the final choice of method, more detailed consideration of the limitations and strengths of particular methods appears in the relevant chapters. Only the more general comments are in order here.

DATA DESCRIPTION AND MODIFICATION

The value of this preliminary stage should not be underestimated. Inspection of the data can facilitate and improve later analyses quite apart from supplying summaries of results. Similarly, there are many data modifications available designed to clarify relationships in otherwise intractable data structures. Questionnaires are the most impressive examples of data formats which benefit considerably from various types of recoding.

COMPARING TWO MEASURES

Undoubtedly the point to emphasize here is the power of visual presentations in identifying idiosyncrasies in relationships. Too often a summary statistic such as the correlation coefficient hides the distorting effect of individual responses or of group variations. A second important comment concerns the widely held misconception regarding the 'special' measures of relationship such as the phi-coefficient. It is seldom appreciated that their 'specialness' is only to do with computational ease. At heart most of them are the product-moment correlation coefficient, and consequently they can be obtained with no difficulty from standard correlation programs.

COMPARING THREE MEASURES

Apart from the use of three-way tables in the analysis of questionnaires this intermediate strategy is relatively unpopular in social research. More often the limitations of two-variable comparisons are overcome by multivariate approaches involving many measures. In general the three-variable case can be treated as a limited instance of many-variable research.

COMPARING MANY MEASURES

Once the number of measures to be analysed exceeds the homely half-dozen there is an almost instinctive reaction to attack the design with factor analysis. Naturally, such an indiscriminate approach records failures, not because of weaknesses in the method but through lack of thought on the part of the analyst. A little more care in ascertaining the precise objective of the analysis will usually indicate whether a predictive method is more appropriate, or even whether the pattern to be sought is not in the variables but in the cases (cluster analysis). Considering the frequency with which social research is concerned with change and prediction it is a little surprising that multiple regression has only recently become a popular method of analysis.

DIFFERENTIATING TWO GROUPS ONLY

It is essential to appreciate the need to separate two-group analyses from those involving more than two groups, particularly since the latter is by far the commonest situation. Chapters 7 and 8 discuss the principles in detail. At this point all that is required is a reminder to check that *only* two groups are to be analysed, or whether the analysis concerns *pairs* of groups from a larger set. Unless special considerations dictate otherwise, it is usually safest to treat two-group analyses as the simplest form of many-group analysis.

DIFFERENTIATING MANY GROUPS

In analysing many groups it is unlikely that all the hypotheses can be adequately tested by a series of pairwise comparisons. Usually, some of the more specific hypotheses fit naturally into one of the many methods available for examining different aspects of group variation. For example, it is often more appropriate to compare individual groups

12

with the others combined, rather than with each in turn. This is a test of atypicality and is especially useful for diagnosing the groups generated by cluster analysis.

One major consideration is whether the groups are to be differentiated on dependent measures taken one at a time, or on many measures taken together. It is also important to clarify the characteristics defining the groups, usually called the independent variables or treatments. Groups may be identified by single measures such as social class, school or attitude type, or a combined classification may apply. In Table 1.1 these are described as one-way or many-way classifications respectively. Many readers will recognize the latter case as an analysis of variance design with nested groups. One possibility in group analysis that is often overlooked is that the groups may be ordered. If this is so, then a trend analysis might be appropriate.

GENERATING GROUPS

Groups feature prominently in social research. Usually their structure is known although their extraction can be awkward if a complicated set of conditions has to be satisfied for membership. Recently, there has been a growth in the popularity of procedures which identify groups without the need for prior definitions. Variously called cluster analysis or numerical taxonomy, these methods are ideally suited to researches which seek to structure samples in terms of homogeneous subgroups. The range of methods available forces the researcher to study the procedures in detail, but their general robustness has already been demonstrated sufficiently well to merit serious consideration as a research strategy. It must be remembered, however, that once generated these groups, or clusters, need to be characterized as would any other groups. Rather more important, though, is the need to validate such classifications as they can be highly sample or method dependent.

It is not suggested that this list of research strategies is exhaustive. Nevertheless, it should help direct the researcher into an appropriate statistical domain. From that standpoint any specific analytical requirements can be more easily isolated and suitable solutions achieved.

1.5 Practical considerations

With the burden of statistical computation removed from the researcher the practical side of research analysis takes a different form. Instead of being an arithmetician, the researcher becomes a clerk. This manifests itself in the extreme care and diligence needed in preparing the data, and in the systematic habits essential to efficient computer usage. It is easy to dismiss these abilities because they appear trivial, but to do so would be foolish. Without a concern for detail and precision, what is usually a quick stage of the research can easily become excessively long and frustrating.

It is not sufficient simply to emphasize the importance of care. The virtues of tidiness, vigilance, and caution are personality features that have to be acquired if they are not already present. The only sure way of developing them is by practice. This means that the researcher must take every opportunity to acquaint himself with the various

13

computing procedures, no matter how time consuming this training might be. Only then will the hidden pitfalls be encountered and overcome. It should not be difficult to generate the necessary enthusiasm because the reward is so great. Once the skills have been mastered research analysis becomes an exciting venture, offering unexpected personal and intellectual satisfaction.

1.6 A guide to statistical texts

Since this book does not set out to explain fully the statistical procedures used, the reader is expected to have access to one or more appropriate statistical texts. Some of the more advanced methods are treated in specialized texts and these are referred to in the relevant chapters. The following texts are suitable as general source-books. Introductory texts (level A) are only intended as preliminary reading for anyone with little or no prior statistical training. They tend to provide descriptive rather than analytical accounts and consequently they are not adequate as reference texts. The basic statistical texts (level B) employ more advanced explanations, but they do tend to cover most of the standard statistical methods and therefore are sufficient for the majority of researches. Advanced texts (level C) need only be consulted by readers interested in the mechanics of the methods. Explanations are usually heavily mathematical and represent a considerable increase in difficulty. However, for multivariate methods such as factor analysis and multiple regression, it is virtually impossible to avoid detailed mathematics if a full understanding is to be achieved. Bennett and Bowers (1976) go part way towards explaining multivariate techniques without using advanced mathematics. But since most readers will not be in a position to develop a complete understanding of some of these more elaborate procedures, they must be prepared to accept a degree of superficiality in some sections of the following chapters.

Level A—Introductory

Brown, G. L., J. R. Amos, and O. G. Mink (1975) *Statistical Concepts: A Basic Program*, Second edition, New York, Harper and Row.

Crocker, A. C. (1974) *Statistics for the Teacher*, Slough, National Foundation for Educational Research.

Robson, C. (1973) *Experiment, Design, and Statistics in Psychology*, Harmondsworth, Penguin.

Sanders, D. H., A. F. Murph, and R. J. Eng (1976) *Statistics: A Fresh Approach*, New York, McGraw-Hill.

Level B—Basic

B1: General coverage

Ferguson, G. A. (1976) *Statistical Analysis in Psychology and Education*, Fourth edition. New York, McGraw-Hill.

Linton, M. and O. S. Gallo (1975) *The Practical Statistician: A Simplified Handbook of Statistics,* Monterey, Brooks/Cole.

14

Guilford, J. P. and B. J. Fruchter (1978) *Fundamental Statistics in Psychology and Education,* Sixth edition, New York, McGraw-Hill.

Glass, G. V. and J. C. Stanley (1970) *Statistical Methods in Education and Psychology,* Englewood-Cliffs, Prentice-Hall.

Bruning, J. L. and B. L. Kintz (1968) *Computational Handbook of Statistics*, Glenview, Scott-Foresman.

Edwards, A. L. (1973) *Statistical Methods*, Third edition, New York, Holt, Rinehart and Winston.

B2: Selected coverage

Siegel, S. S. (1956) *Nonparametric Statistics for the Behavioral Sciences*, New York, McGraw-Hill.

Bennett, S. and D. Bowers (1976) *An Introduction to Multivariate Techniques for Social and Behavioural Sciences*, London, Macmillan.

Level C—Advanced

Winer, B. J. (1970) *Statistical Principles in Experimental Design*, International Student Edition, New York, McGraw-Hill.

Cooley, W. W. and P. R. Lohnes (1971) *Multivariate Data Analysis,* New York, John Wiley.

Overall, J. and C. Klett (1972) *Applied Multivariate Analysis,* New York, McGraw-Hill.

Maxwell, A. E. (1977) *Multivariate Analysis in Behavioural Research,* London, Chapman and Hall.

The same classification by level will be applied to the various specialized texts referred to later in this book.

2. Preparation of Data

Planning and care in design and data collection provide a substantial guarantee of quality in research, but the ultimate test lies in the evaluation. Assuming that statistical analysis is to be applied a quantitative link has to be made between the information collected and the analytical methods. The coding system used will reflect many of the considerations discussed in Chapter 1, but further thought is needed to ensure that all anticipated analyses can indeed be performed. In general, this means that as much as possible of the original information should be retained when recording the data. At the same time the system should minimize the amount of additional work needed to prepare the data for eventual computation. So, for example, the use of tape-recorders makes this transfer time consuming and therefore costly. Where tape-recorded information is used its method of analysis should be decided upon early and a suitable recording format applied. In other instances lack of thought in data recording can introduce irremediable errors. Probably the commonest overall mistake is to assume that statistics can sort out whatever might be in the data. Only with the most meticulous care in data preparation can even a vague approximation to this ideal be achieved.

2.1 Data recording and coding

Methods used for recording the results of research meet the needs of computer coding to varying degrees. Where there is choice the computer coding paradigm should be followed. Certainly intermediate recording systems should be discouraged. A major problem in computerized analysis is the avoidance of errors; the more times data are transferred between coding systems, the greater the risk of introducing errors. Without actually using automatic data recording devices (such as are common in meteorology or agriculture, for example) the minimum number of transfers is one, namely from the respondent to punched cards. Usually one or two intermediate systems are introduced to process and then to code responses. In using standardized tests the responses are marked and a score computed. Clearly, marking presents one opportunity for error. If the resulting scores are written down and *then* transferred to computer coding forms (see Fig. 2.1) a further likelihood of introducing errors arises. A better method would be to record the scores directly onto coding forms reducing the number of transfers to two. In many situations even greater accuracy (and incidentally, less effort) can be achieved by designing the research instrument so that supplied responses can be punched onto computer cards without incorporating a coding stage. Questionnaires, attitude scales, and multiple-choice tests are the commonest examples of single-transfer coding. Many other methods such as inventories and checklists, interaction schedules and preference reports can usually be constructed so that answers are numeric making direct punching feasible.

Even survey questionnaires can often be treated in this manner. Consider questions relating to the size of institutions. These occur frequently and normally a category rather than an exact figure suffices. Indeed, to ask for precise numbers tends to deter respondents since not only does the question become considerably harder to answer, it may be that a 'correct' answer does not actually exist.

What is the size of the school in which you teach?

NUMBER OF PUPILS	under 500	500– 999	1000– 1499	1500 or more	not known			C12
ANSWER CODE	1	2	3	4	9		Answer →	

Given suitable instructions it is a simple matter for the respondent to select the appropriate answer code and to place it in the box indicated. More involved questions can be split into parts. Questions with a large number of possible responses, particularly open-ended questions, need careful piloting so that relevant response categories can be identified and offered. Whenever single-transfer coding is practicable, its use is recommended.

Multiple responses are a feature of questionnaires that tend to cause problems in data coding. Typically, a question asks which of a set of possibilities apply and the respondent is allowed to select as many as he wishes. Few analysis packages contain facilities for handling these variable length lists and their use is discouraged. Possible alternatives are to treat each possibility as a separate YES/NO question, to ask for a fixed number of responses, or to ask for ratings or rankings of all or a specified number of the choices.

Data coding becomes a relatively straightforward task if the recording system has been properly designed. Using data coding forms all the items of information for an individual are coded together as a sequence of numbers. For most computer programs it is desirable to start this sequence with a case identification number. By far the simplest method is to use sequential numbering starting at one and continuing as far as the sample size demands. Data coding forms usually contain 80 columns corresponding to the 80 columns of standard computer cards. The number of rows is not important since each row merely represents one computer card. Should the amount of information for each case be so large that it cannot be contained within 80 columns (i.e., 80 characters) then additional cards are used as needed. It is advisable to repeat the case identification number on each card although card numbers are rarely of use. Most of the conventions for coding data are little more than clerical common sense.

OVERALL AIM

The overall objective in coding is to space the numbers so that the same item of information appears in the same card-columns for all cases. This is called *fixed-format coding*.

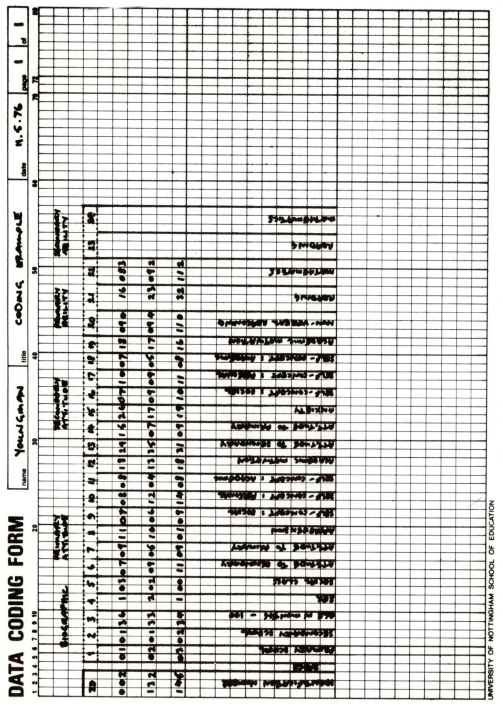

Fig. 2.1 *Computer coding form example.*

When values have a varying number of digits *all* the values for that item must be coded using the maximum width. Identification numbers, for example, will usually start at 1. If the largest number is in the 100's then the maximum width is three digits and therefore all identification numbers have to be in three-digit form, 001, 002, 076 and so on. The same applies to scores, intelligence quotients, and decimal values. For the latter, if two decimal places are considered sufficient, then all values are rounded or extended in coding to have two places.

ORDER

Normally the identification number comes first, but the remaining information need not be in any particular order. Nevertheless, it is much easier to remember the coding arrangement if similar types of data are kept together. Biographic data tend to be coded first, followed by the rest grouped by analysis or type. The identification number should not contain additional information such as sex or school which is intended for use in later analysis. Any item likely to be used for cross-tabulation or group extraction must be treated as a separate variable and coded accordingly.

SPACING

Fixed-format coding does not require spaces to separate values although the judicious use of spaces within the card can be helpful, particularly in checking punching (see Section 2.5). Certainly a single space after the identification number can be useful. Not only does it clearly distinguish the case number, but it can also be used later to carry extra information should data need to be added to the card. Patterns in data coding reduce the risk of errors and therefore it is generally advisable to code using the same number of columns per item. At times this can be rather awkward, particularly if it means overflowing onto a second card per case. In general, however, to mix single-column, double-column and even wider values does tend to increase the chance of making mistakes in the instructions needed to describe the data layout. Tidiness is a substantial virtue in computing.

WHOLE NUMBERS

Most data values are whole numbers, integers, and therefore decimal points are not required so long as the integer pattern applies to all cases. If decimal values do occur they should be treated with care.

DECIMAL POINTS

A decimal point is a character and as such requires a column for coding, just as it does in typing. Scores of around 100 with two decimal places would therefore need six columns.

19

By maintaining a fixed number of decimal places for all cases the decimal point always appears in the same column. Consequently a very quick check that punching is not 'off-punched' (i.e., displaced to the left or right) is to hold the pack of cards up to the light. If all the decimal points are correctly positioned it should be possible to see daylight through the three holes representing each point.

POSITIVE AND NEGATIVE VALUES

As in standard arithmetic notation, only negative signs are essential. The minus should never be embedded within a number, so minus one is coded -1, or -01, or -1.0, but never 0–1.

DICHOTOMOUS DATA AND ZERO CODES

Many measures have two possible responses—YES/NO, present/absent, male/female—and traditionally these are coded 1/0. However, should missing values exist the zero code is a convenient way to signal missing data. In that case zero should be avoided in the main coding if at all possible. Usually 1/2 coding is just as convenient for dichotomous data.

EXAMPLE

Figure 2.1 shows a possible coding system for three individuals measured on a range of data pertinent to the problems of primary/secondary school transfer.

Identification number: Three columns are needed since the maximum is 200. The space separates it from the data.

Primary school: For 11 schools a two-digit code is needed.

Secondary school: For three schools one column would suffice. To preserve uniformity two-column coding is used here.

Age (in months): When a continuous measure is needed the normal method using years and months must be modified. Decimals are awkward; changing to months is simple. With 10-year-olds this produces a three-digit number but since each one has a 1 in the first position it is redundant. Subtracting 100 produces age over 100 months.

Sex: Missing data do arise making 1/2 coding preferable to 1/0 coding. The space produced by allowing two columns but not punching the zero in the first column (the leading zero) will help subsequent checking.

Social class: Parental occupation is classified using the Registrar-General's grouping (Office of Population Censuses and Surveys, 1970) to produce four categories. Missing or unclassifiable information is coded 00.

Primary and secondary attitude: Scores on these scales are potentially two-figure values although scores below 10 do arise.

20

Primary and secondary ability: Data standardized to a mean of 100 inevitably produce three-digit values. The trick used for age (subtracting 100) cannot be applied and therefore three-column coding is needed. By placing primary and secondary ability data together a reasonably tidy pattern is maintained.

2.2   Treatment of missing data

The most acceptable solution to the problem of missing information is not to have any. This may seem fatuous, but in practice all other solutions are to some degree distortions of the truth. In social research, especially, absence of information tends to be associated with a certain type of behaviour which in itself may be significant. In educational research, failure to collect information is usually caused by absenteeism or even truancy. Both of these behaviours are atypical and may constitute important effects within the research. With questionnaire surveys, no matter what method of distribution is used, it cannot be assumed that non-response is a random characteristic. One solution that has been suggested is to examine late respondents since they often display similar attitudes to non-respondents. In general, every effort should be made to secure missing information even though substantially greater cost in both time and energy may be involved. Failing that, whatever information *is* available should be examined to ensure that the residual sample remains representative of the target population.

Analytical procedures for handling missing data vary, but as far as coding is concerned, all that is required is a suitable unique signal code. By far the most convenient solution is to preserve the zero code for this purpose; it is both simple and consistent. However, should zero occur (and the stress is on actual occurrence, not *theoretical* possibility) within the data as a legitimate value, then an alternative code must be used. When zero is not available, substitutes tend to be chosen from $-1, 9, 99, 999$, and so on. The values mostly require at least two columns, and consequently even cases with complete data must be coded in the same format to maintain the pattern. It must be appreciated that the code only signals the missing data. Statistical treatments depend on the analyses employed and indeed certain methods cannot handle omissions at all. These considerations are dealt with in the appropriate method chapters.

2.3   Modifications to data

Raw responses seldom satisfy all analysis requirements and some form of recoding tends to be necessary eventually. Questionnaires almost invariably need a certain amount of *regrouping of categories* to enable relationships to be identified (see Chapter 10). Even score data may not meet statistical assumptions. Many statistical texts state that a normal distribution is a prerequisite for using most parametric statistics although empirical studies (e.g., Keselman and Toothaker, 1974) have tended to question this assertion. Nevertheless, instances do arise where it becomes advisable to *transform the score distribution* before performing a particular statistical analysis. Possibly the commonest transformation is *standardization* to a common mean and variance. In analyses where comparable variances are essential standardization is done automatically, often through using the product-moment correlation coefficient. Factor analysis and multiple linear regression fall into this category. Other techniques, and cluster analysis is probably the most prominent, do *not* standardize but leave the decision in the hands of the analyst. The decision must be made following careful consideration of the research implications.

Situations often arise where the amount of pertinent information is so large that analysis of the measures singly does little to produce an overall picture. Checklists, inventories, and attitude scales are instruments typically prone to this difficulty. One solution is to carry out a secondary scoring to condense the original data into fewer measures. *Reduction* of this kind can be achieved by using an appropriate multivariate analysis such as factor analysis, or simply by partitioning the items into subscales (see Chapters 10 and 11). As long as sufficient care is taken over the preliminary data coding, many extensions and refinements are available should they be needed later.

Many disciplines, especially economics, employ a vast range of transformations such as quotients and indices which require detailed explanation before they can be correctly used. The only reservation that needs to be made concerns the effects of such recodings. Traditional transformations such as combining categories, standardization or factor scoring have a substantial background of research analysis which helps to protect against spurious effects. Where evidence in this area is lacking then either the analyst should examine the statistical effects independently, or alternatively, even greater effort should be made to cross-validate any findings based on these transformations.

2.4 Preparing data for the computer

If sufficient care has been taken over the recording and coding of raw data, the rest should be both simple and quick. The data coding form rows correspond to computer cards although these rows should not be confused with the *apparent* rows on a computer card (Fig. 2.2).

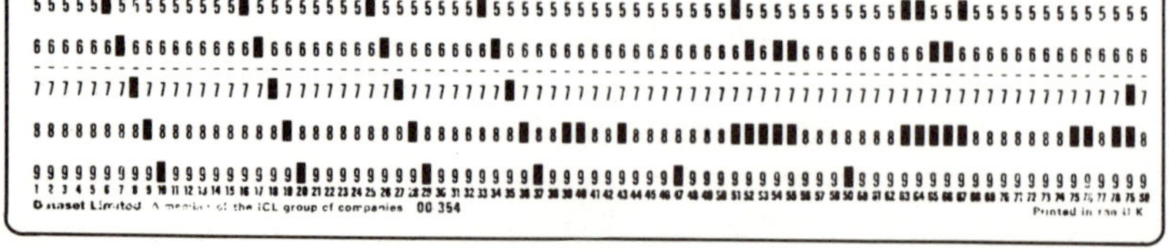

Fig. 2.2 *Computer card showing ICL and IBM character sets. Numerals, letters, and standard punctuation characters are the same for all computer codes. The remainder of the card shows the representations for five common characters in ICL 1900 code, IBM029 (EBCDIC), and IBM026 (BCD).*

A computer card carries the information *printed* across the top. The holes punched in the various horizontal positions are the computer input representations of that information. A hole in row numbered 4 represents the digit 4 and so on. Letters and special characters such as punctuation marks and mathematical symbols are represented by two or even three holes in the relevant column. Thus 'w' has holes in rows 0 and 6. While these hole representations are standard for digits and letters, the patterns for some of the special characters are not. Whenever these characters are needed care must be taken to ensure that the card punch matches the computer to be used. Raw data seldom raise problems since the coding used is almost invariably numeric. Thought is needed in preparing the operation system control cards which do tend to incorporate non-standard characters.

Card punching is little different from typing. Given sufficient attention to accuracy the preparation of small datasets (up to 200 cards) should cause no difficulty. When large amounts of information are to be punched, or if the format is awkward as may be the case with direct punching of questionnaires, it is usually advisable to use professional operators. Most establishments which take computing seriously do see this provision as an essential part of the service. Where card punching is not available, commercial agencies can be used. Prices vary but a cost of around 4 pence per full card (1978 prices), with *pro rata* reductions for shorter cards, should be expected. To insure against loss or damage, a duplicate set should be obtained and stored separately from the main pack.

2.5 Data checking

Valid statistics demand accurate data and therefore checking is an essential stage in computer usage. The frequency of errors on punched cards is too often underestimated. In monitoring the preparation of his reading research data Fawcett (1977) discovered error rates of around 1 per 1000 characters, equivalent to about 1 card in 12. Commercial services should produce lower rates. Verification, effectively punching each card twice, virtually eliminates all errors apart from any in the coding. The best protection is care; allied with that there are certain procedures which can be followed to sift out a substantial proportion of errors.

LISTING

No cards should be subjected to any analysis before being listed. A numbered listing enables a check on the number of cards to be made. It is amazing how often statisticians are incapable of accurate counting! Listing also allows certain more obvious features to be spotted.

As Table 2.1 shows, tidy coding produces a clear pattern; any breaks in this pattern indicate errors. So the short card starting 002 is presumably a punching error that was not removed. The correct version follows. Assuming that ten cases exist the presence of two cards for case 002 implies that the card count is wrong. The jump from 008 to 010 suggests that case 009 is missing.

The coding format leaves blanks in columns 4 and 9 with all punching stopping at

Table 2.1   Example of data listing showing errors

	Column	
	1 2	
	12345678901234567890	
1	001 1025 103095088	
2	002 2122 102	E
3	002 2122 102100114	
4	003 3019 099086107	
5	004 2120 1251061111	E
6	005 2022 116190095	E
7	006 1125 107102099	
8	07 2022 095107124	E
9	008 3019 120120124	
10	010 U024 116093098	E

column 18. Two cards violate this pattern. Case 004 is too long, quite likely the result of having repeated digits. The card starting 07 should read 007. 'Off-punching' is a common error and it can usually be detected easily if spaces exist. Another frequent source of error that a listing can expose is mispunching through failing to depress the numeric key, or by punching two numbers in one column (multipunching). Non-numeric characters result and these can often be seen (case 010).

TABULATION

Errors remaining after the initial visual inspection are likely to range from invalid characters, through impossible values, to incorrect values. By obtaining a frequency tabulation non-numeric characters will be traced since these are usually fatal, stopping the run. Also any values which logically should not occur become apparent. In Table 2.1 case 005 records 190 in columns 13, 14, and 15. For standardized data such a value is quite likely impossible. Almost certainly the score should be 109, reversals are a common error. Whenever incorrect scores remain theoretically acceptable, tracing becomes much more difficult.

STATISTICS

In many instances some of the basic statistics such as means and standard deviations are already known. These values can be confirmed by running a suitable program. The standard deviation is particularly susceptible to errors since it is based on squaring numbers.

CONTRADICTION

A final check that may apply involves testing that different items of data are not contra-dictory. For example, subtest scores should usually match totals. It is also common for a particular response on one question to preclude certain answers to others. Program BACH (Appendix 1) can be used to define impossible attributes and therefore any case recording them must contain errors.

Unfortunately, no matter how meticulous the care taken to protect against errors, no system is foolproof. Throughout all analyses vigilance is essential. The relevant computing adage here is 'know thy data'.

References

Fawcett, J. R. (1977) *The Use of Reading Laboratories and other Procedures in Promoting Effective Reading among Pupils aged 9–15*, Unpublished Ph.D thesis, University of Nottingham.

Keselman, H. J. and L. E. Toothaker (1974) 'Comparison of Turkey's T-method and Scheffé's S-method for various numbers of all possible differences of averages contrasts under violation of assumptions', *Educ. and Psychol. Meas.*, **34**, 511–519.

Office of Population Censuses and Surveys (1970) *Classification of Occupations 1970*, London, HMSO.

3. Computer Usage

Before statistical analyses can be computed both a machine and suitable programs need to be available. Most establishments concerned with research are able to meet these requirements and individuals involved in research analysis should be able to gain access to such facilities, usually without charge but occasionally on payment of a nominal sum. Even so, considerable mystique and fear seem to be associated with computing. Admittedly the statistical side does demand careful study, but no one need worry about computer usage. The procedures are essentially clerical and invariably a wealth of supporting advice and documentation is at hand if required. Patience is probably the main requirement. Once the local system has been mastered through a combination of care and practice, then attention can turn to the more important element in research analyses, the programmed methods themselves.

3.1 Programs and packages available

The past decade has seen a rapid growth in the range of computing facilities available to social researchers. There are two distinct features in this development. At the specialist level there have appeared centres of expertise capable of handling particular needs. Generally, both programs and advice are included and anyone working in the associated areas tends to experience little difficulty. At the other extreme, there exist a number of large packages intended to satisfy a substantial proportion of social research demands. BMD (Dixon, 1970) was one of the first of these major packages although SPSS (Nie *et al.*, 1970; Nie *et al.*, 1975) has since become more widely available. Veldman's (1967) book *FORTRAN Programming for the Behavioral Sciences* contains programs which have been regularly used by social scientists. More recently the OSIRIS package (Rattenbury and Van Eck, 1973) has begun to achieve some popularity. Development is gradual, though, and more novel techniques such as cluster analysis and multidimensional scaling, tend to be covered by specialist programs. The CLUSTAN suite (Wishart, 1969) offers a wide range of classification methods while multidimensional scaling is handled by a number of separate programs (e.g. Roskam and Lingoes, 1970; Guttman, 1968; Kruskal, 1964). Other techniques such as Automatic Interaction Detection performing segmentation rather than classification (Sonquist and Morgan, 1973) or multiple classification analysis (Andrews *et al.,* 1973) are rather more restricted in their application.

As far as the researcher is concerned the important point is that no matter what analysis is required, a program providing that facility is likely to exist somewhere. With luck, one of the more comprehensive packages will perform all the desired methods making the preparation of data and analysis specifications much simpler. One drawback

26

of the large packages is that increased flexibility does tend to complicate usage. More decisions are needed, for example, about data input, type of analysis or output content. For the experienced user this raises few problems. However, for many social scientists computer usage is a relatively rare activity and the extensive documentation alone may act as a deterrent. A remedy has been to produce smaller packages with fewer facilities, often those relevant to a particular discipline. An early one of this kind was Hallworth and Brebner's (1965) program intended for use in educational research. The present author has himself compiled a linked series of programs (Youngman, 1976) suitable for conducting the most commonly used social research analyses. The package, PMMD, is gradually achieving a wider circulation so that anyone can fairly easily either access or acquire it (see Appendix 1). Most aspects of computer usage will be described with reference to PMMD, SPSS and the most recent version of BMD, renamed BMDP (Dixon, 1975).

3.2 General procedures

The preliminary stages of data preparation and gaining access to appropriate programs may take rather a long time but after that the process is much more productive. Normally a considerable amount of computer analysis can be performed in a few weeks once the procedures have been mastered. If anything, the main difficulty is to resist the temptation to try virtually every technique available.

Before the actual computing starts it is essential that an accurate record of the data coding should be produced. The complicated coding often used in surveys tends to demand a highly detailed *codebook*. Most researches are less involved and a relatively simple *variable list* should suffice. It gives a column by column description of the data cards, together with names, variable numbering and brief coding details. Table 3.1 shows a variable list suitable for the data coded earlier (see Fig. 2.1). Every card column is carefully identified and described. The label in column F of the table is an abbreviated form of the full name and can be supplied to certain programs for labelling computer output. Most programs do not contain a labelling facility, instead the variables analysed are numbered sequentially. In that case it is vital that a record of the numbering for different analyses should be kept. Columns C, D, and E (more if necessary) are useful for that purpose. Data format specifications are described in the next section; sometimes it helps to record the individual variable formats as part of the variable list as shown in column H. Obviously, detailed specifications of variables such as test scores and attitude scales need to be recorded separately. Nevertheless, some of the more general information including maximum values and missing data codes can also be profitably included in the variable list. When completed it provides a quick but valuable reference document for all subsequent analyses.

Running programs is heavily dependent on the local computing installation but in general the input structure will tend to be as follows:

A.   OPERATING SYSTEM INSTRUCTIONS.

B.   Data and analysis specifications.

C.   Data cards.

D.   Further analysis specifications.

E.   OPERATING SYSTEM INSTRUCTIONS.

The outer parts of this sandwich are the ones most likely to vary from installation to installation. Where a standard operating system such as IBM's OS or ICL's GEORGE 3 is used these variations will be minimal. Many establishments prefer to develop their own structure for computer input and output and then there is little uniformity. Fortunately, users of standard packages usually require few special facilities and as a result production of the operating system instruction cards should be a simple task, particularly after the first one or two runs. For the remaining sections of the input the specifications depend upon the package or program used, not the installation.

All computing requires a working familiarity with a certain amount of *documentation* and the dual nature of the input instructions means that two sets of documents need to be studied. Good documentation will make this a quick and efficient process but even

Table 3.1   Variable list for the sample data

A	B	C	D	E	F	G		H
			Variable					
Item	*Column*	*A1*	*A2*	*A3*	*Label*	*Description*		*Format*
1	1–3	ID	ID	ID	ID	Identification number	[1–830]	I3,
	4						(blank)	1X,
2	5–6	1			PRIM	Primary school	[1–11]	F2.0,
3	7–8	2			SECY	Secondary school	[1–3]	F2.0,
4	9–10	3			AGE	Age in months	[minus 100]	F2.0,
5	11–12	4			SEX	Sex	[1 = M/2 = F]	F2.0,
6	13–14	5			CLAS	Social class	[1–4/0 = NA]	F2.0,
7	15–16	6	1		JASS	Attitude to secondary	[max 11]	F2.0,
8	17–18	7	2		JAPS	Attitude to primary	[max 11]	F2.0,
9	19–20	8	3		JAPH	Apprehension over transfer	[max 12]	F2.0,
10	21–22	9	4		JSCS	Self-concept: social	[max 12]	F2.0,
11	23–24	10	5		JSCP	Self-concept: personal	[max 14]	F2.0,
12	25–26	11	6		JSCA	Self-concept: academic	[max 12]	F2.0,
13	27–28	12	7		JMOT	Academic motivation	[max 24]	F2.0,
14	29–30	13	8		SASS	Attitude to secondary	[max 40]	F2.0,
15	31–32	14	9		SAPS	Attitude to primary	[max 20]	F2.0,
16	33–34	15	10		SANX	Anxiety	[max 36]	F2.0,
17	35–36	16	11		SSCS	Self-concept: social	[max 12]	F2.0,
18	37–38	17	12		SSCP	Self-concept: personal	[max 14]	F2.0,
19	39–40	18	13		SSCA	Self-concept: academic	[max 12]	F2.0,
20	41–42	19	14		SMOT	Academic motivation	[max 24]	F2.0,
21	43–45	20			JNVR	Non-verbal reasoning	[100]	F3.0,
22	46–48	21			JRED	Reading—unstandardized	[max 42]	F3.0,
23	49–51	22			JMAT	Mathematics	[100]	F3.0,
24	52–54	23			SRED	Reading–unstandardized	[max 161]	F3.0,
25	55–57	24			SMAT	Mathematics	[100]	F3.0

(Bracketed groupings in column G: PRIMARY — items 7–13; SECONDARY — items 14–20; PRIMARY — items 21–23; SECY — items 24–25.)

where the quality is less satisfactory it is essential that an effort is made to understand the procedures *before* starting, not when problems arise. There is little point in discussing *operating system instructions* because of their variability. Primarily, their purpose is to identify the user and the particular computer run, to call the program to be used, and to request any special facilities needed such as named files, extra long times, or card output. The important features of computer analysis are the data and analysis specifications and these are outlined in the next two sections.

3.3 Data format specification in FORTRAN

The need to vary the spacing of data on computer cards eliminates the possibility of having standard input formats. Instead, most programs require the user to supply an instruction indicating how the analysis measures are distributed across each card. Since the vast majority of statistical packages are written in the FORTRAN language this section explains the construction of FORTRAN format statements only. The elements used may look complicated at first (they are in fact features of the FORTRAN language) but in essence they operate in a similar manner to algebraic symbols. Once they are understood their use becomes automatic. They allow considerable flexibility in data coding and analysis and therefore effort spent in mastering the principles is a rewarding investment.

DATA FORMAT TERMINOLOGY

Record: A block of information, usually an 80-column card.

Sample: Those records comprising one case.

Field: A set of adjacent columns identifying one value.

Width: The number of columns forming the field.

Descriptor: An expression describing the form of a field.

Type: Three types of descriptors are commonly used.

Separator: Punctuation element separating descriptors. A comma is used unless a bracket or solidus is needed.

Solidus: Oblique stroke (/) transferring control to a new card.

Repeater: Integer indicating repetition of a descriptor.

Data format statement: The complete data description, a series of descriptors and separators enclosed in round brackets. It indicates how each successive column of the data record is to be read by the computer.

Field descriptors

Of the many types of descriptor available in the FORTRAN language only three are commonly used.

I-type refers to integer data.
F-type refers to continuous data.
X-type refers to data to be ignored.

Any descriptor has an associated width and possibly a repeater. F-descriptors have an additional qualification indicating the number of decimal places. In general, all variables are identified by F-descriptors even though they may be integer. The I-descriptor tends to be used for identification numbers only.

Repetition

Where an analysis requires a series of equally spaced scores to be identified then a descriptor can be repeated simply by prefixing the appropriate number. Thus 4I1 identifies four single-column integer values. For a single occurrence (that is, no repetition) the initial 1 can be omitted, as in algebraic notation, I1, I2, etc.

The I-descriptor

rIw where: r is the number of times to be repeated and w is the width of each field. This descriptor is almost always used to identify case numbers. Its associated width (I4, for example) gives the number of columns the index number occupies. Normally only the first incidence of a case number is identified and so if multiple cards are needed for each case all subsequent case numbers must be skipped (see later). In certain programs, particularly where binary data are input (see PMMD/CARM, for example), I-descriptors may be needed to describe variables as well as case numbers.

The F-descriptor

$rFw.d$ where: r is the number of repetitions, w is the width of the field, and d is the number of decimal places.

Apart from the initial I-descriptor for the index number data format statements mostly contain a series of F- and X-descriptors. The F-descriptor tends to be used to identify *all* analysis variables regardless of whether they are continuous or categoric. For *whole numbers* this entails specifying no decimal places (i.e., $d = 0$). A three-digit integer score would be described F3.0.

For *decimal values* there are two possible approaches. The simplest approach is to code the data as they look, always bearing in mind that for every case, any particular measure should appear in the same card columns. So values:

2.0	1.25	5.625	10.5

would be standardized to occupy six columns

02.000	01.250	05.625	10.500

The descriptor would be F6.3 since the values each occupy six columns (remember that the decimal place needs a column), and there are three decimal places.

It is possible to code data omitting the decimal points but the method is not recommended. Keeping the point not only increases accuracy, it also enables the position of the punched point to be checked by holding the pack of cards up to the light. If all the points are correctly positioned it should be possible to see straight through the pack.

INTEGER SCORES: use Fw.0 (i.e., $d = 0$)
DECIMAL SCORES: use Fw.d (d = number of decimal places).

Example

A card contains the following data:

Col. 1–4   a case number
Col. 5 and beyond   five single column scores followed by ten two-column scores (all without decimal places), then a four-column score with two decimal places.
format: (I4,5F1.0,10F2.0,F4.2)

The X-descriptor
wX   where w is the number of columns to ignore.
The X- or skip descriptor is used to indicate that certain columns of the computer card are to be ignored, either because they are blank, or because they contain data not needed for the current analysis. The number of columns to be skipped comes *before* the X (note this difference from the I and F types), so that 5X means skip five columns. No repeater is used with the X-descriptor. To skip a single column use 1X.

Example

A data card contains:

a four-column identifier	(I4)
irrelevant data in the next six columns	(6X)
12 three-digit scores to be analysed	(12F3.0)
four blank columns	(4X)
four two-digit scores for the analysis	(4F2.0)

The complete data format description then is:

$$\text{(I4,6X,12F3.0,4X,4F2.0)}$$

The Solidus: /
The solidus is a control signal that causes the computer to start reading a new record or card for a particular case. Its presence is only required when more than one card is used for each case. Two placed together have the effect of missing out a data card for every case.

Example

Each subject has four cards:

Card one has a three-column index number, and biographical data for analysis by a different program.
Card two contains 16 two-digit scores from column 11 onwards.
Card three contains 12 three-digit scores from column 11.
Card four contains four two-digit scores in columns 11–12, 13–14, 15–16, 17–18.

The data format statement reads:

$$(I3/10X,16F2.0/10X,12F3.0/10X,4F2.0)$$

Checks for data format statements

Possibly the greatest likelihood of error in computer usage lies in the data format statement. Fortunately, there are two checks that enable the user to reduce the chance of introducing an error.

Check 1:   number of variables

Most programs require the user to specify the number of variables (excluding the initial identifier) for analysis. The data format statement should be checked to ensure that the number of variables specified matches the number identified by the descriptors within the format statement.

Example

The following statement purports to define an analysis on 35 specified variables. Does it?

$$(I4,6X,12F2.0,F1.0,3F3.0,6X,F1.0,2F2.0/4X,F3.1,1X,2F2.0,5X,F1.0,F2.0//10X,10F2.0)$$

No.   (Why?)

Check 2:   column span

Every descriptor includes an associated width value. For instance:

F5.2	spans	5 columns
2F5.2	spans	10 columns (2×5)
16X	spans	16 columns
I3	spans	3 columns

A data format statement must successively describe all card columns, starting at the first and continuing until a new card is indicated (either by '/' or by ')'). Therefore, by totalling the width values of all the field descriptors in a data format statement, it is possible to check that the value tallies with the column span on the data cards themselves.

Example

The width values of the descriptors in card one of the previous example can easily be tabulated:

Descriptor	Width value	Cumulative column span
I4	4	4
6X	6	10
12F2.0	24	34
F1.0	1	35
3F3.0	9	44
6X	6	50
F1.0	1	51
2F2.0	4	55

So the final data value required for the analysis should be in column 55. (This does *not* exclude the possibility that other data *not* needing analysis are present in columns 56+.)

Together these two checks enable a reasonably exhaustive check on the data format statement to be made. However, prevention is better than cure, and if data recording is kept as tidy as possible (i.e., all variables in the same number of columns each) a lot of unnecessary effort can be saved.

3.4 Analysis specifications

Program structures reflect the statistical philosophies of their writers and inevitably differences appear. Generalizing fiercely, there are two main schools. On one hand, the scientifically inclined have favoured programs requiring sparse but precise specifications. The other extreme is not necessarily unscientific, but rather its representatives have tended to be user-oriented. Both input and output have been designed to counter an assumed fear of numbers by using literal specifications and elaborate output. The two philosophies are not mutually exclusive, but in general, where choice exists, the more parsimonious programs are to be preferred. A very simple justification for this preference is that fewer instructions mean fewer errors. An excessive desire to assist users does tend to require a large number of specification cards, too often resulting in errors of omission or misordering. Should the choice not exist, the analyst must be aware of the need for extra care with some of the more innocuous looking packages.

Most programs fall between the two extremes, sometimes requiring only one or two specification cards, but occasionally needing extra instructions for repeated analyses or non-standard facilities. Taking PMMD, SPSS (Nie, *et al.,* 1970) and BMDP (Dixon, 1975) as examples, the simplest form of analysis specification can be seen in program PMMD/CATT. This is a relatively standard program for means, standard deviations and product-moment correlations. Its input structure is:

A. Parameters and title card.
B. Data format statement.
C. Data cards.
D. Blank card to terminate.

There are effectively two cards to prepare, A and B, of which the data format statement has already been described in the previous section.

PARAMETERS AND TITLE CARD

The single card giving details of both the data and the analysis required is constructed as follows:

Col. 1– 4   *NV*   number of variables.
Col. 5– 8   *NS*   number of subjects.
Col.   9   *KF*   number of format cards.
Col.   10   *KD*   data source (0 = cards/1 = file).
Col.   11   *KK*   output (1 = all/2 = no correlations).
Col.   12   *KT*   test type (0 = none/1 = Scheffé/2 = t/3 = Tukey).
Col.   13+   TITLE (any characters can be used).

Its structure is typical of most PMMD programs, and indeed many others. Details of the specific facilities (for example the between-groups test coded in column 12) are given in a program document. Having studied it, completion of the card is automatic.

EXAMPLE

A single dataset of 125 cases is to be analysed to obtain means, standard deviations, and product-moment correlations for eight measures. Since only one group is to be input any between-groups testing is inapplicable. The data format statement is sufficiently tidy to be contained on a single card. The data themselves are on cards. The CATT parameters are:

$$NV = 8 \quad NS = 125 \quad KF = 1 \quad KD = 0 \quad KK = 1 \quad KT = 0$$

The parameter card is
followed by

> 000801251010   GROUP ONE STATISTICS
> (whatever the format is)
> the data cards
> one blank card

Programs often allow a number of datasets (groups, for example) to be analysed on the same rum. To do so sections A, B, and C are repeated for each dataset. The blank card D indicates that no more datasets follow. The test facility (*KT*) on CATT enables differences between successive datasets to be tested by any of the methods indicated.

The original BMD package (Dixon, 1970) requires similar specifications to those for PMMD, but the latest version BMDP (Dixon, 1975) has verbalized instructions. The main operations for a particular program are defined in a paragraph specification; more detailed qualifications, statistics or output for example, are indicated via parameters to these paragraphs. BMDP does not offer a program directly comparable to PMMD/CATT. The popular means, standard deviations and correlations analysis, is supplied by program BMDP/P8D. This is more general than PMMD/CATT since it also handles missing data. Table 3.2 (pages 36 and 37) summarizes the instructions for this program.

The increased complexity of this set of specifications stems from the greater range of facilities offered, particularly those enabling data manipulations to be performed. The following cards would generate the same analysis described earlier;

column	1	10
	PROBLEM	TITLE IS 'GROUP ONE STATISTICS'./
	INPUT	VARIABLES ARE 8.
		CASES ARE 125.
		FORMAT IS '(whatever the format is)'./
	PRINT	MEAN.
		VAR./
	END/	
	data cards go here	
	FINISH/	

Although the use of verbal instructions makes the content of the analysis explicit, care is needed over the punctuation, particularly with the full stops and slashes needed at various points.

Both PMMD and BMDP comprise independent programs designed to handle specific analyses. The third package, SPSS, generalizes research needs much further by incorporating all possible analyses within the same structure. The researcher indicates which analyses are required by means of a procedure card and its associated options. So as well as studying the control instructions summarized in Table 3.3 (page 38) it is also necessary to refer to the procedure and option details given in a separate part of the SPSS manual. Correlational analysis is offered by the PEARSON CORR subprogram. Its specifications are too protracted to list here, but essentially the user indicates similar analysis and output needs as those already presented for the PMMD and BMDP programs. The example analysis would be specified as shown on page 39. Here the increased generality demands even greater care on the part of the user to ensure that cards are defined accurately, entered in the correct order, or are not omitted.

Table 3.2 Specifications for the BMDP correlation program P8D

PROGRAM CONTROL CHART

Paragraph name	Parameter name	Assumed value Blank	Comment	Type and max. size	Reference
PROB (req'd)	TITLE	Blank	Problem title	Literal, 160 char.	IV.6
INPUT (req'd, 1st prob. only)	VARIAB	None/pp	Number of input variables	Number	IV.7
	FORMAT	None/pp	Input data format	Literal, 800 char.	IV.7
	CASE	E-o-f/pp	Number of input cases	Number	IV.7
	UNIT	5/pp	Input unit number	Number	IV.7
	REWIND	Yes/pp	Rewind input data unit	Logical	IV.8
	CODF	None	Input Save File identification	Literal, 8 char.	IV.8
	CONTENT	None	Input Save File identification	Literal, 8 char.	IV.9
	LABEL	None	Input Save File identification	Literal, 40 char.	IV.9
VARIAB (optional)	ADD	Zero/pp	Number of variables added through transf.	Number	IV.20
	NAME	X(subscript)/pp	Variable names, one for each variable	Literals, 8 char. each	IV.10
	USE	All variables	Variables to be processed	NAMEs or numbers	IV.10
	LABEL	None/pp	One or two case label variables	NAMEs or numbers	IV.10
	ROW	All USE vars./pp	Row variables to be processed	NAMEs or numbers	P8D.5
	COL	All USE vars./pp.	Column variables to be processed	NAMEs or numbers	P8D.5
	MISS	None/pp	Missing value codes for each variable	Numbers	IV.9
	MAX	None/pp	Maximum limits for each variable	Numbers	IV.9
	MIN	None/pp	Minimum limits for each variable	Numbers	IV.9
	BEFORET or AFTERT	BEFORET/pp	Variables checked before or after transf.	Logical	IV.20
	WEIGHT	No weight var./pp	Variable containing case weights	NAME or number	P8D.6

Table 3.2 (continued)

	Name or X(subscript)		Program Control Language transformations		
TRANSF (optional)		None			IV.13
SAVE (optional)	UNIT	None	Output Save File unit number	Number	IV.24
	NEW	Not new	Used when Save File is new	Logical	IV.25
	CODE	None	Output Save File identification	Literal, 8 char.	IV.24
	CONTENT	CORR/pp	One or more: DATA, COVA, CORR	Literals	P8D.6
	LABEL	Blank	Output Save File identification	Literal, 40 char.	IV.25
PRINT (optional)	COVA	No/pp	Print covariance matrix	Logical	P8D.7
	CORR	Yes/pp	Print correlation matrix	Logical	P8D.7
	FREQ	Yes/pp	Print frequency table	Logical	P8D.7
	MEAN	No/pp	Print matrix of means	Logical	P8D.7
	VAR	No/pp	Print matrix of variances	Logical	P8D.7
	SUMWTS	See P8D.7	Print weight matrix	Logical	P8D.7
CORR (optional)	TYPE	CORPAIR/pp	One or more: ALLVALUE, COVPAIR, CORPAIR; or COMPLETE	Literals	P8D.7
END (req'd)			End of control information for problem		IV.3
FINISH (req'd unless data input is from cards and INPUT CASE is not specified)			End of deck setup		IV.3

Key: pp = previous problem
IV = Program Information section
E-o-f = end-of-file

Caution: Don't forget slash (/) at the end of each paragraph, and period at the end of each sentence.

Table 3.3 General specifications for SPSS analyses

This structure relates to the first edition of SPSS. The second edition (Nie *et al.*, 1975) operates a slightly modified format.

Control-card order for running with BCD data files.

Card status	Control field	Remarks	
Optional	RUN NAME		
Conditional	FILE NAME	Required if an SPSS system file is to be generated.	
Required	VARIABLE LIST		
Conditional	SUBFILE LIST	Required if there is a subfile structure.	
Required	INPUT MEDIUM		Data definition cards
Required	# OF CASES		
Required	INPUT FORMAT	The order of these cards is arbitrary.	
Optional	MISSING VALUES		
Optional	VAR LABELS		
Optional	VALUE LABELS		
Conditional	PRINT FORMATS	Required for 'A' type variables, otherwise optional.	
Conditional	PROCESS SBFILES	Used only for files with subfiles.	
Required	*PROCEDURE CARD**		Task definition cards for first task
Optional	OPTIONS		
Optional	STATISTICS		
Required	READ INPUT DATA		
	(Cards containing the data for cases appear here when the data is being input from cards.)		
	(The next set of task definition cards appears here if desired.)		
	PROCESS SBFILES		Task definition cards for subsequent tasks
	*PROCEDURE CARD**		
	OPTIONS		
	STATISTICS		
Required	FINISH		

*To be replaced by the desired procedure card such as CROSSTABS, REGRESSION, MARGINALS, etc.

column	1	16
	RUN NAME	GROUP ONE STATISTICS
	VARIABLE LIST	VAR001 TO VAR008
	INPUT MEDIUM	CARD
	# OF CASES	125
	INPUT FORMAT	FIXED (whatever the format is)
	PEARSON CORR	VAR001 TO VAR008 WITH VAR001
		TO VAR008
	STATISTICS	1
	READ INPUT DATA	
	data cards go here	
	FINISH	

3.5 Special considerations in computer usage

Even after the initial novelty has worn off, computer analysis remains vastly different from traditional statistical computation. The speed and versatility together tend to increase the amount of analysis carried out. As a result errors become more frequent, and quite likely more serious because of the interdependent nature of the various stages in data analysis. In the final stages, the large number of analyses performed can make interpretation and presentation of the results a complicated and often ill-considered task. One frequent side-effect of computing is the desire to acquire some expertise in FOR-TRAN programming to extend even further the scope of research analysis. A wealth of texts and courses is available (e.g., Calderbank, 1969; Organick, 1966; Veldman, 1967) although the FORTRAN manual appropriate for the local installation will also be needed. These and many more are the sort of problems data analysts are likely to encounter. Error tracking and analysis presentation are without doubt the commonest. Interactive computing may become an important consideration as it develops.

ERROR TRACKING

Any brief discussion of this topic must be unsatisfactory because of the numerous possibilities as well as the wide variations between computers. In general, the analyst must assume that an uncompleted analysis indicates a data or control card error since program or system faults are rare. Even more important, the results themselves should be scrutinized to ensure that they make sense—the computer can appear to have completed an

39

analysis successfully but still have produced garbage. Assuming that the data checking procedures described earlier (Section 2.5) have been followed errors tend to occur most often in the format statement. Again, carrying out the two checks—number of variables and number of columns—should obviate these errors. Of the remaining errors those in the operating system control cards are commonly caused by requesting certain facilities in the program parameters (file input or card output, for example) but failing to do so in the system specifications. Other system errors are more obvious, particularly running out of time or print.

Most errors in program parameters fall into two types. Mispunching of parameter or specification cards can introduce either impossible or incorrect values for certain parameters. These in turn can cause failure, or wrong analyses. Careful checking of the parameter cards should identify mispunches. The other type of parameter error is violating the limitations of a program. Restrictions are sometimes necessary and are given in the program documents. Trying to input too many variables is a common error; it will either produce incorrect results or more often halt the analysis through overflowing computer storage allocations.

The best guide to where an error lies is in the printout produced. By checking through to see where mistakes first occur some indication of the probable cause can be obtained. This is particularly so for those programs requiring a number of specification cards. Since programs usually output results as they are computed, the error card should be one somewhere after the last successful part of the analysis.

INTERPRETATION AND PRESENTATION OF RESULTS

The ease of carrying out very elaborate analyses does exaggerate the problem of understanding the full implications of results. Probably the best safeguard against incorrect or unsatisfactory interpretation is to ensure that a clear grasp of the basic sample statistics is obtained first. Scatter plots and distribution charts are particularly useful. On no account must the program output be used by itself. The relevant program document may give guides to interpretation, and possibly further references. Further study is essential since the results of difficult or apparently contradictory analyses can only be appreciated if the methods themselves are understood.

The presentation of results is another area where an excessive dependence is placed upon program output. A program has to meet the needs of many users and will therefore tend to include far more information than any individual requires. For example, although accuracy is usually to four decimal places, it is rare to need more than two for means and standard deviations or three for correlations. The analyst must accept that summary tables will have to be produced incorporating only the essential parts of the program output. Certainly, huge sections of printout should never be photocopied and presented as valid statements of results. The precise format for presentation varies for different methods. Guidelines can easily be obtained by referring to articles using the same methods. Later sections of this book offer examples for the methods covered.

INTERACTIVE COMPUTING

One further consideration in computer usage involves the mode in which the computing is performed. In most instances the analysis is defined completely before it is submitted to the computer. This is usually referred to as batch processing. Normally this is an effective and convenient way of working, but there are situations where it can be helpful and even necessary to define a later part of an analysis on the basis of earlier results. In data recoding, for example, combination of codes cannot be performed until actual code distributions are known. Then there are certain analytical methods which are essentially sequential. Multiple regression analysis requires the construction of optimal models; these are optimized using information from previous models.

At the moment most statistical packages available assume batch operation but an interactive version of SPSS (called SCSS) is being implemented on certain larger computers. The University of Michigan, famous for its development of the interactive Michigan Terminal System, MTS, is also working on an interactive statistical package called MIDAS. It seems likely that such facilities will proliferate and data analysts may need to learn new ways of working. However, interactive computing, or 'talking to the machine' as it is sometimes affectionately called, does not remove the need to think carefully about analyses. It is an expensive form of computing and time spent designing anticipated analytical routes beforehand can save valuable time within the interactive session.

3.6 A guide to program availability

Although a comprehensive guide to program packages is out of the question, it is possible to provide a worthwhile summary since a small number of packages accounts for a substantial proportion of the analyses performed by social scientists. Without doubt SPSS (Nie *et al.*, 1970; Nie *et al.*, 1975) is the most popular choice where it is available. A frequent alternative is the Biochemical Computer Programs package of which the most recent version is BMDP (Dixon, 1975). Smaller installations often cannot cope with the large size of these two packages. The present author's own suite of programs, PMMD (Youngman, 1976) has helped overcome this problem for certain British universities and polytechnics. A recent introduction from America, OSIRIS (Rattenbury and Van Eck, 1973), is still gaining popularity and is therefore a potential candidate for increased usage. Two other widely used packages are available in book form. They are a general behavioural science package (Veldman, 1967) and a range of multivariate programs (Cooley and Lohnes, 1971). Each chapter in this book ends with a guide to the availability of the methods discussed in these six packages. The key used is as follows:

P PMMD Programmed Methods for Multivariate Data.
S SPSS Statistical Package for the Social Sciences.
B BMDP Biomedical Computer Programs (Dixon, 1975).
O OSIRIS University of Michigan (Rattenbury and Van Eck, 1973).
V Veldman, D. J. (1967) *FORTRAN Programming for the Behavioral Sciences*.
C Cooley, W. W. and P. R. Lohnes (1971) *Multivariate Data Analysis*.

One final comment is in order regarding the notion of a computer program. As electronic calculators have become more powerful, so many of the statistical methods only available hitherto on large machines are now provided by these small hand calculators. Much of the discussion of statistical analysis and interpretation in the remainder of this book applies equally well to these devices.

References

Andrews, F. M., J. N. Morgan, J. A. Sonquist, and L. Klem (1973) *Multiple Classification Analysis,* Second edition, Ann Arbor, Institute of Social Research, University of Michigan.

Calderbank, V. J. (1969) *A Course in Programming in FORTRAN IV*, London, Chapman and Hall.

Cooley, W. W. and P. R. Lohnes (1971) *Multivariate Data Analysis*, New York, John Wiley.

Dixon, W. J. (ed.) (1970) *BMD: Biomedical Computer Programs*, Berkeley, Calif., University of California Press.

Dixon, W. J. (ed.) (1975) *BMDP: Biomedical Computer Programs*, Berkeley, Calif., University of California Press.

Guttman, L. (1968) 'A general technique for finding the smallest coordinate space for a configuration of points', *Psychometrika*, **33**, 469–506.

Hallworth, H. J. and A. Brebner (1965) *A System of Computer Programs for Use in Psychology and Education*, London, British Psychological Society.

Kruskal, J. B. (1964) 'Non-metric multidimensional scaling: a numerical method', *Psychometrika*, **29**, 115–129.

Nie, N. H., D. H. Bent, and C. H. Hull (1970) *Statistical Package for the Social Sciences*, New York, McGraw-Hill.

Nie, H. N., C. H. Hull, J. G. Jenkins, K. Steinbrenner and D. H. Bent (1975) *SPSS: Statistical Package for the Social Sciences*, New York, McGraw-Hill.

Organick, E. I. (1966) *A FORTRAN IV Primer*, New York, Addison-Wesley.

Rattenbury, J. and N. Van Eck (1973) *OSIRIS: Architecture and Design*, Ann Arbor, Institute of Social Research, University of Michigan.

Roskam, E. and J. Lingoes (1970) 'MINISSA-1, a FORTRAN IV(G) program for smallest space analysis of square symmetric matrices', *Behavioral Science*, **15**, 204.

Sonquist, J. A. and J. N. Morgan (1973) *Searching for Structure*, Ann Arbor, Institute for Social Research, University of Michigan.

Veldman, D. J. (1967) *FORTRAN Programming for the Behavioral Sciences*, New York, Holt, Rinehart and Winston.

Wishart, D. (1969) *CLUSTAN 1A: User Manual*. St. Andrews, Scotland, University of St. Andrews Computing Laboratory.

Youngman, M. B. (1976) *Programmed Methods for Multivariate Data*, Version 5, Nottingham, University of Nottingham School of Education.

4. The Demonstration Dataset

By far the most fruitful approach to discussing data analysis is to relate theory and procedures to research examples at every possible opportunity. Rather than select from the research literature the strategy used will be to demonstrate analyses on one genuine educational research dataset. Not only does this introduce a more realistic situation, but also the gradual accumulation of knowledge about this dataset will help in the specification and interpretation of subsequent analyses. In order to pursue this overall policy some of the analyses performed will be rather artificial and certainly sometimes superfluous to the research needs. On no account should one impute that the whole armoury of statistical methodology is essential for all research analysis! As Chapter 1 attempted to argue, *the research problem and the data together* determine the statistical approach, not the data alone.

4.1 The research problem

Data are collected in order to investigate a particular research problem. In the case of the demonstration dataset the broad aim was to investigate the difficulties experienced by pupils transferring from primary to secondary education. The two major dimensions in this problem are the schools and the children. Since funds were severely limited attention was directed almost exclusively towards the latter. Potential difficulties in school transfer were interpreted as being both personal and academic and therefore a wide range of attitude and performance assessments was required. Many features of the sample were predetermined partly by the problem (this fixed an age level), further by the need to select schools within the Local Education Authority sponsoring the research. Most of the refinements to the basic design are more appropriately discussed in relation to the respective analyses. However, one aspect that does warrant mention at this point is the longitudinal nature of the study. Various measures were applied over a period of two years to monitor *changes* rather than *levels* of attitude or performance. Although a common feature of social research its statistical treatment often leaves much to be desired. In its entirety the design enables many facets of school adjustment to be studied as well as other problems incidental to the main aim of the research.

4.2 Sample

Like most English counties the one in question contained both urban and rural populations not necessarily showing the same characteristics. Consequently two samples, one of each type, were studied although only the urban one is considered here. It comprised the bulk of the intake to three comprehensive schools. A potential sample size of over 800 pupils stabilized at 454 members through transfers to other schools and absences during the initial testing sessions. Boys and girls are equally represented but a social class imbalance exists because of the heterogeneous nature of the city. The professional occupations are under-represented in spite of selecting the schools to be as representative as possible of social backgrounds.

4.3 Data

The information collected has already been outlined in discussing data preparation (Section 2.1). The three main areas—biographic data, attitude and performance—produce a total of 24 measures.

BIOGRAPHIC

No attempt was made to obtain a detailed biographic description of each child. Apart from essential information such as age, sex, and school, the only other item in this category was socioeconomic status. The Registrar General's classification (Office of Population Censuses and Surveys, 1970) was used with classes I and II (professional and managerial) combined, class III split into non-manual and manual, and classes IV and V (semi-skilled and unskilled) combined producing four categories in all.

INTELLECTUAL

Non-verbal reasoning was tested once only, in June of the transfer year, using the National Foundation for Educational Research test 28, BD (Pidgeon, 1965). Achievement in reading comprehension was assessed in the primary school using the Gap Reading Test (McLeod, 1970). The need to allow a sufficient time interval before retesting achievement (two years) necessitated a new choice of test, and in the secondary school a recently developed comprehension test (Lunzer and Gardner, 1977) was used. The age range of the Basic Mathematics Test DE (NFER, 1974) did allow it to be used on both occasions. In addition to measuring these achievement levels, change scores were also computed using procedures described in Chapter 12.

ATTITUDE TO SCHOOL

Inventories in this area tend to be unsuitable for use outside of the intended application. It was therefore decided that two inventories should be constructed to assess attitudes to school before and after transfer. Each inventory was subjected to oblique factor analysis (see Chapter 10) to produce subscales. The Prospective Attitude to Transfer inventory comprised 34 YES/NO questions forming three subscales measuring attitude to secondary school, attitude to primary school, and apprehension over transfer. The Retrospective Attitude to Transfer inventory (24 items rated on a four-point scale) formed three similar subscales except that the third was better interpreted as anxiety about school. Statistics for all these scales are given in Table 4.1.

Table 4.1   **Means, standard deviations, and reliabilities for the attitude, personality, and motivation scales**

	Scale	Items	Mean	Standard deviation	Reliability (alpha)	N
	PROSPECTIVE					
1	Attitude to secondary school	11	9.01	2.12	.75	641
2	Attitude to primary school	11	8.20	2.64	.81	641
3	Apprehension	12	6.36	3.01	.78	641
	RETROSPECTIVE					
4	Attitude to secondary school	10	29.36	4.45	.75	456
5	Attitude to primary school	5	12.08	3.07	.70	456
6	Anxiety	9	21.76	4.35	.75	456
	SELF-CONCEPT					
7	Self-concept social	6	7.40	2.46	.65	641
8	Self-concept personal	7	10.30	2.72	.62	641
9	Self-concept academic	6	6.50	2.33	.57	641
10	Academic motivation	24	15.78	3.73	.72	456

Internal consistency reliabilities are measured by Cronbach's Alpha (see Chapter 11). The obtained figures ranging from .70 to .81 are perfectly acceptable.

PERSONAL ADJUSTMENT

The two areas of adjustment deemed important were motivation and self-concept. For the former Entwistle's Academic Motivation Inventory (Entwistle, 1968) was used. This is a 24-item scale with demonstrated reliability and validity over the relevant age-range (Nisbet and Entwistle, 1969). Self-concept raised more awkward problems and again the unsatisfactory nature of existing scales prompted the construction of a new inventory. It comprised 19 items (e.g., 'other children pick on me') each one rated under one of three headings: YES, SOMETIMES, NO. Once more oblique analysis resulted in three identifiable scales, self-concept social, personal, and academic. Reliabilities for scales of an introspective nature do tend to be lower than those for object-directed scales and therefore the obtained values of around .6 are acceptable for use as part of a battery.

    The contents of the unpublished scales are given in appendices to this chapter.

Appendix 4.1   Prospective Attitude to Transfer Scale

This questionnaire is to find out what you think
about your present school and about the new school
you will be going to next September.
READ EACH SENTENCE CAREFULLY.
Put a circle round 'YES' if you agree with the sentence.
SCALE   Put a circle round 'NO' if you do not agree with it.

SCALE	No.	Statement		
3	1	I am worried about going to a new school	YES	NO
2	2	This school is great	YES	NO
2	3	My teachers are interested in me	YES	NO
1	4	I shall be happier when I am at the new school	YES	NO
3	5	I am worried about the subjects I have not done before	YES	NO
3	6	Work at the new school will be too hard for me	YES	NO
1	7	My new school will be great	YES	NO
1	8	I am looking forward to the new school	YES	NO
1-	9	The new school is far too big	YES	NO
1	10	I think a different teacher for each subject is a good idea	YES	NO
1	11	I am looking forward to joining some clubs at the new school	YES	NO
1-	12	The new school will be boring	YES	NO
1	13	The new school will be all right	YES	NO
2	14	School is all right	YES	NO
3	15	I am worried about losing things in the new school	YES	NO
2	16	Teachers are nice to me most of the time	YES	NO
3	17	I am scared to ask teachers for help if I do not understand	YES	NO
2-	18	Teachers at the new school will be nicer than they are here	YES	NO
3	19	I am scared of being bullied by the older children at the new school	YES	NO
3	20	I shall be scared among so many children I do not know	YES	NO
3	21	Tests and exams will make me nervous	YES	NO
1-	22	I will hate the new school	YES	NO
1	23	Teachers at the new school will be all right	YES	NO
3	24	I am afraid of getting lost in the new school	YES	NO
2-	25	I dislike teachers	YES	NO
3	26	I think there is a lot of bullying in the new school	YES	NO
3	27	They have lots of tests and exams in the new school	YES	NO
2-	28	This school is too small	YES	NO
2-	29	I hate this school	YES	NO
3	30	I get worried about school work	YES	NO
2	31	This school is the right size	YES	NO
1-	32	I shall dislike the teachers at the new school	YES	NO
2-	33	This school is boring	YES	NO
2	34	I like this school	YES	NO

SCALE 1:   Attitude to Secondary School
SCALE 2:   Attitude to Primary School
SCALE 3:   Apprehension

 - indicates items to be reversed for scale scoring.

Appendix 4.2 Retrospective Attitude to Transfer Scale

This questionnaire is to find out what you think about school.
There are no right or wrong answers and your teacher will not
see what you put.
READ EACH SENTENCE CAREFULLY.
You will see that there are 4 columns on the right.
IF YOU DEFINITELY AGREE WITH THE SENTENCE, tick column 1.
IF YOU MOSTLY AGREE - tick the second column.
IF YOU DON'T REALLY AGREE - tick the third column.
IF YOU CERTAINLY DON'T AGREE WITH THE SENTENCE - tick column 4.

SCALE			STRONGLY AGREE	AGREE	DISAGREE	STRONGLY DISAGREE
2	1	I wish I was still at junior school				
1	2	I enjoy doing homework				
1-	3	This school is boring				
3	4	I am scared of being bullied by the older children				
2-	5	My junior school wasn't very good				
3	6	I get worried about school work				
1	7	I think wearing school uniform is good				
3	8	I am worried about losing things				
1	9	The teachers here are interested in me				
1	10	This school is great				
3	11	I am scared among so many children I do not know				
2	12	The teachers at my junior school were nicer than the teachers here				
3	13	I am scared to ask the teacher for help if there is something I do not understand				
1-	14	The teachers are always picking on me				
2-	15	I am glad to have left the junior school				
1	16	The teachers here are all right				
2	17	I miss having one teacher all the time				
3	18	I think there is a lot of bullying at this school				
3	19	I worry about exams and tests				
1-	20	I hate this school				
3	21	The new subjects are worrying me				
1	22	Lessons at this school are really interesting				
3	23	I am worried about having things stolen				
1-	24	I wish I had gone to a different school				

SCALE 1 : Attitude to Secondary School
SCALE 2 : Nostalgia for Primary School
SCALE 3 : Anxiety over school

Minus (-) indicates items to be reversed for scale scoring

Appendix 4.3 Self-concept in school

READ THESE QUESTIONS CAREFULLY.
Answer them as honestly as you can by putting a tick in the column you agree with.

SCALE   YES   SOMETIMES   NO

SCALE			YES	SOMETIMES	NO
3-	1.	I forget how to do things after we've been told			
2-	2.	It's no use relying on me			
1	3.	I find it easy to get on with other children in the class			
1	4.	Other children like playing with me			
2-	5.	I don't understand what I am supposed to do in class			
1	6.	I am popular			
1	7.	I have lots of friends in the class			
2-	8.	People are disappointed with me			
3-	9.	I wish teachers would explain things better			
1	10.	Other children like working with me			
2-	11.	It's hard to be me			
3	12.	I can generally work things out for myself			
1	13.	Other children often choose me as their leader			
2-	14.	I have hardly any friends in the class			
3	15.	I am good at most things			
3	16.	School work is easy			
2-	17.	Other children don't seem to take much notice of me			
3	18.	The teacher thinks I'm good at school work			
2-	19.	Other children pick on me			

SCALE 1 Self-concept : Social
SCALE 2 Self-concept : Personal
SCALE 3 Self-concept : Academic

Minus (-) indicates items to be reversed in scale scoring

References

Entwistle N. J. (1968) 'Academic motivation and school attainment', *Brit. J. Educ. Psychol.*, **38**, 181–188.

Kaiser, H. F. and J. Rice (1974) 'Little Jiffy Mark IV', *Educ. and Psychol. Meas.*, **34**, 111–117.

Lunzer, E. A. and W. K. Gardner (1977) *The Effective Use of Reading*, London, Schools Council.

McLeod, J. (1970) *Manual: Gap Reading Comprehension Test*, London, Heinemann.

National Foundation for Educational Research (1974) *Basic Mathematics Test DE*, Number 248, London, Ginn.

Nisbet, J. D. and N. J. Entwistle (1969) *The Transition to Secondary Education*, London, University of London Press.

Pidgeon, D. A. (1965) *Non-verbal Test BD*, London, Ginn.

Part 2
Analytical
procedures

5. Initial Descriptions of the Data

There is no doubt that far too little inspection of data occurs before the more substantial analyses are embarked upon. Admittedly tables and charts of scores are not especially revealing. What they do provide is an insurance against making unwarranted and even rash statements later on. In the first instance carrying out the data checking procedures outlined earlier (Section 2.5) should guarantee that results are at least correct. More importantly, information on distributions is essential for the valid interpretation of most multivariate analyses. Since the effort required to generate distribution plots and simple descriptive statistics is so little there can be no excuse for failing to obtain these preliminary descriptions of the dataset.

5.1 Frequency tables and charts

The raw frequency tabulations identify the codes actually occurring and at the same time they enable the distributions of these codes to be seen. A variety of other distribution statistics may also be given depending on the program used. Most data tabulation programs give overall percentage responses together with means, standard deviations, and sigmas. Table 5.1 presents a typical frequency tabulation output for a selection of the transfer data measures. The plotted asterisks show the shape of the distributions.

The distribution information for age clearly emphasizes the need to discover the *actual* occurrence of codes rather than the theoretical possibility. Since the sample was taken from one year group, in theory twelve age codes should appear. The presence of the three codes 23, 27, and 28 at the lower end of the range indicates that some under-age children feature in the sample. This could affect standardization procedures as well as disturbing the shape of the main distribution. As one would expect approximately equal frequencies occur for the remaining age codes producing a uniform distribution. A further benefit in knowing actual incidences of codes is seen in the two primary school attitude measures. Both record a zero score and, therefore, care needs to be taken over the treatment of missing data, particularly if these two measures are to be analysed with social class for which missing values were coded zero.

In social research many variables tend to be normally distributed even if only in a highly distorted manner. The two attitudes to secondary school measures, one prospective the other retrospective, are particularly interesting in demonstrating the very common phenomenon of *curtailment*. The primary school scale was incapable of discrimination at the top end with the result that 56 per cent of the sample obtain the maximum score or one less. At the secondary school level this drawback was overcome by allowing greater variation in responses; a four-point scale was used rather than a simple YES/NO answer. Consequently, the curtailment effects disappear although the distribution

Table 5.1 Frequency distributions for a selection of the demonstration dataset measures

CODE	N	%	C%	
				Variable 3 (15 codes) OVERALL TOTAL = 454 AGE IN MONTHS MINUS 100

CODE	N	%	C%	
23	1	0	0	*
27	1	0	0	*
28	3	1	1	***
30	30	7	8	*****************************
31	39	9	16	************************************
32	30	7	23	*****************************
33	51	11	34	**
34	34	7	42	*********************************
35	46	10	52	***
36	30	7	58	*****************************
37	43	9	68	***
38	36	8	76	***********************************
39	45	10	86	**
40	34	7	93	*********************************
41	31	7	100	******************************

MEAN		35.412
STANDARD DEVIATION		3.440
SIGMA		3.447

Variable 6 (12 codes) PRIMARY ATTITUDE TO SECONDARY SCHOOL

CODE	N	%	C%	
0	1	0	0	*
1	2	0	1	**
2	5	1	2	*****
3	10	2	4	*********
4	10	2	6	*********
5	12	3	9	***********
6	19	4	13	******************
7	35	8	21	**********************************
8	48	11	31	***
9	60	13	44	**
10	134	30	74	**
11	118	26	100	***

MEAN		8.949
STANDARD DEVIATION		2.211
SIGMA		2.216

Variable 8 (13 codes) PRIMARY APPREHENSION OVER TRANSFER

CODE	N	%	C%	
0	3	1	1	***
1	15	3	4	**************
2	33	7	11	*******************************
3	43	9	21	**
4	31	7	28	*****************************
5	60	13	41	***
6	56	12	53	***
7	46	10	63	***
8	34	7	71	*********************************
9	46	10	81	***
10	41	9	90	**
11	30	7	96	****************************
12	16	4	100	***************

MEAN		6.410
STANDARD DEVIATION		2.655
SIGMA		2.661

Table 5.1 (continued)

CODE	N	%	C%	

Variable 13 (25 codes) SECONDARY ATTITUDE TO SECONDARY SCHOOL

12	1	0	0	*
16	2	0	1	**
17	2	0	1	**
18	4	1	2	****
19	4	1	3	****
20	7	2	4	*******
21	5	1	6	*****
22	6	1	7	******
23	5	1	8	*****
24	20	4	12	********************
25	23	5	17	***********************
26	40	9	26	*****************************
27	29	6	33	******************************
28	31	7	39	**********************************
29	49	11	50	***
30	39	9	59	***************************************
31	29	6	65	*****************************
32	39	9	74	***************************************
33	29	6	80	*****************************
34	32	7	87	********************************
35	29	6	94	*****************************
36	15	3	97	***************
37	8	2	99	******** MEAN 29.355
38	5	1	100	***** STANDARD DEVIATION 4.463
39	1	0	100	* SIGMA 4.473

Variable 15 (26 codes) SECONDARY ANXIETY

10	2	0	0	**
11	1	0	1	*
12	4	1	2	****
13	7	2	3	*******
14	7	2	5	*******
15	8	2	6	********
16	15	3	10	***************
17	34	7	17	**********************************
18	30	7	24	******************************
19	36	8	32	************************************
20	29	6	38	*****************************
21	47	10	48	***
22	40	9	57	**
23	44	10	67	**
24	32	7	74	********************************
25	29	6	80	*****************************
26	31	7	87	*******************************
27	16	4	91	****************
28	14	3	94	**************
29	8	2	96	********
30	10	2	98	**********
31	1	0	98	*
32	3	1	99	*** MEAN 21.744
33	4	1	100	**** STANDARD DEVIATION 4.349
34	1	0	100	* SIGMA 4.358
35	1	0	100	*

Note: frequency charts are curtailed at 50.

remains biased towards the high scorer (that is, negatively skewed—see Section 5.3). The apprehension and anxiety scales, variables 8 and 15, are more symmetrically distributed, suffering less from both curtailment and skewness.

The format of Table 5.1 is essentially that of the computer printout although generally computer output is not suitable for presenting the results of analyses. Both of the standardized tests, non-verbal reasoning and mathematics, record over 50 codes making some form of combination necessary to help inspection and analysis. The actual method of combination used needs careful thought to ensure that the categories produced make sense. With continuous scales such as these there is little difficulty since the range can easily be split into intervals. Where the codes represent nominal data only related categories can validly be put together. Once the combined frequencies have been

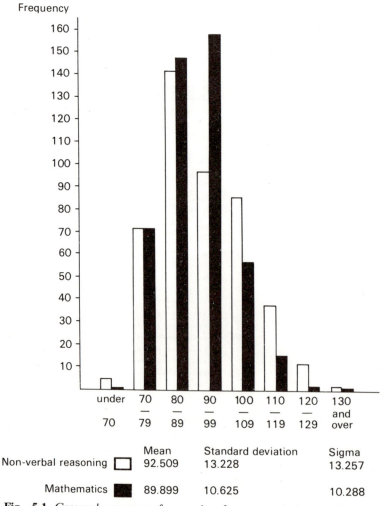

	Mean	Standard deviation	Sigma
Non-verbal reasoning ☐	92.509	13.228	13.257
Mathematics ■	89.899	10.625	10.288

Fig. 5.1 *Grouped response frequencies for non-verbal reasoning and mathematics.*

produced the results can be displayed in a variety of forms. Most introductory statistics texts cover these methods in detail although histograms and frequency polygons are probably the most popular. Figure 5.1 shows one possible approach plotting two scores together so that any differences can be seen. Since both measures are standardized to the same mean and similar standard deviations they are comparable. The histogram does suggest that non-verbal reasoning records a lower level of performance and shows greater spread.

5.2 Measures of tendency

Visual inspection reveals many of a variable's characteristics but certain summary statistics are needed to enable more general observations to be made. Percentages, for example, facilitate comparisons of unequal-sized groups by relating frequencies to a fixed number, 100. For fixed groups, as in the distributions of Table 5.1, percentages add little to the raw frequencies until cross-tabulations are required (see Section 6.2). Cumulative percentages, however, can be helpful particularly in the derivation of other measures such as the median. This is one of a number of measures of location giving the position of the sample distribution along the variable continuum.

The *median* is that code or score with 50 per cent of the responses on either side. It tends to be used to summarize a distribution where analyses based on ranking are applied. The *mean*, or more correctly the arithmetic mean, is obtained by summing a set of scores and then dividing by the number of values. It indicates the overall level of scoring but need not itself appear as a recorded score. The third commonly used summary statistic is the *mode*, the most frequently occurring code or value. Unlike the median and the mean, the mode cannot be considered a measure of central tendency. Many distributions can be sufficiently irregular or non-normal for the mode to occur at any point on the recorded range. On the other hand, the mode does possess the advantage not necessarily held by the other two measures of always being an authentic code.

The distributions in Table 5.1 only give the mean scores but the median and mode are easily calculated; for age, 42 per cent of the cases record 34 or less, 52 per cent 35 or less, and therefore the median must be 35 or 135 months. This corresponds almost exactly with the mean of 35.4. The mode, the commonest code, is 33. Since the uniform distribution implies that the mode could have occurred anywhere from 30 to 41, it is obvious why the mode cannot necessarily be used as an average measure. For variable 6, primary attitude to secondary school, the mean, median, and mode are 8.95, 10, and 10 respectively. Here the median and the mode agree, but differ markedly from the mean. Looking at the shape of the distribution reveals a pronounced bias towards the high scores. Skewed distributions of this kind will record median scores higher than the mean. Applications of the three measures depend on both the data and the intended analyses. Severest restrictions concern nominal data. Since no inherent order exists neither the median nor the mean can be used leaving the mode as the only statistic for summarizing response tendencies. If there is ordering but no valid assumption can be made regarding the intervals then the median is appropriate. Only when the steps between codes are equal is it legitimate to use the mean as a central measure. In practice, however, this assumption is made in many instances where its justification is dubious but its use convenient. With rating scales, for example, it is unlikely that the graduations are treated equally by respondents, but the mean score can often be used to plot group profiles. So long as an appropriate statistical analysis is employed eventually, at the descriptive stage all that is really required is that the summary statistic should be interpretable.

One important area of application for measures of tendency is in the treatment of missing data. Traditionally, the mean is used as a substitute particularly in certain multi-variate analyses. Where the observed scores are integer a drawback with the mean is the almost inevitable presence of a decimal value. If the substitution is to be made in existing coding the need to allow extra columns to accommodate the decimal part may be awkward or even impossible. The choice may then be between the median and the mode. Since the former can itself have a decimal part (rarely, though, with large samples) the mode could turn out to be the most satisfactory solution. If it is used, care must be taken to ensure that it is representative of response patterns, and not just a quirk of the coding.

5.3 Measures of spread and shape

Social research is probably more concerned with variations in features rather than levels of incidence. Almost all measures of variation assume a relationship between scores and it follows that these statistics must be based on data of at least ordinal association and preferably interval. Of the statistics available few are widely used. The most direct but also the least useful is the *range*, the difference between the highest and lowest scores. The *semi-interquartile range* is a modification of the range and can be helpful. The quartiles are those values with 25 per cent of the cases above or below them. So for secondary school anxiety, variable 15, the lower quartile is 19, and the upper one 25. The interquartile range is the difference between them, 6, and therefore, the semi-interquartile range is 3, half of that figure. Its interpretation derives directly from its definition; approximately 50 per cent of the sample will fall in one semi-interquartile range of the median. In the case of the anxiety measure the median is 22 and the range 19 to 25 inclusive contains 56 per cent of the sample

The two other commonly used measures of spread relate to the mean rather than the median. Both involve deviations from the mean $(x-\bar{x})$, the difference between each score x and the variable mean $\bar{x}$. Clearly this value can be positive or negative and if all the obtained values of $(x - \bar{x})$ are totalled the result is zero. This is not particularly helpful. One solution is to forget about the sign of the difference and total the *absolute* deviates $|x - \bar{x}|$. Averaging the sum of these deviations produces the *mean deviation*. It is the average amount by which the recorded values differ from the mean. An alternative approach to the problem of the direction of deviations results in the *standard deviation* the most commonly used measure of spread. It incorporates $(x - \bar{x})^2$ rather than the absolute value. It's computational formula:

$$s = \sqrt{\frac{1}{N} \Sigma (x - \bar{x})^2}$$ (5.1)

frequently causes confusion because the divisor N is sometimes replaced by $(N - 1)$. The explanation for this is that while Eq. (5.1) is perfectly adequate as a measure of dispersion for a *sample* often it is useful to be able to *estimate* an equivalent statistic for the *population* from which the sample was drawn. If Eq. (5.1) is used it tends to underestimate the population parameter, it is biased. On the other hand replacing N by $(N - 1)$ produces an estimate which can be high or low, but it is an *unbiased estimate*. In most statistical work it is preferable to work with the unbiased estimate often called sigma for identification purposes. As far as the analyst is concerned it can usually be assumed that any programmed method incorporates the appropriate form. Where standard deviations are output the program documentation should give their computational formula.

Since both the standard deviation and sigma are obtained by squaring and square-rooting differences it follows that they are in the *same units as the original scores*. It also follows that modifying each score by adding or subtracting a fixed value (taking 100 off the age in months, for example) leaves both statistics unchanged. Multiplying scores by a constant has the effect of multiplying the standard deviation or sigma by the same number. Any interpretation of the standard deviation tends to work from an assumed underlying normal distribution. Given that assumption it is possible to predict the proportions of a sample expected to lie within certain standard deviation multiples of the mean:

$$\bar{x} \pm 0.5 \quad S \text{ contains } 38.3\%$$
$$\bar{x} \pm 0.67 \, S \text{ contains } 49.7\%$$
$$\bar{x} \pm 1 \quad\; S \text{ contains } 68.3\%$$
$$\bar{x} \pm 1.96 \, S \text{ contains } 95.0\%$$
$$\bar{x} \pm 2 \quad\; S \text{ contains } 95.4\%$$
$$\bar{x} \pm 2.24 \, S \text{ contains } 97.5\%$$
$$\bar{x} \pm 3 \quad\; S \text{ contains } 99.7\%$$

The first estimate provides a particularly simple way of splitting a range so that approximately one-third of the sample falls in each section; the second gives a quick method for producing one-quarter splits.

Taking one standard deviation either side of the mean for the secondary anxiety measure, variable 15, produces a range from 17.39 to 26.09. From Table 5.1 70 per cent fall within the limits 18 to 26 inclusive which matches very closely the 68 per cent estimate. Applying the same procedure to variable 6, primary attitude, produces a range from 6.74 to 11.16. Notice that here the upper limit exceeds the variable maximum. This is not an error; the phenomenon frequently occurs with skewed distributions. Should the distributions be skewed in the opposite direction towards the low values, it then becomes possible for the standard deviation to be greater than the mean. There is no general rule relating the mean and standard deviation although it is rare for the mean to be the smaller. The extreme skewness of variable 6 also results in a quite different proportion of the sample within one standard deviation of the mean, 87 per cent falling in the range.

The evidence from the charts and statistics of Table 5.1. does suggest that measures of tendency and spread may in some instances give a rather misleading guide to the nature of a distribution. Where distributions are approximately normal their *shape* can be defined in terms of two further measures, *skewness* and *kurtosis*. As its name implies the first gives an indication of the degree to which the scores predominate at one end of

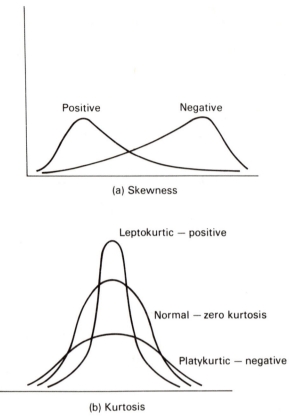

Fig. 5.2 *Diagrammatic representation of skewness and kurtosis.*

the scale. A *positive skew* value arises when a distribution tails off towards the positive direction; that is the scores pile up towards the low end of the scale. *Negative* skew is defined conversely. Figure 5.2(a) shows these features diagrammatically.

Kurtosis measures the peakedness of a distribution and is related to the standard deviation. It differs in that its computation also involves fourth powers of the deviations from the mean as well as squares, thereby exaggerating the influence of extreme scores. *Positive* kurtosis (also called leptokurtic) indicates a more peaked distribution than the normal curve; a *negative value* (platykurtic) implies a flattened distribution. A normal distribution has zero kurtosis. Figure 5.2(b) demonstrates these possibilities.

One final point on the shape of distributions concerns the rare but awkward characteristic of *bimodality*. Most distributions, no matter how distorted, do tend to produce one hump. Unfortunately, on occasions, two or even more humps can appear. These make most of the summary statistics such as the mean and standard deviation very difficult to interpret. Attitude scales are probably the worst culprits. Figure 5.3 records response statistics for one of the MYJOB semantic differentials used in the engineering research described in Chapter 10. Clearly the mode is at scale point 6 but a second local mode occurs at point 4. This probably stems from some respondents using the middle

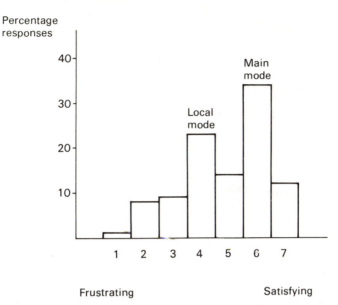

Fig. 5.3 *Bimodal response of a semantic differential.*

point of the scale to indicate indecision or because they felt that both ends of the differential applied equally. Nevertheless a blind application of statistics might lead one to accept the mean value of 4.90 as indicative of dissatisfaction. A more reasonable interpretation would be that most register satisfaction but that some find the scale ambivalent. The effect is quite mild in Fig. 5.3. More extreme bimodality would preclude the use of that measure in any analysis that assumed normality. Factor analysis and regression analysis can be invalidated by the inclusion of such variables. The remarkable but comforting aspect of analysing distributions is that although the repertoire of statistical parameters may seem confusing, in practice a great deal of insight can be achieved simply by plotting responses as shown in Table 5.1. Appropriate summary statistics can then be obtained to corroborate impressions gained from the frequency charts or to enable any more probing analyses to be performed later.

				V	
			O	E	C
			S	L	O
PROGRAM AVAILABILITY	P	S	B	I	D	O
	M	P	M	R	M	L
see Section 3.6	M	S	D	I	A	E
	D	S	P	S	N	Y
frequency tables and charts	P	S	B	O	V	
median, mode	P	S	B	O		
mean, standard deviation	P	S	B	O	V	C

6. Relationships Between Pairs of Measures

The isolation of patterns in data is probably the first stage at which computer analysis becomes almost essential. Only with the smallest of samples or a minimal number of relationships to study is it convenient to use hand computation. Regrettably this switch can tend to induce a rather violent effect on subsequent tactics. Too often the whole range of multivariate analysis is immediately applied without developing any analytical rationale. The preferable approach is to examine pairwise relationships first, not only as a prelude to some more extensive form of analysis, but because many of these direct relationships can be interesting in their own right. Simplifying even further, it does not follow that the only valid methods for investigating patterns are statistical. As with the initial inspection of data so here visual displays serve a valuable function in alerting the analyst to spurious effects or unusual distributions. A recommended procedure would be to produce simple scatter plots initially, to obtain cross-tabulations as summaries of these plots, and only then to analyse these relationships by means of such statistics as chi-square or a correlation coefficient.

6.1 Scatter plots

Most statistics texts do emphasize the need to study the distributions of individual variables but the same importance is not accorded to scatter diagrams. A prominent exception is McCall (1975) who lucidly demonstrates the effects of various features of scatter on correlation coefficients. The situations causing severe distortion of this statistic are by no means rare and anyone not aware of the dangers would be well advised to read McCall's account.

Nevertheless it would be imprudent to overemphasize the value of scatter plots. Many types of data are not amenable to plotting, notably those with very few categories or nominal data. Where the method can be used the procedure is straightforward. Programs available tend to use line-printer plotting methods which may not be sufficiently discriminating to produce clear plots with large samples. With most of these programs the page size limitation of around 50 intervals on each axis almost invariably results in repeated points for samples of more than 200 cases. While this may make the printed output unsuitable for publication as it stands, the detail usually remains acceptable for data analytic purposes. Figure 6.1 shows a typical plot involving two closely related measures, mathematics achievement and non-verbal reasoning. The clear tendency for high mathematics scores (horizontal axis) to be associated with high non-verbal reasoning scores is reflected in the high correlation coefficient of .70 (see Section 6.3). The

Fig. 6.1 *Scatter plot for mathematics and non-verbal reasoning.*

agreement between the visual impression and the quantification of the relationship is so high as to be indisputable. If further information on the relationship is needed a third variable can be introduced by labelling the points. In Fig. 6.1 pairs of scores are plotted as letters rather than points with A, B, and C identifying the three secondary schools. An equals (=) sign indicates that more than one person is located at that point making unique labelling impossible. The introduction of this third variable enables any variations in the overall relationships to be spotted should they exist. In this case there is no reason

63

to expect differences between the schools and indeed the A, B, and C labels are distributed almost uniformly, as far as can be seen.

The benefits of scatter plots are most pronounced when the patterns depicted are not so obvious as in Fig. 6.1. In Fig. 6.2 there does not appear to be any marked degree of association between the apprehension scores, vertically, and mathematics. Yet the correlation coefficient is -0.227 and is highly significant. In retrospect, knowing this correlation figure it is possible to distinguish a slight negative trend since the highest

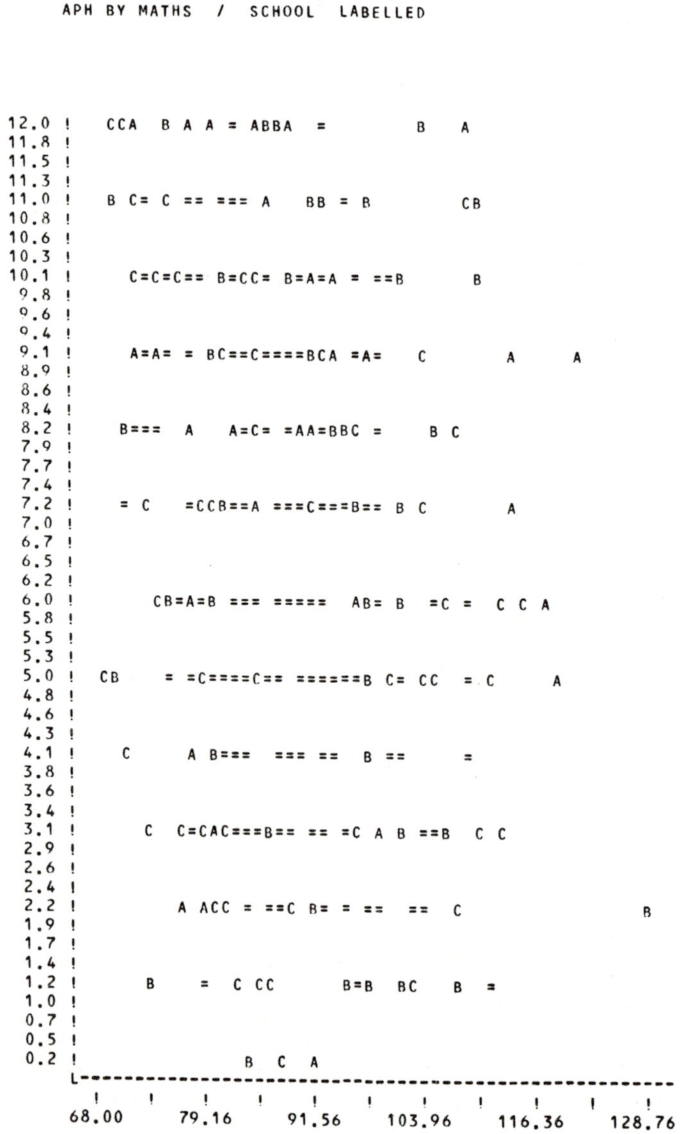

```
                    APH  BY  MATHS   /   SCHOOL   LABELLED



      12.0 !   CCA   B A A = ABBA   =            B    A
      11.8 !
      11.5 !
      11.3 !
      11.0 !   B C= C  ==  === A    BB = B            CB
      10.8 !
      10.6 !
      10.3 !
      10.1 !    C=C=C== B=CC= B=A=A = ==B         B
       9.8 !
       9.6 !
       9.4 !
       9.1 !    A=A= =  BC==C====BCA =A=   C         A      A
       8.9 !
       8.6 !
       8.4 !
       8.2 !   B===   A    A=C= =AA=BBC =     B C
       7.9 !
       7.7 !
       7.4 !
       7.2 !   = C    =CCB==A ===C===B== B C         A
       7.0 !
       6.7 !
       6.5 !
       6.2 !
       6.0 !       CB=A=B === ===== AB= B  =C = C C A
       5.8 !
       5.5 !
       5.3 !
       5.0 !  CB    = =C====C== ======B C= CC  = C      A
       4.8 !
       4.6 !
       4.3 !
       4.1 !   C     A B=== === == B ==     =
       3.8 !
       3.6 !
       3.4 !
       3.1 !    C  C=CAC===B== == =C A B ==B  C C
       2.9 !
       2.6 !
       2.4 !
       2.2 !      A ACC = ==C B= = ==  ==  C              B
       1.9 !
       1.7 !
       1.4 !
       1.2 !   B    = C CC     B=B  BC   B  =
       1.0 !
       0.7 !
       0.5 !
       0.2 !--------------B-C--A-----------------------------------------
          L--------------------------------------------------------------
            !    !    !    !    !    !    !    !    !    !    !    !    !
          68.00     79.16     91.56     103.96     116.36     128.76
```

Fig. 6.2 *Scatter plot for mathematics and apprehension.*

apprehension scores do correspond with the lowest mathematics scores. On the other hand, one feature of the plot that recalls some of McCall's warnings is the presence of the *outlier* labelled B in the bottom right hand section. Is it possible that the correlation has been inflated because of this extreme point? Recomputing the correlation coefficient *without* the outlier reduces the value to -0.218. This is indeed slightly smaller than the original value but not enough to affect the significance because of the large sample size.

Many multivariate methods do demand linearity in the measures used and by far the simplest way to check this requirement is to obtain scatter plots. Any deviations from linearity are readily seen; if necessary the degree of divergence can be assessed using an appropriate statistic. One severe limitation with this tactic is that a large number of measures generates a disproportionately large number of plots. The actual number is given by $M \times (M - 1)/2$ where M is the number of variables. In such circumstances a little judicious selection is called for. Where popular measures are used the relationships may already be known making it only necessary to examine the novel or constructed variables. As a last resort it *may* be sufficient to wait until the multivariate analysis has been performed before specific plots are obtained. Without doubt the general rule is to be wise before the event, not after it.

6.2 Cross-tabulations

In their most basic form cross-tabulations of pairs of measures (also called contingency tables) are very similar to scatter plots, the main difference being their rather condensed format. The advantages arise when the number of categories is small, or is reduced by means of combinations. The resulting summaries of the joint distributions can then demonstrate tendencies which may not be obvious from scatter plots. Rather more important, though, is the fact that tabulated relationships can readily be subjected to statistical analysis to test the significance of a pattern. Moreover, many researches, particularly questionnaire surveys, are analysed solely by means of cross-tabulations followed by significance testing of those tables. Chapter 10 deals specifically with the analysis of questionnaires and many of the points discussed there may apply to other situations requiring cross-tabulations. The present section will consider only the more general procedures summarized in the following list.

Selecting the variables to cross-tabulate.
Specifying the row variable.
Number of categories to use.
Selecting cell contents.
Treatment of missing data.
Combining categories.
Ordering of categories.
Recoding categories.
Three-way tabulations.
Significance testing.

SELECTING VARIABLES TO CROSS-TABULATE

Since the number of possible tables is the same as the maximum number of scatter plots $(M \times (M - 1)/2)$ some selection is usually necessary. The initial frequency tabulations will highlight certain measures worthy of further study. Most category data are suited to tabulations; nominal data can only be tabulated. At the other extreme continuous measures with many values (for example the achievement scores) cannot usefully be tabulated unless score categories are combined. Bearing all these considerations in mind should reduce the required number of tables to a manageable size, an essential limitation given the relatively high cost of computing contingency tables.

SPECIFYING THE ROW VARIABLE

Frequently, research reports present a number of tables together and comparison is much easier if related tables have the same measure in the rows each time. Mostly, there are important reference variables such as sex, school or social class and they become natural candidates for row variables. Where no such priority exists the principle of parsimony says that measures with fewest categories occupy the rows—this makes the tables more compact.

NUMBER OF CATEGORIES TO USE

Tables with more than about six or seven rows or columns tend to produce such small and fluctuating cell frequencies that interpretation can be very difficult. Either do not cross-tabulate measures with a large number of categories or else reduce the table size by combining categories *in a logically consistent manner*.

CELL CONTENTS

It will always be necessary to obtain actual cell frequencies for each table, but in addition it may be useful to present these as some form of percentage. This is particularly true if the row or column totals differ so much as to make comparisons awkward. Assuming that the main variables have been allocated to the rows it follows that the most relevant choice is to have each cell defined as a percentage of the row total. Other possibilities are percentages of the column totals, of the table total, or even of some other total such as a larger sample of which the tabulated set is only a subsample. This latter choice would be appropriate in three-way tabulations.

TREATMENT OF MISSING DATA

Only when percentages are calculated or when some significance test is requested does the presence of missing data matter in cross-tabulations. In most instances these calculations should be performed *excluding* cases with missing or otherwise irrelevant responses. Of the program facilities available for this, probably the simplest and commonest is the one whereby it is possible to exclude specified codes, often by recoding them as zero.

If missing data have originally been coded zero the process is automatic. If not, it is usually possible to employ a recoding facility to allocate the zero code to those categories which need excluding, and at the same time to modify any authentic zero scores so that they are kept in.

COMBINING CATEGORIES

It should never be assumed that the original coding system is inviolate; many situations benefit from some form of coding modification usually resulting in fewer categories. The presence of a large number of categories may preserve detail but it will almost certainly result in very low frequencies for some categories. Usually, these can be profitably combined with *logically similar* categories to clarify a table, and to facilitate significance testing. Continuous measures with a wide range (intelligence, for example) are better partitioned into four or five—roughly equal—frequency steps if cross-tabulation is to be performed. Again most tabulation programs offer a recoding facility that enables combinations to be done automatically once the specifications have been defined.

ORDERING OF CATEGORIES

If there is a logical order in a set of responses this order should be maintained in the coding since it may be possible to test the significance of such a relationship. Even though the product-moment correlation coefficient may not be appropriate other statistics are available for ordered data.

RECODING CATEGORIES

Some situations requiring recoding have already been mentioned. Certainly with questionnaires some modification must be expected. Chapter 10 explains these procedures. Partitioning or dichotomizing are other possibilities.

THREE-WAY TABULATIONS

A natural extension of simple two-way tables is to look at relationships in terms of a third variable. Thus it might be useful to examine the association between apprehension and intelligence for boys and girls separately. This could be achieved by specifying a standard table relating apprehension and intelligence, but adding the further qualification that only boys or girls are to be included. Clearly, since sex records two codes, two tables would be needed. Because of the proliferation of tables three-way tabulation inevitably causes it should be restricted to measures with very few categories. Occasionally, a definite need may compel an application of the technique to more elaborate variables.

SIGNIFICANCE TESTING

The culmination of cross-tabulation is usually some form of significance test on the table structure. The conditioned reflex is to use chi-square analysis. Although the method does apply validly to the majority of tables it may be that some other measure of association such as Fisher's exact probability test, Kendall's S-method or even one of the many correlation coefficients may be more appropriate. Choice of a suitable technique depends on the precise aim of the test as well as the nature of the data constituting the table. Section 6.3 looks at a selection of measures of correlation, some of which can be used with contingency tables.

EXAMPLE

Certain of these considerations can be readily demonstrated using the transfer test data. Others are treated in more detail in Chapter 10. The social class measure provides a useful example since it records missing responses and it also has an irregular distribution. The overall response frequencies can be seen in the row totals of Table 6.1(a). Almost 200

Table 6.1   Cross-tabulation of social class and apprehension

(a)   **Frequencies in cells**

							Apprehension score								
		0	1	2	3	4	5	6	7	8	9	10	11	12	TOTALS
Social class code	0	0	11	11	17	12	28	23	26	17	18	14	14	7	198
	1	0	2	2	4	2	3	1	3	0	0	1	0	0	18
	2	1	0	2	7	3	5	10	3	1	6	8	0	0	46
	3	2	2	15	14	12	20	19	10	13	18	12	13	8	158
	4	0	0	3	1	2	4	3	4	3	4	6	2	1	33
	5	0	0	0	0	0	0	0	0	0	0	1	0	0	1
TOTALS		3	15	33	43	31	60	56	46	34	46	41	30	16	454

(b)   **Percentages of each row in cells**

							Apprehension score								
		0	1	2	3	4	5	6	7	8	9	10	11	12	TOTALS
Social class code	0	0	6	6	9	6	14	12	13	9	9	7	7	4	198
	1	0	11	11	22	11	17	6	17	0	0	6	0	0	18
	2	2	0	4	15	7	11	22	7	2	13	17	0	0	46
	3	1	1	9	9	8	13	12	6	8	11	8	8	5	158
	4	0	0	9	3	6	12	9	12	9	12	18	6	3	33
	5	0	0	0	0	0	0	0	0	0	0	100	0	0	1
TOTALS		3	15	33	43	31	60	56	46	34	46	41	30	16	454

codes are missing while at the other extreme only one code 5 occurs. In cross-tabulating against apprehension the large number of categories for apprehension makes interpretation difficult even using row percentages (Table 6.1b).

The most sensible modification to the social class coding is to eliminate the zero codes and to subsume the isolated code 5 into code 4. Little detail is lost, the recoding simply redefines the last code as manual, and a suitably small number of codes results. The rather low frequency of 18 for code 1 may cause problems later in chi-square testing, particularly if too many codes are kept for the column variable in the table. This suggests that it may be better to split apprehension into three new codes rather than four. Referring to its distribution given earlier in Table 5.1 three roughly equal partitions arise if the splits are made after scores of 4 and 7. Thus scores 1–4 need to be recoded as new code 1, 5–7 as 2, and 8–12 as 3. Table 6.2 presents the same data as Table 6.1, but using the recoded scoring rather than the original. It now becomes clear that the relationship between social class and apprehension over transfer is by no means random. Even without significance testing there are plainly differences in the apprehension scores recorded by the four social class categories. Closer inspection suggests that the pattern might even be progressive since category 1 has only one high score yet category 4/5 registers half of its scores at the highest apprehension level. Given that the coding for *both* variables is ordered, this hypothesis can be tested later when various measures of association are discussed. The present need is to demonstrate the clarification gained from careful recoding of the tabulated measures. More detailed examination of the effect of recoding and an example of the use of three-way tabulations appear in Chapter 10.

6.3 Measures of association

A common misunderstanding in statistics is that contingency tables are analysed by chi-square leaving the various correlation coefficients for use with columns of paired scores. In fact, the two methods of presentation are equivalent, contingency tables are simply handy summaries, particularly when few codes are involved. The important considerations in applying any of the many measures of association are data type and the hypothesis under test. The point about the research hypothesis is that what looks at first

Table 6.2 Cross-tabulation of recoded social class and apprehension

Chi-square significances are for individual rows (row 1 only, $P<.01$ **) and for the overall table ($P <.05$ *).

			Apprehension score				
			0–4 1	5–7 2	8–12 3	TOTALS	CHI-SQUARES
Social	1	1	10	7	1	18	9.56 **
class	2	2	13	18	15	46	0.83
code	3	3	45	49	64	158	0.52
	4/5	4	6	11	17	34	2.81
TOTALS			74	85	97	256	13.73 *

Table 6.3 Tests of association for different levels of measurement

Nominal data	Ordered data	Continuous data
Fisher's exact	phi	phi
McNemar's test	Kendall's S	product-moment correlation
chi-square	Kendall's tau	
contingency coefficient	Spearman's rho	
Cramer's V		

to be a situation needing a test of association may be more appropriately analysed by some form of difference test. So a cross-tabulation of school against level of apprehension could be tested for association by chi-square, but a more valid approach would be to apply one-way analysis of variance to test for variations between the schools.

INDEPENDENCE

Frequent mention is made of the need for samples in certain analyses to be independent. This might seem a contradictory requirement in a test of association and indeed it does *not* infer that the two attributes cannot be correlated. Rather one of the measures should not directly affect the other otherwise there is no point in testing an association. The commonest instance introducing dependence is a test–retest or before and after analysis. Most likely situations of this kind require a difference test anyway. Less obvious examples occur when a response to one of the measures to some degree predetermines responses to the other, either by restricting choice or through some implicit connection.

It is a mistake, however, to assume that responses to two items on an inventory cannot be tested for association using chi-square because they seem psychologically related. The whole point in applying a chi-square test to the resulting 2×2 contingency table would be to confirm this apparent association. One rule of thumb that does hold is that if individuals appear twice in a table, then the table is not independent. Except for the special test–retest designs mentioned above, most researches involve independent samples. An outline of the tests available follows. More detailed consideration is given in many statistics texts, especially Siegel (1956).

Most methods can be used with data of a higher level of measurement (i.e. to the right) but it may not be advisable to do so since information can be lost. For example, Kendall's S-method tests whether a progressive relationship exists in an ordered table; to use chi-square would preclude statements about order.

NOMINAL DATA

The absence of ordering in data restricts the choice of association measure largely to *chi-square* or one of its derivatives. Chi-square is a measure of the amount of deviation from random expectation in a table. Should the obtained value be sufficiently high for the null hypothesis to be rejected it would follow that the data exhibited tendencies for certain joint responses to predominate. The *size* of chi-square cannot be interpreted as an indication of the degree of association, only that a relationship exists. Should it be necessary to assess the strength of association, for example in comparing two tables, the *contingency coefficient C*, or Cramer's *V*, can be used.

$$C = \sqrt{\frac{\chi^2}{\chi^2 + N}} \qquad (N = \text{number of cases}) \qquad (6.1)$$

The coefficient ranges from 0 to 1 with high values indicative of strong relation-ships. One important feature of *C* is that it can never actually achieve the value of 1 for a given table. The maximum possible value is

$$C_{max} = \sqrt{1 - \frac{1}{n}} \qquad (6.2)$$

where *n* is the smaller of the number of rows or columns. In a 3×2 table, $n = 2$, and therefore this limit is $\sqrt{0.5} = 0.707$. A natural consequence of this restriction is that the contingency coefficient can only validly be used to compare tables of the same size. Cramer's *V* overcomes the size limitation of *C* since it ranges from 0 to 1 regardless of table size.

$$V = \sqrt{\frac{\chi^2}{N \times m}} \qquad (6.3)$$

where: m is the smaller of $(NR - 1)$ or $(NC - 1)$.

Should a program not test the significance of a chi-square value, it will be necessary to use tables with the degrees of freedom equal to the number of rows minus one multi-plied by the number of columns minus one, $(NR - 1) \times (NC - 1)$. An extension of chi-square not often reported enables the *significance of rows* to be assessed by comput-ing chi-square for each row using the standard expression.

$$\chi^2 = \sum \frac{(O - E)^2}{E} \qquad (6.4)$$

with the degrees of freedom $(NC - 1)$. It should only be performed *after* a significant table chi-square has been found, to locate specific relationships. Chi-square is a direct function of *sample size* so that if all cell frequencies are doubled, so is chi-square. It follows that significance levels may be raised if larger samples are used, assuming similar response patterns obtain. Very few restrictions apply to chi-square. The data need not be normally distributed, a popular misconception. Cell sizes are important and the general recommendation is that no more than 20 per cent of the cells should have *expected* frequencies of less than 5, none less than 1 (Siegel, 1956). Confusion sometimes arises over expected and observed frequencies. Clearly small *observed* frequencies are legiti-mate since they arise from strong association. The conditions apply to the expected frequencies, given by

$$E = \frac{R \times C}{N} \qquad (6.5)$$

71

where R and C are the row and column totals (usually called marginal totals) for the cell in question.

Rather more stringent restrictions apply to 2×2 tables. No cell may have an expected frequency of less than 5. Furthermore, chi-square should not be used to test tables containing fewer than 20 cases, instead Fisher's exact probability test should be applied. *Yates's correction* for continuity is recommended for 2×2 tables and most programs do incorporate it. The *Fisher exact probability test*, as its name implies, enables the exact probability associated with a particular table to be calculated. If A, B, C, and D

A	B
C	D

$N = A + B + C + D$

represent the cell frequencies, the probability is given by

$$P = \frac{(A + B)!(C + D)!(A + C)!(B + D)!}{N!\, A!\, B!\, C!\, D!} \tag{6.6}$$

For a given table, it is necessary to compute this value *plus the probabilities for all the more* extreme forms of the table. These have the same marginal totals, but the smallest cell frequency is progressively reduced by one until it is zero.

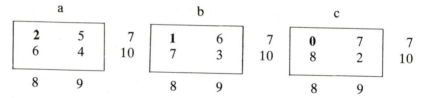

Adding together all those probabilities gives the chance of obtaining the observed table *or a more extreme one*. The need to compute factorials severely restricts use of the Fisher

Table 6.4 **Fisher test of association between secondary school anxiety and nostalgia for primary school** (10% sample)

		Nostalgia for primary		
		LOW < 12	HIGH ≥ 12	Totals
Secondary anxiety	LOW < 23	18	11	29
	HIGH ≥ 23	5	11	16
	Totals	23	22	45

FISHER EXACT PROBABILITY = 0.0471 *
CHI-SQUARE = 2.783 (NS)

test to small tables. Most of the available programs apply the test to samples of 50 or less and this is probably the largest acceptable figure. Table 6.4 tabulates secondary anxiety and primary nostalgia for a 10 per cent sample of the transfer data. Fisher's exact probability is 0.047, marginally significant whereas the chi-square value of 2.783 is not. This difference largely derives from the continuity correction being needed for chi-square. If it had *not* been applied a significant chi-square of 3.918 would have resulted. The demonstration emphasizes the importance of using Fisher's test for small samples.

The above discussion applies to independent tables. Should the two attributes in a table be *dependent* McNemar's test of changes (Siegel, 1956) is appropriate for 2×2 tables, otherwise use Cochran's Q-test (Siegel, 1956).

ORDERED DATA

Ordered data differ from continuous data in that although an increasing progression exists across the codes, the intervals between adjacent codes are not assumed to be comparable. Tests available for analysing this type of data include those already discussed for nominal data, together with others specifically designed to test the ordering of an association. The case of 2×2 tables is rather meaningless in this context since with only one interval they can equally well be considered as nominal or continuous.

The two commonest methods used are the rank-order correlation coefficients developed by Spearman, *rho*, and Kendall, *tau*. A modification to the latter method, Kendall's *S*, is also useful since it is possible to test its significance by referring to the normal curve. Spearman's *rho* is derived directly from the product-moment correlation coefficient (see later) and if no ties occur rho can be computed using a product-moment correlation program on the ranked scores. Should two or more cases record the same score the associated ranks must be averaged before the standard program can be used. Kendall's *tau* differs in that it employs a measure of disarray, *S*, comparing an obtained value with the maximum possible. Both rho and tau range from -1 to $+1$ although for any set of paired scores rho will be the larger. Nevertheless both reject the null hypothesis at the same level of significance. In the absence of any fundamental reasons for choosing either, the data analyst's preference tends to be for Kendall's tau, primarily because of its more consistent treatment of ties. Any moderately-sized sample (over 50, say) will record repeated scores and these need to be handled appropriately. An added benefit with tau is its ability to be used on dichotomous data.

Kendall's S-method is closely related to tau except that a normal deviate is produced rather than a correlation coefficient (Ferguson, 1976). An interesting demonstration of its use arose from the transfer data. Cross-tabulating the recoded forms of social class apprehension over transfer produces a chi-square value which is significant at the .05 level (Table 6.2). Knowing that both these measures are ordered it is tempting to conclude that a continuous relationship exists. Unfortunately that would not be a valid interpretation of chi-square. Applying Kendall's S-method which *is* designed to test ordering results in an S-value of 3241 with a standard deviation of 1118.95. The associated normal deviate is obtained by dividing these two values, i.e.,

2.896. This is a highly significant value ($P<0.01$) and therefore it is now legitimate to conclude that there is a progressive pattern in Table 6.2, such that lower apprehension levels tend to be associated with higher social class.

CONTINUOUS DATA

The assessment of relationships among continuous variables has an ambivalent character, its apparent simplicity hiding many complications. Initially, there is little difficulty since the Pearson product-moment correlation coefficient can be used for most continuous measures. There are fewer restrictions than is generally accepted. Certainly the two measures *do not need to be normally distributed*, they merely need to have similarly shaped distributions. Another frequently quoted requirement is *homoscedacity*, the property whereby one of the variables to be correlated has the same variance for all values of the other. This is only necessary if the correlations are to be used for predictions since that technique assumes a constant standard error. When the correlation coefficients are obtained for other purposes such as factor analysis homoscedacity is not essential (DuBois, 1965). A further unnecessary qualification on the use of product-moment correlations concerns the modification to the basic formula recommended for use with various special types of data, particularly where dichotomies are involved. For example, where both measures are dichotomies, the *phi-coefficient* is advocated. In fact all the variants of Pearson's are only computational simplifications. In general, computational ease is irrelevant in computing and as a result any standard product-moment correlation program can be used to obtain the appropriate statistic. The result must be identical. One researcher actually justified not carrying out a certain analysis because the phi-coefficient program was not available, presumably amidst a surfeit of product-moment programs!

The serious problems in the use of correlation coefficients arise at the interpretation stage. Considerable space has already been devoted to the vital role of scatter plots in interpretation (Section 6.1). The possible effect of *outliers* has been specifically highlighted; even with 454 cases removing one outlier reduced a correlation from -0.227 to -0.218. *Small samples* are more susceptible to distortion and the concensus of opinion tends to favour samples of at least 30 cases. *Significance testing* is also affected by sample size. The standard error of a population correlation coefficient is given by:

$$SE_{\bar{r}} = \frac{1 - \bar{r}^2}{\sqrt{N - 1}} \qquad (6.7)$$

where $\bar{r}$ is the hypothesized population parameter. Mostly the parameter value is 0.0 implying a null hypothesis of no correlation in the population from which the sample is drawn. Applying the formula with $\bar{r} = 0.0$ and for 101 cases produces a standard error of .1. Given that this standard error is normally distributed for large samples a rough rule of thumb is that a sample of around 100 cases requires a correlation of .2 before significance is achieved. If a correlation of .2 is only just significant, implying that a relationship quite likely exists, how is a *strong* relationship characterized? Two main guidelines exist. Firstly, the amount of *explained variation* between the two correlated

74

measures can be calculated by *squaring the coefficient*. Under this test the importance of very high correlations is readily confirmed; one of .9 accounts for 81 per cent of the co-variation. Intermediate values necessarily attract a more reserved interpretation since the co-variation associated with a correlation of .7 is only 49 per cent. The second guide

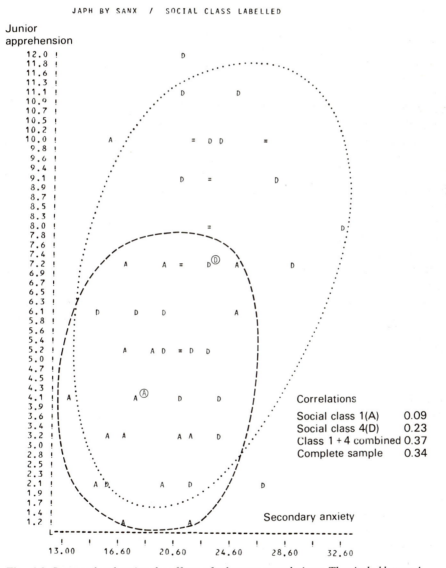

Fig. 6.3 *Scatter plot showing the effects of subgroup correlations. The circled letters A and D give the means for the two groups on the two measures. The differing distributions, particularly in the mean scores, result in an inflated correlation for the combined sample.*

75

to the importance of a correlation coefficient applies to a different use of the statistic, namely *prediction*. A non-zero correlation between two measures does imply that one can be predicted from the other, even if not very accurately. An estimate of the accuracy is given by:

$$SE_y = S_y\sqrt{1 - r_{xy}^2}$$
(6.8)

where SE_y is the standard error of the predicted y score.
          S_y is the standard deviation of the actual y score.
          r_{xy} is the correlation between the two sets of scores x and y.

The implications of this assessment are even stronger than those issuing from the explained variance test. Here a correlation of .7 produces a standard error of prediction of $\sqrt{1 - 0.49} = 0.71$ times the standard deviation. That is the prediction is only .29 of a standard deviation better than pure guesswork.

Of the remaining qualifications to the interpretation of the correlation coefficient (McCall, 1975) those to do with *differences between correlations* are probably the most relevant. Not infrequently, it is assumed that if one correlation is significant but another is not, then the difference between them is also significant. A little thought shows this to be plainly a fallacy. Differences are tested by a modified version of the method used to test the significance of a single correlation. Another area where differences may lead to

PROGRAM AVAILABILITY

see Section 3.6

	P M M D	S P S S	B M D P	O S I R I S	V O E L D M A N	C O O L E Y
Relationships Between Pairs of Measures						
scatter plots	P	S	B	O		
cross-tabulation	P	S	B	O	V	
recoding	P	S	B	O		
chi-square	P	S	B	O	V	
contingency coefficient	P	S	B	O		
Cramer's *V*		S				
Fisher exact test	P	S	B			
McNemar and Cochran Q tests						
Spearman's rho		S	B	O		
Kendall's tau	P	S	B	O		
Kendall's *S*-method		S		O		
phi-coefficient	P	S	B	O	V	C
product-moment correlation coefficient	P	S	B	O	V	C

invalid conclusions is in *subgroup analysis*. If correlations are different for various subgroups it can be misleading to combine these groups and then to produce an overall correlation. The essential flaw is that the combined distributions can be very irregular, particularly when extreme groups are used. In Fig. 6.3 two extreme social class groups have been separated from the main transfer sample.

Within group correlations between primary apprehension and secondary anxiety are .09 (class 1) and .23 while combined the figure is .37. The wide separation of these two idiosyncratic groups has produced an artificial correlation which quite likely cannot hold for any legitimate subsample. The complete sample correlation is .34.

Throughout correlational analysis there is the perpetual dilemma of reconciling the limitations of individual coefficients with the considerable scope of large correlation matrices. It is too easy to ignore the simpler situation assuming that methods as powerful as factor analysis or multiple regression are immune to the problems that beset the interpretation of specific correlations. In spite of the huge number of elements in most matrices an analysis is only as good as its constituents. The initial spadework involved in ensuring that a set of associations is valid provides an invaluable foundation for subsequent analyses.

References

DuBois, P. H. (1965) *An Introduction to Psychological Statistics*, New York, Harper Row.

Ferguson, G. A. (1976) *Statistical Analysis in Psychology and Education,* Fourth edition, New York, McGraw-Hill.

McCall, R. B. (1975) *Fundamental Statistics for Psychology*, Second edition, New York, Harcourt, Brace and World.

Siegel, S. S. (1956) *Nonparametric Statistics for the Behavioral Sciences*, New York, McGraw-Hill.

7.   The Analysis of Groups

Most researches involve some analysis of subgroups, whether as a fundamental part of the design or for elaboration of the main analysis. In its simplest form a subgroup is a selection of cases from a larger sample; that sample may itself comprise a set of related groups. In considering analytical approaches almost certainly the first reaction is to visualize two groups and in consequence to assume that the t-test applies. This reaction is unfortunate since the two-group situation is only a special case in subgroup analysis. Even though most multiple-group procedures do reduce down to a form of the t-test in the two-group instance the reverse is not the case. Extending the t-test to more than two groups does not produce the same results. Exactly the same problem arose with correlation coefficients. The general product-moment formula equated to the various special forms, but the latter could not be applied to more elaborate data than that for which they were designed.

The whole field of subgroup analysis has been given considerable attention recently yet large areas of dispute remain. Kirk (1972) has collated a number of important articles on this issue and as such that chapter in his reader provides an excellent account of the problems involved, and some of the suggested remedies. Very briefly, the main steps can be summarized as the need to define and extract valid subgroups, to ascertain that there are differences between these groups, and finally to identify the nature of those differences, both in respect of the groups and the measures. One rather restricted application of the methodology has been outlined in discussing the use of cross-tabulation and measures of association with nominal data. Nominal classes can just as legitimately be conceived as subgroups. The present chapter extends the approach to all types of data.

7.1   The definition of subgroups

In experimental designs the analysis subgroups are explicitly defined. Where an analysis is less structured there may be a large number of groupings worthy of study. Some are of obvious interest, the sex split being a subdivision quite often relevant to educational research. Almost any measure, nominal or continuous, can be used to define a set of subgroups so long as certain statistical requirements are met. The problem is one of escalation and it therefore behoves the analyst to define the initial hypotheses so that the number of subsequent subgroup analyses is kept to a manageable minimum. All too often the blunderbuss technique is used in the vain hope of finding significant differences somewhere amidst a vast sequence of computer printouts.

EXTRACTION OF SUBGROUPS

In addition to the definition of valid subgroups the identification and extraction of those groups may cause difficulties. In the simplest situation where a single classification is to be analysed, the data pack can be arranged so that analyses can be performed on each group in turn. More elaborate designs incorporating a variety of classifications cannot be treated in this manner without an inordinate amount of card sorting. The alternative is to use some automatic procedure for group extraction. Although it may be possible to work from case identification numbers (SPSS and PMMD both allow this) in practice the method is cumbersome. A more elegant tactic is to use appropriate variables for group identification. Generally, the relevant characteristics will have been coded as variables anyway (sex, age, social class, for example), but less obviously analytical features such as school or experimental group should be recorded in the same way.

Once suitable variables have been introduced into the coding the extraction of the associated subgroups becomes a simple matter of identifying each code in turn. A useful elaboration upon this basic method is to use more complicated specifications, either on one classification variable, or even using two or more variables together. The commonest need for the first modification is in partitioning variables with a large number of codes. So groups corresponding to five intelligence levels can be constructed by specifying four intermediate cut-off points. A natural extension of single-variable classifications is one involving two or more measures at once. Thus the intelligence level partition might profitably be extended so that each level is further subdivided by age or sex. For example, a member of the lowest-ability male subgroup would be identified by a double condition:

> male *with* non-verbal reasoning score below 81
> i.e.,   VARIABLE 4 EQUAL TO 1 (male)
>   *and* VARIABLE 20 LESS THAN 81 (low IQ)

Such a system of joint and alternative conditions (derived from set theory) can introduce sufficient flexibility to allow virtually any conceivable subgroup to be defined and extracted. The essential requirement is that all relevant information should be coded as part of the data. The facility is not common but the major packages including PMMD and SPSS do enable such specifications to be made.

STATISTICAL CONSIDERATIONS

The validity of many group structures for statistical analysis will depend largely on the analysis applied. Nevertheless, it is worth considering one or two general features right from the start. *Group size* is especially important since the analysis of small or unequal-sized groups may not be possible without violating assumptions implicit in certain methods. Both analysis of variance and the Tukey tests are intended for use with equal-sized groups and although corrections do exist for slight variations, excessive differences could tend to invalidate the use of those methods.

No clear convention exists for determining *optimum group sizes* the choice being so heavily dependent on the method to be applied. It was mentioned in Chapter 6 that chi-square analysis requires expected frequencies of five per cell and any subdivision of a larger sample would need to relate to this limitation. In testing for differences between subgroups groups of under 10 cases are rarely satisfactory (Petrinovich and Hardyck, 1969). Recalling that the standard error of a sample mean is $\sigma/\sqrt{N}$, for nine cases this amounts to one-third of the population standard deviation. With the non-verbal reasoning scores, for example, the standard deviation of around 13 results is a standard error of over four points. Given that most tests require a difference of two standard errors for significance the necessary difference of eight points is large. In general statisticians tend to recommend the use of subgroups of at least 15 cases.

Variation in group sizes is a similarly contentious issue but Ferguson (1976) does recommend Bancroft's (1968) procedure for handling certain differences. Initial checking is done by applying a suitable chi-square test to the group sizes to assess equality or proportionality. Should the deviations from either of these properties be sufficiently small to be non-significant the appropriate correction can be applied.

One particularly prevalent malpractice in subgroup analysis is the isolation of *extreme groups*. Admittedly the research emphasis might be on atypical characteristics, but from a statistical standpoint the danger lies in the virtual inevitability of producing inaccurate estimates of population parameters. Where extreme groups do need examining separately, the initial significance testing should be carried out *including* the intermediate groups as well. Other hazards in subgroup definition are either specific to particular methods (for example, the need for ordering in trend testing) or else relatively obvious given a little thought about the research implications. So groups should not overlap since interpretation becomes contradictory, a set of groups should bear some consistent relationship to each other, and without being flippant, do not construct vacuous subgroups.

7.2 Confirming variation between subgroups

Discrimination between groups measured on nominal scales has already been discussed in Chapter 6. Ordinal data represent a somewhat ambivalent situation since although nominal or specifically ordinal procedures can be applied, it may also be legitimate to assume sufficient closeness to interval data to employ parametric methods. Semantic differential scales are a typical instance where the ordinal relationship is generally treated as interval for analytical purposes.

There is some disagreement as to whether it is necessary to confirm overall variation between groups before examining specific differences (Linton and Gallo, 1975). The main problem hinges on the fact that where three or more groups are involved, a significance level α (the chance of a Type I error) is associated with *each* pairwise comparison. For NG groups the total number of possible comparisons is $NG \times (NG - 1)/2$. It can be shown that for N independent comparisons the accumulated type I error is:

$$\alpha_N = 1 - (1 - \alpha)^N \qquad (7.1)$$

and this is approximately equal to $N\alpha$. Therefore for five groups $N = 5 \times 4/2$, that is 10.

Consequently α_5 is $10 \times \alpha$. With a typical α of .01 the true α_N becomes .1. Ryan (1959) shows that even where the comparisons are dependent (and this is so for some of the pairwise group comparisons), the α_N is rarely much smaller than for independence. As a result the argument over the need to confirm overall variation centres on this problem of error rates in experiments. In general, Ryan (1959) recommends the use of multiple comparison tests such as Tukey's or Scheffé's. They both operate on *experimentwise error rates* and incorporate overall variance testing. If other tests are used, it may then be necessary to confirm overall variation beforehand.

An interesting but seldom featured extension of analysis of variance is the use of trend analysis to test for progressive differences between ordered groups. Many researches postulate this kind of variation and given that a significant trend can arise without a significant one-way analysis of variance it is important to consider this possibility. Figure 7.1 depicts the relationships between the two methods.

The basic principle is that it is possible to derive a number of alternative estimates of the population variance. If there is no variation between the groups those estimates should agree. In *one-way analysis of variance* two estimates are obtained. A within-groups estimate (W) is calculated by summing the squared variations of individual group members about their respective group means. A second between-groups estimate (B) is

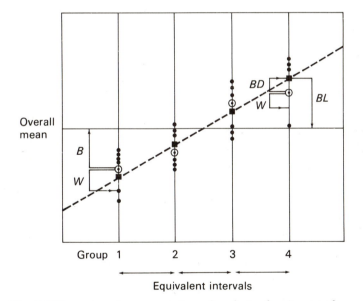

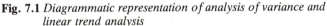

Fig. 7.1 *Diagrammatic representation of analysis of variance and linear trend analysis*

■   *Predicted group mean*

⊙   *Actual group mean*

B   *Between-groups variance estimate* ⎫   *Analysis of variance*
W   *Within-groups variance estimate* ⎭

BD *Between-groups deviation estimate* ⎫   *Trend analysis*
BL *Between-groups linearity estimate* ⎭

●   *Individual scores*

computed by treating each group as entirely located at its mean, and squaring the differences between each mean and the overall mean. Dividing these two estimates produces an *F*-ratio; a sufficiently large value would indicate that the variation within the groups was considerably less than that between the groups, that is, the groups differ.

Trend testing subdivides the between-groups variation even further. For a *linear trend test* two separate components are derived from the regression line linking the ordered groups. This regression line enables a predicted mean to be computed for each group. The sum of squared differences between these predicted means and the overall mean gives a linear between-groups estimate *(BL)*; a similar calculation for the differences between the predicted means and the group means gives the non-linear estimate *(BD)*. These components enable two *F*-ratios to be computed and evaluated:

$$F \text{ linear} = BL/W \qquad df = 1, (N \times NG)$$
$$F \text{ non-linear} = BD/W \qquad df = (NG - 2), (N - NG) \qquad (7.2)$$

A significant linear *F*-ratio would imply that the group scores tended to increase or decrease linearly. Should the non-linear *F*-ratio be significant, the further qualification would be that although the group scores show clustering the variation between the groups was not linear. The specific nature of such a non-linear trend would need further investigation before it could be quantified.

ASSUMPTIONS AND PROCEDURES

Even with carefully constructed subgroups further qualifications apply if analysis of variance is to be interpreted fully. Most textbooks discuss these basic assumptions and an extended account by Eisenhart (1947) appears in Kirk's reader (1972). Essentially the recorded scores should be independent and normally distributed. Variances for each subgroup should be equal and the relationship between subgroups should be additive. In general, equal numbers per subgroup are to be preferred since the corrections for unequal-sized groups may not be wholly satisfactory (see Section 7.1). Mild aberrations from these requirements tend to have little effect on subsequent analyses (Ferguson, 1976) but the implicit model must be borne in mind if extensive inferences are to be made from the analysis results.

The requirements concerning group sizes and interrelationships have already been discussed. The *additivity* assumption is even more stringent than the need for a clear relationship between the groups in that the steps between the groups (whatever they might represent) need to be comparable, otherwise interaction effects in two- or three-way classifications cannot be validly interpreted (see Section 7.4). Variance equality, usually called *homogeneity of variance,* can be assessed by a number of methods. The commonest is probably Bartlett's test (DuBois, 1965) employing a form of chi-square For the variances to be acceptably alike the Bartlett test should *not* be significant. Should this condition not be satisfied it may be possible to proceed with subgroup analysis if a suitable specific comparison test is applied (see Section 7.3).

The same conditions appertain to linear trend tests; it is particularly important that the intervals between the groups should be equal because of the linear regression model incorporated (see Fig. 7.1). Since the various complications of confirming and then locating group differentiation are so inextricably interwoven an application of the procedures to the transfer sample will be left until the end of the following section which deals with the second phase, the identification of specific differences.

7.3 Locating differences between groups

Once variation between the analysis groups has been confirmed, either by analysis of variance or possibly by applying a trend test, most likely more details on the specific nature of the variation will be required. The most direct way of achieving this is to compare each group with every other, a total of $NG \times (NG - 1)/2$ comparisons for NG groups. Tests of this kind, variously called multiple comparisons, or better, *specific comparisons*, are ideal when the number of groups is small, say six or fewer. As the number increases the difficulty is not so much in actually performing the tests, but rather in interpreting and presenting the results. In those circumstances a useful additional test is to compare each group with the rest taken as a whole. Effectively a *test of atypicality*, it can be readily obtained by a slight modification of some of the standard procedures used for specific comparisons, especially the Scheffé test. Indeed, in certain researches where even more complex *combined comparisons* are justified the same procedure will quite likely provide those tests as well. For example, a not uncommon occurrence is the presence in an experiment of a number of treatment groups which need to be compared with two or more control groups. Such a combined comparison is a natural extension of the Scheffé multiple comparisons test.

CHOOSING A SPECIFIC COMPARISONS TEST

Writing about the future of data analysis Tukey (1962) emphasized the vital role of judgement, offering the maxim: 'far better an approximate answer to the *right* question, which is often vague, than an *exact* answer to the wrong question; which can always be precise' (page 14). The embarrassingly large number of methods available for testing group differences is clear evidence of the need to approximate in the absence of conceptual precision. This does *not* mean that choice can be random, only that judgement must be applied so that the test selected is appropriate both to the research problem and to the data.

One of the first research considerations is usually expressed in the form of *a priori* or *a posteriori* comparisons. An *a priori* or planned comparison is designated of interest *before* the analysis. Most texts accept that the t-test or even a 2×2 chi-square analysis can be used (see for example Ferguson, 1976; Linton and Gallo, 1975) although there is dissension (e.g., Petrinovich and Hardyck, 1969). However, as Kerlinger (1973) emphasizes, because of the Type I error considerations it is not possible to perform more *a priori* comparisons than there are degrees of freedom (that is, $NG \times 1$), and the comparisons must also be independent.

The alternative, an *a posteriori* comparison, is sometimes called a post-mortem test. Its rationale is that the experiment itself is the main concern with all possible comparisons deemed of interest. The conceptual difference between the two situations does seem rather artificial since hopefully all researches only include groups that are worthy of examination. Consequently, there will normally be a desire to accept the implications of *all* significant differences which in turn effectively makes them *a posteriori* comparisons. Therefore, the normal preference should be for a test which controls experiment-wise error rates. The t-test does *not* do this; of those than do, the Scheffé, Tukey, Neuman–Keuls, and Duncan tests are most widely used.

An interesting approach to resolving the problem of choice has appeared recently in a series of articles examining the error rates for various tests over a large number of applications to random data (e.g., Petrinovich and Hardyck, 1969; Toothaker, 1972; Keselman and Toothaker, 1974; Keselman, 1976). The Petrinovich and Hardyck study offers a comprehensive assessment of the methods under a variety of conditions both meeting and violating the traditional assumptions. It is impossible to summarize adequately their findings here but the authors themselves eventually express a preference for either the Scheffé or the Tukey tests. Both produce acceptable Type I and Type II error rates although the Tukey method is possibly more sensitive. The authors particularly stress the need to use samples of at least 10 members to have any chance of detecting real differences. The later study by Keselman and Toothaker (1974) compares the Scheffé and Tukey tests and offers useful additional advice. On the whole the Tukey test does tend to give a more accurate Type I experimentwise error rate and Petrinovich and Hardyck strongly support the use of experimentwise error rates. The only clear exception to the rule favouring the Tukey test is where group sizes and variances are both unequal and where the larger variances are associated with the smaller groups, a relatively uncommon occurrence. Petrinovich and Hardyck moderate their preference for experimentwise error rates in the sole instance of exploratory studies. On condition that subsequent research reverts back to the more stringent approach they accept Block's (1960) support for using individual comparison error rates (such as the t-test may offer) in the early stages of problem investigation.

One novel feature of the Keselman and Toothaker (1974) study was the inclusion of a number of combined comparisons in addition to all possible pairwise differences. The results for these tests indicate a slight preference for the Scheffé method, and therefore this would appear to be the most suitable procedure for testing atypicality. Other considerations in multiple comparisons testing are beyond the scope of this book. An illuminating account of the whole area is given in an article by Ryan (1959) which is also reprinted in Kirk's (1972) reader.

THE CHI-SQUARE TEST FOR PLANNED COMPARISONS

Little mention is made of the use of 2×2 chi-square analysis in the same *a priori* test situations for which the t-test may be appropriate. The procedure is eminently simple. A convenient cut-off point is defined and 2×2 frequency tables are compiled by counting the numbers in each of the two groups above and below that figure. Usually it is legitimate to take the population mean as the separation point. Having obtained the 2×2 table either the normal chi-square is evaluated, or better still, for relatively small groups Fisher's exact probability is computed.

The method is particularly suitable where the discriminating measure is dichotomous since the 2×2 table would reduce to the standard chi-square analysis. This would apply regardless of whether or not the dichotomy was defined as 1/0. Depending on the coding system employed ordinal or even nominal data may be amenable to this type of analysis, an advantage over the t-test which cannot be used for nominal data. Surprisingly few packages offer the facility automatically although it can usually be obtained by manipulating the standard chi-square procedure available in most packages.

AN APPLICATION OF SPECIFIC COMPARISON TESTS TO TRANSFER SUBGROUPS

One aim of the transfer research was to identify variations in transfer arrangements between schools and, if possible, to relate these to the children's reactions to school transfer. Examining differences in secondary school attitude to the new school (variable 13) constitutes a typical subgroup analysis situation. Table 7.1 presents the complete sequence of tests involved but it does not follow that all are necessarily pertinent to any particular research analysis.

Taking the steps in turn, the Bartlett homogeneity of variance test is not significant. If it had been, it might have been preferable to have used the Scheffé specific comparison test rather than Tukey's method. One-way analysis of variance confirms that there are differences in attitude between the three secondary schools. The linear trend test, like many statistics, can usually be *computed* but that does not imply that it can always be *interpreted*. Here, unless there exists some good reason to assume an ordering of the three schools (for example, an increasing commitment to pre-transfer liaison) the significant linear trend of Table 7.1 *must* be ignored, it cannot be interpreted. This highlights a general point in computer data analysis in that one should never assume that all

Table 7.1   Analysis of differences in attitudes for the three secondary schools
(Atypicality test results are given in the diagonal)

VARIABLE 13: *Attitude to secondary school*

(a) BARTLETT HOMOGENEITY OF VARIANCE TEST	χ^2	= 1.419	$P = 0.503$	NS
(b) ONE-WAY ANALYSIS OF VARIANCE	BETWEEN	= 98.195		
	WITHIN	= 19.618		
	F-RATIO	= 5.006	$P = 0.007$	**
(c) LINEAR TREND TEST	LINEAR	= 121.313		
	WITHIN	= 19.618		
	F-RATIO	= 6.184	$P = 0.013$	*
(d) NON-LINEAR TREND TEST	DEVIATION	= 75.077		
	WITHIN	= 19.618		
	F-RATIO	= 3.827	$P = 0.048$	*

(e) SPECIFIC COMPARISONS (TUKEY) AND ATYPICALITY TEST (SCHEFFÉ)

		MEAN	SD	COMPARISONS 1	2	3
SCHOOL 1	($N = 148$)	30.29	4.22	9.80**		
SCHOOL 2	($N = 147$)	28.78	4.35	−4.19**	3.63	
SCHOOL 3	($N = 159$)	29.01	4.64	−3.55*	0.64	1.46

computer printout is of value. Programmers try to offer comprehensive facilities even though the applicability of some may be limited. This reservation applies to the linear trend test in this instance.

Specific comparisons are those tests which compare each group (school) with the remainder in turn. The simplest way to present them is in the form of a matrix giving the test results (in this case Tukey Q-values) and significance levels. In such a system the diagonal is meaningless since a group cannot be compared with itself. Instead the atypicality test result using Scheffé's method is inserted. For this particular analysis the only significant specific differences are between School 1 and both the others; the mean scores show the difference to be a more positive attitude. The atypicality test result reiterates this finding.

Table 7.2 offers a revealing demonstration of the various possibilities associated with the various tests confirming variation. It summarizes the analysis of secondary school anxiety and self-concept differences for groups comprising five non-verbal reasoning ability levels. Four specific comparison tests are applied, the t-test (T), a 2×2 chi-square (X), Tukey's method (Q) and the Scheffé test (S). The three levels of significance .01, .05 and .10 are indicated by bold type, upper case, and lower case letters respectively. The right hand column gives the significance of the overall variation tests and it is these that pinpoint the different possibilities. Table 7.2(b) exemplifies the situation where the one-way analysis of variance is not significant but the linear trend test is. The group means confirm a tendency for greater anxiety to be associated with lower ability (low numbered groups). Notice that neither of the experimentwise comparison tests (Scheffé and Tukey) isolates any specific differences but both of the individual comparison tests do, and at the .01 level.

In Table 7.2(c) an opposing situation occurs in that in spite of the absence of any kind of overall variation the comparison group 2 with group 4, is identified as significant by three of the four methods. If this had involved the two extreme groups it might have been possible to interpret the result; it is difficult to explain why only intermediate ability groups should differ in social self-concept and it is, therefore, almost certainly a chance result. Once more the t-test produces liberal significance but more interesting is the marginal chi-square significance (1 versus 4) which no other method locates. No obvious justification appears in the mean scores (7.72 and 7.32), the reason being that the 2×2 chi-square tests the substantially different hypothesis that the distributions, not average levels differ. In fact 61 per cent of group 1 score above the population mean while only 46 per cent of group 4 do.

The next level of variation is where most of the differentiation involves one group and Table 7.2(d) offers a good example. The separation of group 1 is so marked that both the one-way variance and linear trend tests are significant. Given the clear ordering of these five groups the close agreement between the two tests is to be expected. The Scheffé atypicality test also shows this isolated position of group 1 and the specific comparisons with the other four groups confirm it. Again the t-test is excessively generous since the Tukey and Scheffé tests, and indeed chi-square, suggest that the major difference is between group 1 and the two highest ability groups, 4 and 5. Table 7.2(e) extends the pattern of (d) with both extreme groups clearly separated. The test results

Table 7.2 Self-concept differences for five IQ levels tested by four specific comparison methods

(a) The five groups based on non-verbal reasoning scores (VARIABLE 20)
  GROUP 1 (N = 92) up to 80
  GROUP 2 (N = 77) 81 – 87
  GROUP 3 (N = 107) 88 – 95
  GROUP 4 (N = 89) 96 – 104
  GROUP 5 (N = 89) 105 and over

(b) *Secondary Anxiety* VARIABLE 13

DIFFERENCES BETWEEN GROUPS

GROUP	MEAN	SD	1	2	3	4	5	TESTS	
1	22.36	4.26	-					Bartlett	-
2	21.82	4.54	-	-				One-way	-
3	22.18	4.74	-		-			Linear	*
4	21.03	4.12	TX	-	t	-		Non-linear	-
5	21.24	3.81	Tx	-	-	-	-		

(c) *Self-concept: Social* VARIABLE 14

			1	2	3	4	5		
1	7.72	2.44	-					Bartlett	-
2	8.30	2.09	t	-				One-way	-
3	7.78	2.24	-	-	-			Linear	*
4	7.36	2.24	x	TXQ	-	-		Non-linear	-
5	7.82	2.19	-	-	-	-	-		

(d) *Self-concept: Personal* VARIABLE 15

			1	2	3	4	5		
1	8.71	2.56	S					Bartlett	-
2	9.48	2.32	T	-				One-way	*
3	9.55	2.47	T	-	-			Linear	**
4	9.74	2.37	TXQs	-	-	-		Non-linear	-
5	9.82	2.28	TXQS	-	-	-	-		

(e) *Self-concept: Academic* VARIABLE 16

			1	2	3	4	5		
1	5.68	1.84	**S**					Bartlett	-
2	6.61	1.68	**TXQS**	-				One-way	**
3	6.41	1.74	**TXQ**s	-	-			Linear	**
4	6.78	1.84	**TXQS**	-	-	-		Non-linear	*
5	7.60	1.75	**TXQS**	**TXQS**	**TXQS**	**TXQ**s	S		

KEY
Significance levels: Heavy type (**) $p < 0.01$
                        Upper case (*) $p < 0.05$
                        Lower case (?) $p < 0.10$
                        - not significant

Tests
T   t-test
X   chi-square
Q   Tukey
S   Scheffé
Diagonal gives Scheffé atypicality test only

are unanimous, bearing in mind the general qualification that the t-test overestimates and the Scheffé test is very conservative with respect to Type I error.

The general conclusions to be drawn from these analyses are substantially in line with the earlier discussions regarding the need to use tests based on experimentwise error rates, the t-test being particularly dangerous without clear research justification for its use. A rather surprising but valuable feature is the robustness of the 2×2 chi-square. Quite often there may be reservations about the suitability of certain data for parametric testing. In the above examples the chi-square test results correspond very closely with those for Tukey's method suggesting a similar efficiency which could extend to data for which Tukey's method is inappropriate. The importance of relating statistical findings to the research framework was neatly demonstrated in the single significant comparison of Table 7.2(c). Suspicion is an essential element in all statistical interpretation and not just the extreme situations such as those exposed by significant Bartlett test results.

PRESENTATION OF SUBGROUP ANALYSIS RESULTS

An appropriate format for the presentation of analysis results has the dual benefit of helping the reader as well as making interpretation that much easier. Subgroup analysis tends to generate a large amount of statistical data particularly when many variables or groups are included. Tabulation of these results may be necessary, but some form of graphic representation is usually a more efficient means of summarizing results. The standard method is a *profile chart* giving the mean scores of each group on all the measures of interest (Fig. 7.2a).

The problems are immediately apparent. As the number of groups or measures increases so the clarity of the features is diminished. This is especially so where the measures show little similarity since the high variation associated with some will necessarily result in compression of the scale for measures with less variation. On the ability measures, for example, the groups range over one standard deviation on either side of the mean; most measures record less than half a standard deviation variation. Nevertheless, using scale plotting based on standard deviations together with careful choice of line textures can produce sufficient definition to expose the salient features. In Fig. 7.2(a) the wide ability spread is implicit in the group structures. The opposing profiles of the two extreme groups are easily distinguished and are quite revealing. The top ability group's negative attitude to the secondary school before transfer suggests a general satisfaction with any educational *status quo*; the low ability groups are possibly operating under the assumption that any change can only be an improvement!

The ordering of variables in Fig. 7.2(a) does imply some relationship but where the pattern is broken the clarity of presentation does suffer. So the apprehension and anxiety measures (8 and 15) are negatively related to most of the rest and consequently the group profiles tend to cross over. Reordering the measures can help to eliminate these interferences. Figure 7.2(b) takes the process of modification even further. In addition to reordering, the relative standing of each group with respect to the mean is based on Scheffé atypicality tests, not straight scores. These *atypicality charts* obviously lose detail but they can help expose patterns. The opposing profiles of the two extreme groups are

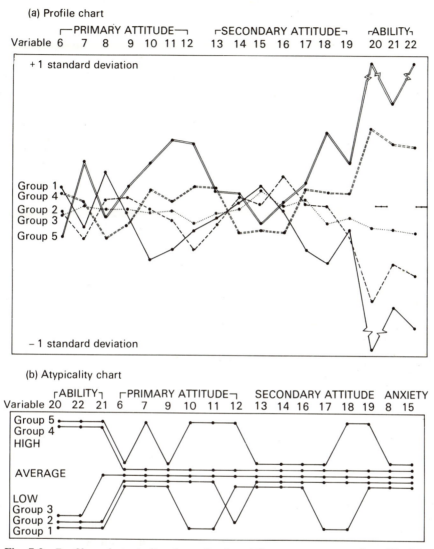

Fig. 7.2 *Profile and atypicality charts for five ability groups measured on 17 of the transfer variables. The profile plot of (a) is simplified in (b) to take into account only significantly high or low deviations. In both instances points are linked for ease of interpretation. Since adjacent measures are related, this is acceptable.*

clearly defined, both in terms of areas of difference and similarity. If the number of groups is sufficiently small (say four or five), it may also be possible to extend this basic method to incorporate between-group significant differences. Figure 7.3 shows a *difference chart* representing all significant between-groups differences as a gap of two or more units. The same distance between a group and the variable mean indicates significant atypicality as tested by Scheffé's method, the black triangles giving the limits for this.

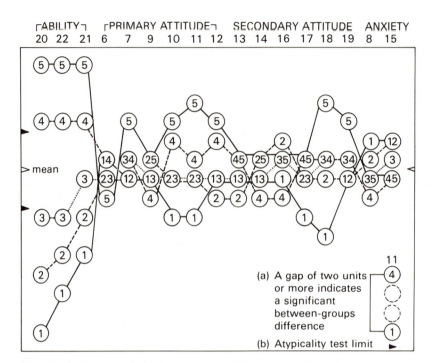

Fig. 7.3 *Difference chart for the five ability groups. The five groups are identified by inserting appropriate numbers inside the circles. Where no discrimination occurs, a single circle may be used to represent two groups to maintain clarity.*

Although the simplicity of the atypicality charts is lost, patterns of group differentiation over all the variables are easily seen.

7.4 Multiple classifications

When the joint effects of two or more features need to be examined the basic one-way classification needs subdividing even further. Two-way classifications are quite common and although there is no theoretical limit to the degree of splitting possible, in practice excessive refinement raises problems in both computation and interpretation. Particularly important are the subgroup sizes since the statistical techniques that test variation in multiple classifications are primarily designed for equal-sized cells. Small deviations can be corrected for but not without loss of reliability in the analyses.

A typical example of a situation where further qualification might be important is offered by the secondary school analysis presented in Table 7.1. Attitude differences between the three schools were found to be significant but how far does this generalization *extend*? For example, is it equally true of boys and girls? It must be appreciated that this is not the same as asking the two *separate* questions 'Are there school differences?' and 'Do boys and girls show different attitudes?' To test the *joint* hypothesis that School

Table 7.3 Two-way analysis of variance for school by sex

Variable 13: SECONDARY ATTITUDE TO SECONDARY SCHOOL

Analysis of variance summary table

Source of variation	Mean square	Degrees of freedom	F-ratio	Probability Two-way	(One-way)
Total	19.876	453			
Between total	111.831	5			
Between schools	77.364	2	4.1042	0.0168*	(0.0154*)
Between sexes	96.735	1	5.1318	0.0225*	(0.0073**)
School/sex interaction	153.846	2	8.1616	0.0006**	
Within total	18.850	448			

TOTAL NUMBER OF CASES	454
NUMBER OF LEVELS FOR A	3
NUMBER OF LEVELS FOR B	2

Of the two probability values given, the two-way figure is the usual analysis of variance output. Since this value may have been adjusted to accommodate unequal-sized groups, it is better to carry out one-way analyses for the various levels. These results are bracketed.

1's better attitude applies to both boys and girls each school needs subdividing by sex producing $3 \times 2 = 6$ groups in all. The results shown in Table 7.3 represent a standard two-way (also called two-factor) analysis of variance. The variation within the sample is split into four components—within the groups, between the schools, between the sexes, and finally the joint variation called the *interaction*. It is only this latter variation that necessitates the use of two-way analysis of variance. The between-school differences were tested using one-way analysis of variation (Table 7.1) and between-sex differences could have been tested in the same way. Moreover, if the cells are not equal-sized these one-way differences should not be assessed from the two-way table because of the corrections applied. Table 7.3 gives the results of both approaches. The discrepancy in the between-sex variation stems from the correction method used in many two-way analysis of variance programs (e.g., Veldman, 1967) whereby the mean for each level of a classification is simply the average of the subcells, no account being taken of the differing cell sizes (see Table 7.4). The highly significant interaction effect in Table 7.3 ($P<0.01$) implies that the relative attitude scores of the boys and girls are *not the same for all three schools*. Table 7.4 gives the mean scores for the six subgroups and this differentiation is clear. In Schools 1 and 3 the girls score higher while the reverse applies for School 2. Notice that this latter result contradicts the overall finding that girls tend to show higher secondary attitude scores than boys ($P <0.05$).

As with the analysis of single classifications so here the final step is to examine the specific group differences. In general, the same procedures apply although one slight modification is recommended. Cicchetti (1972) suggests an improved estimate of the degrees of freedom for what he calls *unconfounded comparisons*. These are comparisons of groups in the same row or column of the interaction table. All other comparisons are

Table 7.4   Significance of differences between analysis of variance levels and cells

Variable 13   SECONDARY ATTITUDE TO SECONDARY SCHOOL

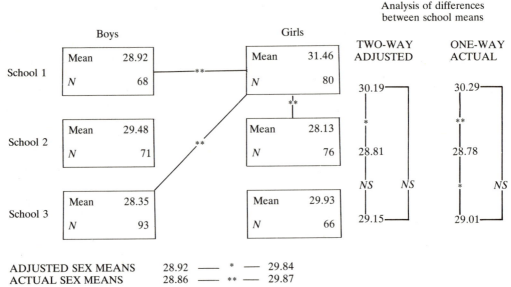

| ADJUSTED SEX MEANS | 28.92 —— * —— 29.84 |
| ACTUAL SEX MEANS | 28.86 —— ** —— 29.87 |

Of the 15 possible between-cell comparisons only the three indicated are significant (Tukey's method). The importance of using one-way analyses of actual means for differences between levels is highlighted by the discrepancy in the between-schools analysis.

confounded. In applying Cicchetti's procedure to the standard Tukey method two additional steps are required. Firstly, the number of unconfounded comparisons is calculated:

$$NU = NA \times NB \times (NA + NB - 2)/2 \qquad (7.3)$$

where NA, NB = number of levels in A, B.

This *NU* value is then used to obtain the corrected (fewer) degrees of freedom from Cicchetti's table (Cicchetti, 1972; Linton and Gallo, 1975). In fact the table is not needed since the new degrees of freedom are simply:

$$df \text{ (unconfounded)} = \text{the integer part of } [0.999 + \sqrt{2 \times NU}] \qquad (7.4)$$

Table 7.4 shows the results of using Tukey's method for all the comparisons. Only three are significant, one of which is confounded (School 1 girls versus School 3 boys) the other two being unconfounded. The table also records the significances for the between-level comparisons of both the two-way analysis adjusted means and the one-way actual means. The results agree for the sex classification ($P < 0.05$) but the between-school analysis does produce discrepancies in certain of the specific comparisons made. Once more this emphasizes the need to carry out tests of between-level differences using one-way procedures rather than by means of the adjusted multiple-classification methods.

7.5 Further considerations in subgroup analysis

While many subgroups analysis procedures have general applicability, occasionally extensions are necessary to meet the needs of specific researches. *Experiments* are the commonest instance where standard approaches may not be entirely satisfactory since assumptions such as independence often cannot be met. A number of excellent specialist texts describe those modifications (for example, Winer, 1970; Lewis, 1968). Another type of development has risen out of the move towards *multivariate methods,* particularly for the purposes of classification and discrimination. Chapter 9 is specifically concerned with these methods. Finally, in spite of the demonstrated robustness of most subgroup analysis procedures, researchers may still feel that *non-parametric tests* are more appropriate. Only one of these tests, the 2×2 chi-square has been described. Others such as the Mann–Whitney U-test, the Sign test and Cochran's Q-test (Siegel, 1956) may be applicable in certain situations.

PROGRAM AVAILABILITY see Section 3.6	P M M D	S P S S	B M D P	I R I S	V O S D M A N	C O O L E Y
The Analysis of Groups						
subgroup extraction	P	S	B	O		
one-way analysis of variance	P	S	B	O	V	
linear trend test	P	S	B			
homogeneity of variance test	P	S	B			
atypicality test	P	S				
Scheffé test	P	S				
Tukey test	P	S				
t-test	P	S	B	O		
two-way analysis of variance	P	S	B	O	V	
unconfounded/confounded comparisons	P					

References

Bancroft, T. A. (1968) *Topics in Intermediate Statistical Methods,* Ames, Iowa, The Iowa State University Press.

Block, J. (1960) 'On the number of significant findings to be expected by chance', *Psychometrika,* **25**, 369–380.

Cicchetti, D. V. (1972) 'Extension of multiple range tests to interaction tables in analysis of variance', *Psychological Bulletin,* **77**, 405–408.

DuBois, P. H. (1965) *An Introduction to Psychological Statistics*, New York, Harper and Row.

Eisenhart, C. (1947) 'The assumptions underlying the analysis of variance', *Biometrics,* **3**, 1–21, *in* Kirk, R. E. (1972).

Ferguson, G. A. (1976) *Statistical Analysis in Psychology and Education,* Fourth edition: New York, McGraw-Hill.

Kerlinger, F. N. (1973) *Foundations of Behavioral Research*, Second edition, New York, Holt, Rinehart and Winston.

Keselman, H. J. (1976) 'A power investigation of the Tukey multiple comparisons statistic', *Educ. and Psychol. Meas.,* **36**(1), 97–104.

Keselman, H. J. and L. E. Toothaker (1974) 'Comparison of Tukey's T-method and Scheffé's method for various numbers of all possible differences of average contrasts under violation of assumptions', *Educ. and Psychol. Meas.,* **34**, 511–519.

Kirk, R. E. (ed.) (1972) *Statistical Issues: A Reader for the Behavioral Sciences*, Monterey, Brooks/Cole.

Lewis, D. G. (1968) *Experimental Design in Education*, London. University of London Press.

Linton, M., and O. S. Gallo (1975) *The Practical Statistician: A Simplified Handbook of Statistics*, Monterey, Brooks/Cole.

Petrinovich, L. F. and C. D. Hardyck (1969) 'Error rates for multiple comparison methods: Some evidence concerning the frequency of erroneous conclusions', *Psychological Bulletin,* **71**, 43–54, *in* Kirk, R. E. (1972).

Ryan, T. A. (1959) 'Multiple comparisons in psychological research', *Psychological Bulletin*, **56**, 26–47.

Scheffé, H. (1959) *The Analysis of Variance*, New York, John Wiley.

Siegel, S. (1956) *Nonparametric Statistics for the Behavioral Sciences*, New York, McGraw-Hill.

Toothaker, L. E. (1972) 'An empirical comparison of the permutation t-test', *Brit. J. Math. Stat. Psychol.,* **25**, 83–94.

Tukey, J. W. (1962) 'The future of data analysis', *Annals of Mathematical Statistics,* **33**, 1–67.

Veldman, D. J. (1967) *FORTRAN Programming for the Behavioral Sciences*, New York, Holt, Rinehart, and Winston.

Winer, B. J. (1970) *Statistical Principles in Experimental Design*, New York, McGraw-Hill.

8. Relationships Between More Than Two Measures

In both chi-square analysis and analysis of variance it seemed reasonable that further subdivisions of the data should increase the power of the methods to expose significant effects. It was suggested that practical problems such as group size and interpretation made these extensions generally undesirable. Clearly, instances can arise where a more probing analysis is necessary and the main reason for not elaborating methods such as chi-square is that a whole area of statistical analysis has been developed to cope with researches involving many measures. More specifically, *multivariate analysis* is concerned with the *joint* effects of relatively large numbers of variables. This differs from the use of methods such as subset analysis to analyse many variables in that in the examination of between-groups differences each measure is dealt with *separately*, regardless of how many measures are involved. If it is felt that a particular effect is caused by the interaction of a range of attributes then some form of multivariate analysis would be more appropriate.

8.1   Using multivariate methods

From the research standpoint the use of multivariate statistics invokes largely the same considerations as does the application of univariate methods. The choice of a particular technique is determined by the nature of the hypothesis to be tested. Most multivariate methods do have univariate counterparts and as long as this is appreciated there should be little difficulty in selecting the appropriate technique. Without doubt the most widely used is factor analysis which is essentially an extension of the correlation coefficient Rather surprisingly, the other commonly used univariate method, subgroup analysis, has not experienced an equivalent popularity at the multivariate level although the situation is beginning to change. Chapter 9 is concerned with methods of that kind. The present chapter covers the two commonest multivariate methods, factor analysis and multiple linear regression.

A major problem in the discussion of all these methods is that the advanced mathematical techniques they necessarily employ make explanations of the computations involved difficult for most readers although Bennett and Bowers (1976, level B) supply a good background account. Since the correct usage of these methods is considerably more important than an understanding of their internal workings the following descriptions will ignore most computational details. References will be made to suitable sources where necessary. The grading system described in Section 1.6 will be used to indicate level of difficulty.

SELECTION OF VARIABLES

The apparently mechanistic nature of multivariate methods does not imply that their use is therefore automatic. It is essential that the analysis specifications should be defined with careful regard to the hypotheses and to the data. Since the constituent measures operate together it follows that the inclusion of inappropriate measures can distort an analysis even though the error may not be obvious. Each multivariate method carries its own requirements regarding the suitability of variables for analysis but two general considerations prevail, suitability and tautology.

The *suitability of variables* for inclusion in a particular analysis depends largely on the computational procedures the method employs. Both factor analysis and multiple linear regression are based on correlation coefficients and therefore similar conditions apply. Nominal measures cannot be used as they stand; a modification which can often obviate this limitation is to use dummy variable coding (see Section 8.3). Dichotomous data are frequently handled by these methods although a degree of wariness is needed to ensure that other requirements are met. Most higher level data, ordinal, interval or ratio, are suitable, but again only so long as secondary criteria are also satisfied.

The most important of these additional conditions concerns the linearity of measures and it particularly applies to methods based on correlation coefficients. Associated with the linearity criterion is the need for completeness. Missing data codes cannot themselves be used as part of an analysis since the coded values have no quantitative meaning. Occasionally, cases without data can be partially removed from the analysis (by means of the code) but the tactic is unreliable at best, and more often than not actually impossible. The individualized nature of cluster analysis and multiple prediction, for example, demands complete data. The most acceptable approach is to remove cases with missing data from an analysis preferably testing the reduced sample to ensure that representativeness is maintained.

Tautology in an analysis presents a more elusive danger. The general requirement is that an analysis should not be predetermined by the special nature of any of the constituent variables. Probably the commonest instance of this error is where a number of seemingly different measures are constructed from the same basic data. A variety of accuracy or error scores may be obtained from performances on a single psychological test; in econometrics the same data may be used to generate a range of indices. In situations such as those where the foundation of one measure necessarily defines others a degree of interdependence is introduced which could prevent the intended aim of the analysis being realized. Certainly, it is hardly ever legitimate to include both subtest and total scores in a multivariate analysis unless the objective is specifically to examine the relationship between them. Usually the interdependence of variables is obvious; where it is not it may be advisable to check using multiple linear regression (see Section 8.3).

Without careful selection of the constituent measures an analysis can often provide no more than would a simple inspection of the variables themselves. To perform a factor analysis on distinct sets of measures can only result in a replication of this initial disparity. Similarly if one variable is dominant, either by virtue of abnormally high correlations or because of excessive variance, a comparable bias will tend to appear in any subsequent analysis incorporating that variable. Mostly the problem of tautology is one of degree, but being aware of the danger can prevent time and effort being spent on futile analyses. No consideration given to the selection of variables is ever wasted; it can only improve the structure and the interpretation of the eventual analysis.

8.2   The application of factor analysis

The abuses of computer analysis are nowhere more evident than in the numerous misguided applications of factor analysis. A combination of expedience and misunderstanding has led to the technique being applied to many situations where other multivariate methods would have been more appropriate, or even to problems readily soluble by simple univariate statistics. In spite of the power of factor analysis *within* its sphere of application, that of detecting and quantifying patterns of variables, this domain is not so wide as is often assumed. Frequently, the relationships between variables can be more effectively analysed using prediction techniques or classification procedures. Most research texts discuss general applications of factor analysis. For a more extended account, those by Rummel (1967, level A; 1970, level B) are particularly informative, additionally so because they also give very accessible descriptions of the method itself. Bennett and Bowers (1976, level B) describe different types of factoring. Any greater detail tends to require mathematical presentations such as are offered by Horst (1965) and Harman (1967), both of which are level C texts.

As a structuring technique factor analysis has a number of general areas of application. Probably the commonest are those of *understanding* and *reduction*. When many measures are needed to examine a research problem the resulting large number of correlations makes it virtually impossible to assess their importance by inspection. By applying factor analysis to this kind of problem it becomes possible to identify patterns within the variables. These patterns can then be related to current theories, or they can be used to generate new theories and associated hypotheses. Alternatively, there are situations where the information available is considered too extensive and some form of reduction is needed. Typical examples are during the exploratory stages of research, or in the analysis of inventories to produce scales (see Chapter 10). Understanding and reduction are clearly two quite different uses for the method and it would be unreasonable to assume that identical conditions apply to both. In general, the application of factor analysis invokes a small number of principles which hold regardless, together with certain considerations which have to be moderated to satisfy specific needs. There are also a few highly specialized features which tend to become part of the analytical folklore of their respective disciplines. They will not be dealt with here but the analyst should be aware of this possibility of further qualifications to the method.

At the risk of arousing suspicion by insistence it should be emphasized that the following account is intended to demonstrate the operation of the method rather than to explain its mechanics. Too often factor analysis is presented on an esoteric tactic almost akin to a confidence trick. In fact it comprises little more than an alternative perspective on the more familiar correlation matrix. The most convincing way of showing this seems to be to subject the transfer data to the various steps involved, drawing in the methodological principles as they arise. These can then be summarized in a more cohesive manner afterwards.

Table 8.1 Correlation matrix for attitude and ability variables (Decimal points omitted from all correlations)

	6	7	8	9	10	11	12	13	14	15	16	17	18	19	20	21	22
6 JASS	100																
7 JAPS	−15	100															
8 JAPH	−34	09	100														
9 JSCS	15	09	−10	100													
10 JSCP	17	18	−28	41	100												
11 JSCA	18	29	−30	32	45	100											
12 JMOT	04	40	−03	10	30	42	100										
13 SASS	09	18	−14	11	17	25	24	100									
14 SAPS	−07	14	05	06	03	02	−05	−38	100								
15 SANX	−14	08	34	−09	−17	−17	−08	−23	27	100							
16 SSCS	04	−03	−13	36	23	17	−01	11	03	−20	100						
17 SSCP	14	08	−22	17	36	21	14	18	−05	−27	37	100					
18 SSCA	06	17	−19	17	23	44	36	40	−17	−35	22	28	100				
19 SMOT	07	21	−12	05	17	31	52	49	−17	−23	06	19	52	100			
20 JNVR	−09	16	−12	04	21	26	26	11	−01	−12	−02	15	32	19	100		
21 JRED	04	22	−15	−01	30	24	30	14	−01	−16	06	13	25	23	48	100	
22 JMAT	00	20	−23	07	25	28	28	17	−04	−19	00	15	33	24	70	63	100

Variables used in regression analysis but not factor analysis

	6	7	8	9	10	11	12	13	14	15	16	17	18	19	20	21	22
3 AGE	09	05	−06	05	02	03	−02	07	−05	−09	10	11	07	11	−09	06	−02
4 SEX	04	−25	−18	13	03	02	−18	−11	09	−14	08	05	02	−11	−06	−20	−09

FACTOR ANALYSIS TO STRUCTURE TRANSFER ATTITUDES AND ABILITY

Having probed the significance of specific features of the personality and ability of children during primary/secondary transfer, the only way the more involved relationships can be studied is by means of a suitable multivariate analysis. Factor analysis would be appropriate for identifying patterns of attitude and ability over the two-year period. The matrix of intercorrelations between the 17 pertinent variables (Table 8.1) provides a starting point for this examination and it is immediately clear that visual inspection is out of the question. Altogether there are 136 correlation coefficients. One approach is to select important variables and to inspect the correlations for them. Given the orientation of the research it seems sensible to examine the correlations for secondary attitude to secondary school, and an ability measure such as mathematics. Rather than scan the relevant row and column of Table 8.1, a neater approach is to plot the correlations. The two variables can be represented as right-angled axes. For any other variable the pair of correlations with those two can be plotted as a point suitably positioned relative to these axes. Figure 8.1(a) shows this for all 17 variables and certain patterns are immediately apparent. The three ability measures 20, 21, and 22 are separated from the rest. Similarly, the two negative attitudes, apprehension and anxiety, fall outside the main grouping. So do the two primary school attitude measures, variables 7 and 14. It is exactly this kind of patterning that factor analysis is designed to achieve and indeed Fig. 8.1(a) represents a crude form of factor analysis. It is even possible to quantify the structure since the location of any measure is defined by:

$$V_j = r_{j,22}V_{22} + r_{j,13}V_{13} \quad (j = 1, NV) \tag{8.1}$$

(a) Correlations relative to junior mathematics and secondary attitude to secondary school

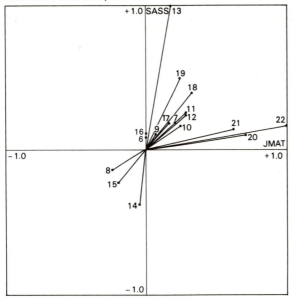

(b) Correlations relative to secondary social self-concept and secondary motivation

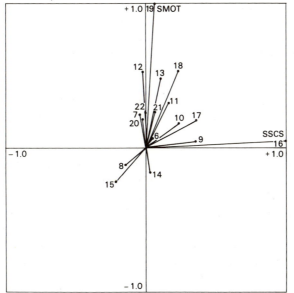

Fig. 8.1 *Correlation plots for 17 transfer variables relative to selected pairs.*

where $r_{j.22}$ is the correlation between variable j and variable 22. There is nothing sacro-sanct about the choice of variables 13 and 22 to summarize the correlation matrix. Figure 8.1(b) shows the same procedure applied to two of the secondary attitude measures, variable 16, self-concept social, and variable 19, academic motivation. In the first example the two selected variables had a near zero correlation between them and that allowed more of the information from the matrix to be represented than if two closely related measures such as mathematics and non-verbal reasoning had been used. For variables 16 and 19 the correlation is .06, again low enough to extract maximum detail. Figure 8.1 (b) is definitely different from Fig. 8.1(a), but not completely so. Variables 8 and 15 show little change. The ability measures 20, 21, and 22 have moved, but they are still together. Overall, the effect has been to clarify relationships involving attitude and self-concept by achieving better discrimination. This has been done by concentrating upon slightly different features of the correlation matrix. Nevertheless, both representations are valid statements of the initial correlation data. Once this is appreciated, the extension into the more analytical methods of factor analysis should be readily appreciated. Essentially, they involve elaborations of the simple relationship expressed in Eq. (8.1):

$$V_j = a_{j1}F_1 + a_{j2}F_2 + \ldots + a_{jm}F_m + d_jU_j \qquad (8.2)$$

where

m is the number of factors ($m \leqslant NV$)
$F_i, i = 1, m$ represent the factors
a_{ji} is the weighting of variable j on factor i
d_jU_j is a specific element for that variable

The factors F_i are themselves combinations of the variables rather than single elements as in Eq. (8.1). The many methods of factor analysis derive from applying different values to the specific term $d_j\,U_j$, and from the manner in which the factors are formed from the constituent variables.

One of these methods, *principal components analysis,* is in turn the starting point for many others. In it the $d_j\,U_j$ term is defined as zero, the factors, or rather components are required to be independent of each other (orthogonal) and the weightings a_{ji} are constructed so that each component in turn accounts for as much of the remaining variance in the correlation matrix as possible. Figure 8.2(a) uses the same system as Fig. 8.1 to represent the 17 variables, but showing the first two principal component weightings rather than two selected variable correlations. The axis values are the weightings or loadings for each variable on the components; they are effectively correlations between the variables and those two components. The exact values are presented later in Table 8.3. Notice the strong similarity between this and Fig. 8.1(a). Variables 20, 21, and 22 cluster together; variable 7 is quite close to them; variables 8, 14, and 15 occupy almost identical positions. The most prominent difference is the tendency for the points in the principal components plot to be further from the origin. Recalling that the joint variation of two variables is obtained by squaring the correlation coefficient, it follows that the larger distances from the origin imply greater variances because the distances are related to the weightings which in turn are correlations. Since the main feature of the principal

100

(a) First two principal components (both reflected)

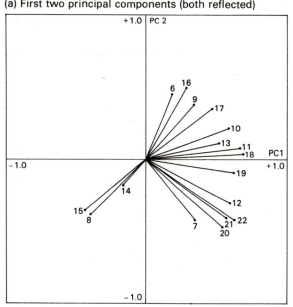

(b) Two largest varimax factors

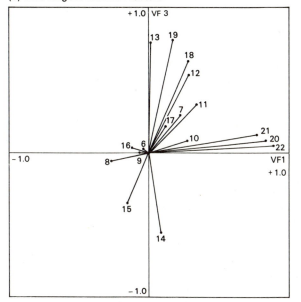

Fig. 8.2 *Plots of two principal components and two varimax factors.*

components method is the need to maximize variation for each component, the wider scatter is as one would expect. In fact the first principal component accounts for 25 per cent of the overall variance (see later).

101

Although factor analysis may be required to maximize variation in as few components as possible, more often the need is to clarify the relationship between variables. The most popular method of achieving this is to apply a modification called *rotation* to the principal components solution. The term rotation derives from the mathematical procedure used to transform the factor equation (8.2). Instead of simply selecting reference variables as in Fig. 8.1, the reference axes are constructed by rotating the principal components. Many types of rotation exist. They can be conveniently classified into orthogonal methods where the rotation must maintain independence between factors, and oblique methods where this requirement is relaxed. Of the *orthogonal methods* the one that has achieved greatest popularity is Kaiser's (1958) varimax criterion. It incorporates the principle that only very high or near-zero correlations can be reliably interpreted. Since the weightings of Eq. (8.2) are generally correlations between variables and factors it follows that these should be similarly high or low. Figure 8.2(b) shows the two largest varimax factors for the same 17 variables. The horizontal axis, factor 1, clearly isolates the three ability measures with their loadings in excess of .75. No others reach .30. The second largest, factor 3, is not so extreme but it does have a large number of near-zero correlations. Once more, however, the affinity with the simple correlation plots of Fig. 8.1 is clearly evident. Factor 1 corresponds to the junior mathematics axis. Factor 2 tends to be dominated by those measures that were closest to the secondary motivation axis of Fig. 8.1(b) namely variables 12, 13, 14, 18, and 19.

In *oblique rotations* the factors can be correlated. This is a particularly valuable quality when the variables for analysis are themselves closely related. The orthogonality restriction would tend to result in a small number of general factors; allowing factors to be related has the effect of producing finer discrimination. Eliciting scales from inventories or questionnaires frequently benefits from oblique factoring (see Chapter 10). Figure 8.3 shows two representations of an oblique analysis of the 17 transfer measures using Kaiser's Little Jiffy method (Kaiser, 1970; Kaiser and Rice, 1974). The first of these two plots is the equivalent of those in Figs. 8.1 and 8.2. It gives the correlations between the variables and factors and is called the *factor structure* matrix. For oblique factors the angle between them, θ, can be determined from the relationship:

$$\text{correlation between factors} = \cos\theta \qquad (8.3)$$

The correlation of .52 between the first two oblique factors would imply an angle of 59° and Fig. 8.3(a) inclines the two factors at that angle. Variables still have to be plotted using right-angled projections. The clustering of variables about the two oblique axes can be seen but the significance of individual measures is less obvious because of the angle. For this reason interpretation of oblique factors is usually obtained from the *factor pattern* matrix (Fig. 8.3(b)) which gives the a_{ji} coefficients of Eq. (8.2) and enables the variables to be computed. However, they are *not* correlation coefficients as the structure matrix loadings are.

In general terms the factor pattern matrix allows the relationships between the variables forming a cluster or factor to be seen. However, the loadings cannot be interpreted as correlations, nor can they be used to evaluate the relative contributions of variables to factors. On the other hand the factor structure matrix quantifies the degree

(a) Oblique structure showing 59° axes and right-angled
projections for loadings

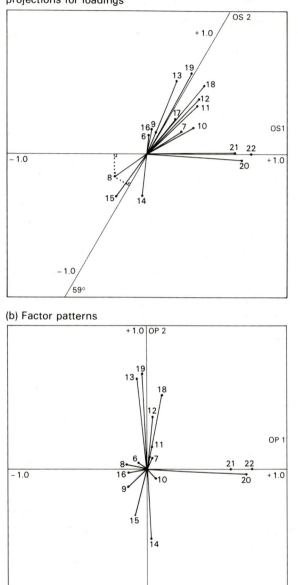

(b) Factor patterns

Fig. 8.3 *Plots of first two oblique factors.*

of association of a variable with a factor in terms of its correlation. As a result the
patterning of the separate variables tends to be obscured.

A comparison of the varimax and oblique solutions shows that although the two

103

analyses generate similar factors, the oblique structure does seem closer to the variable groupings. Both of the varimax factors fall slightly outside the plotted clusters, a result of the forced orthogonality. Just in case this final extension of the basic method appears to have left the original data behind, reference to the correlation plots of Fig. 8.1 should confirm the essential similarity. The ability factor of the varimax and oblique analyses is the mathematics axis of Fig. 8.1(a). The academic attitude factor closely matches the vertical axis of Fig. 8.1(b), secondary motivation. Applying factor analysis has simplified the rather laborious process of plotting correlations, but is has not distorted the original relationships as given in the correlation matrix. The remainder of this section presents some of the main considerations in carrying out and interpreting factor analyses.

SELECTING A METHOD

The different methods have largely been developed as general solutions to the problem of structuring data and therefore it is not possible to specify definite choices for particular applications. Normally other studies in the same area of research will have suggested the suitability of certain methods; the researcher may wish to maintain that tradition, or possibly to assess the power of other methods to provide new insights. It is this background of research, together with some theoretical justification, that has led to the use of oblique methods for constructing scales. Similarly the need to maximize differences adds weight to the use of orthogonal techniques in cognitive structuring.

SPECIFYING THE VARIABLES

The first consideration must be the theoretical justification for including variables in an analysis. No analysis can exceed the quality of its input and too often the blunderbuss tactic prevails so that any vaguely pertinent measure is included. Such an approach can only hide the structure of the more important variables. Initially, therefore, any doubt should lead to a measure being withheld; if necessary it can be added later to see whether any beneficial change results. As well as guaranteeing a valid analysis, this preliminary screening will help considerably in the eventual interpretation.

The need for constituent variables to be linearly independent has been mentioned. Should dependence be suspected without being obvious, a simple method of checking is to obtain the multiple correlation coefficient for each variable with all the rest (see Section 8.3). If the value is 1.0 for any variable then that variable can be constructed from the rest and is therefore linearly dependent. Some factor analysis programs compute and output the multiple correlations as part of the method, otherwise a separate multiple regression analysis must be done to check. Certain other requirements such as linearity may not be met by the raw data, but it could be that a suitable simple transformation of the data obviates this difficulty. On no account must the number of variables exceed the number of cases since this will nullify the mathematical procedures used to transform the correlation matrix.

While most methods are largely automatic occasionally it may be necessary to specify a communality estimate for each variable to replace the self-correlations in the

104

matrix diagonal. The *communality* is the proportion of a variable's variance accounted for by the factor analysis solution and it cannot be known beforehand. A number of possible estimates are advocated (Harman, 1967) including the highest correlation for a variable or its reliability. The latter is necessarily greater than the final communality. Rather more support exists for using the squared multiple correlation for each variable with the rest. The value can be readily computed within the factor analysis program and knowing that it is consistently less than or equal to the communality can be helpful.

HOW MANY FACTORS?

The rotation procedure is applied to a smaller number of factors than there are variables and the final factor pattern depends heavily upon this reduced number. Consequently, the specification of the number of factors is of vital importance. As with most statistical decisions both theoretical and analytical criteria are available. The prime theoretical consideration would be whether there was evidence to suggest a certain number of factors or dimensions. Analytical guides are more varied. Crawford (1975) summarizes a discussion of these as the need for a factor matrix to have few factors, to account for a large proportion of the overall variance, and to have at least three high loadings per factor in conjunction with a large number of near zero loadings.

To appreciate the first two criteria it is necessary to understand factor variance. Table 8.2 lists the variances associated with all 17 principal components for the 17 transfer measures. As has already been mentioned, the first and largest component

Table 8.2   Variance associated with successive principal components

Component	Eigenvalue	Percentage variance	Cumulative variance
1	4.27	25.11	25.11
2	1.97	11.61	36.72
3	1.65	9.68	46.40
4	1.50	8.80	55.20
5	1.15	6.76	61.96
6	0.85	5.00	66.96
7	0.77	4.55	71.52
8	0.70	4.14	75.65
9	0.65	3.84	79.49
10	0.61	3.61	83.10
11	0.57	3.36	86.46
12	0.53	3.14	89.60
13	0.48	2.80	92.40
14	0.38	2.25	94.66
15	0.35	2.08	97.73
16	0.31	1.83	98.56
17	0.24	1.44	100.00
TOTALS	17.00	100.00	

accounts for 25 per cent of the overall variance. Succeeding components account for less and less by virtue of the extraction method. The total variance in the correlation matrix is equal to the number of variables since they are standardized to unit variance. The variance for any individual component is measured by its eigenvalue and this in turn is obtained by squaring the variable loadings for that factor. Table 8.3 gives the factor loading matrices for three different analyses. The eigenvalue for the first principal component can easily be computed:

$$E_1 = 0.19^2 + 0.35^2 + 0.40^2 + \ldots + 0.63^2 = 4.27$$

Since the overall variance is equal to the number of variables, 17, the proportion accounted for by the first component is 4.27/17.0 = 25.1 per cent. Each component adds to the overall variance explained but the problem becomes one of deciding when to stop. If the total variance of 17.0 were distributed equally over the 17 possible components then each would attract one-seventeenth, that is 1.0. This in turn implies that the eigenvalue would be 1.0. Components with *eigenvalues greater than 1.0* therefore account for

Table 8.3 Principal components and varimax factor matrices

(Variables loading over .50 on the varimax factors are asterisked. This enables the difference between the five-factor and four-factor solution to be seen. Particularly noticeable is the separation of an anxiety factor when only four factors are rotated. It comprises the three variables JAPS, JAPH, and SANX.)

	A Principal components					B Five varimax rotated factors					C Four varimax rotated factors				Sum of squares communality		
	1	2	3	4	5	1	2	3	4	5	1	2	3	4	A	B	C
6 JASS	−19	−46	−01	19	63	−12	00	05	04	82*	−04	31	03	−44	68	69	29
7 JAPS	−35	42	−22	−47	04	14	04	−11	70*	−23	22	21	27	64*	57	58	58
8 JAPH	40	38	03	−43	−36	−22	−17	−14	08	−72*	−27	−34	−05	55*	62	62	49
9 JSCS	−34	−39	−45	−24	−09	−10	65*	−14	25	16	−08	72*	00	05	54	54	53
10 JSCP	−59	−21	−42	−04	10	23	51*	−08	36	36	28	69*	09	00	58	58	56
11 JSCA	−67	−08	−23	−19	26	19	32	06	58*	36	28	58*	33	11	61	61	54
12 JMOT	−60	30	02	−39	22	20	−01	19	76*	04	29	23	55*	40	65	66	60
13 SASS	−52	−11	49	−27	−02	00	10	69*	34	04	01	08	76*	−11	60	60	60
14 SAPS	17	18	−70	−06	09	04	11	−73*	15	−04	09	27	−55*	42	56	57	56
15 SANX	44	36	−32	−29	16	−22	−29	−55*	19	−25	−16	−16	−36	58*	54	53	52
16 SSCS	−29	−50	−26	−09	−53	−04	82*	10	−10	−09	−12	60*	04	−19	69	70	41
17 SSCP	−47	−36	−13	03	−32	15	63*	22	02	09	11	51*	19	−24	47	48	37
18 SSCA	−70	−04	23	−12	−15	28	30	54*	35	04	28	27	63*	−08	58	58	55
19 SMOT	−62	09	39	−33	08	12	02	58*	55*	03	16	11	78*	10	66	65	66
20 JNVR	−54	47	−10	41	−18	84*	04	05	12	−06	83*	01	09	02	72	73	70
21 JRED	−57	40	−10	37	−02	76*	03	05	19	09	78*	08	12	00	63	63	63
22 JMAT	−63	43	−07	46	−08	88*	04	09	15	07	88*	05	14	−05	80	81	80
sum of squares	4.3	2.0	1.6	1.5	1.1	2.5	2.1	2.1	2.3	1.6	2.6	2.5	2.6	1.7			
factor variance (%)	25	12	10	9	7	14	12	12	14	10	15	15	15	10			
cumulative variance (%)	25	37	46	55	62	14	27	39	52	62	15	30	45	55			

more than chance variation and can be considered significant. Applied to the analysis of Table 8.2 this would entail accepting five components covering 62 per cent of the total variance. Generally, this criterion tends to result in about $NV/3$ factors accounting for around 70 per cent of the variance. Among the various alternative criteria that have been proposed Crawford (1975) suggests an index of interpretability but he admits that this frequently equates to the eigenvalues–greater-than-one criterion anyway.

Occasionally the importance of specific variables may take precedence over general criteria. Just as the variance of a factor can be computed by squaring the loadings, so the contribution of the factors to a variable's variance is given by the communality. In this case the loadings of all the factors on an individual variable are squared and summed. Table 8.3 gives the communality values for all three analyses. Those for the five principal components and the five varimax factors are necessarily the same (apart from rounding errors) because they involve the same five components. Reducing the number of factors lowers the variable communalities. Should any of these become unacceptably low then more factors may be needed. Variable six, for example, suffers in the reduction from five to four varimax factors while the three ability measures, variables 20, 21, and 22 are hardly affected.

However, most writers on factor analysis agree that there is no simple answer to the problem of how many factors to extract. Rummel (1970) discusses the point in detail and offers a range of strategies. He concludes by saying that while it is generally preferable to err on the side of extracting too many factors, only repeated analysis can confirm which factors are general and which are specific to a particular design.

INTERPRETING FACTORS

Factors are interpreted from the matrix of factor-variable correlations for orthogonal methods and from the factor pattern matrix for oblique rotations. Table 8.3 shows the factor-variable intercorrelations (loadings) for three analyses. Traditionally, for orthogonal analyses, loadings of over .50 are taken to define a factor while those over .30 can be used to add detail. Since these are correlations it follows that high *negative* loadings are equally important; they imply that *low* scores on a variable are associated with that factor. Few programs actually test the significance of factor loadings but Kerlinger (1973) does offer suggestions here. These include taking standard significance levels as for a correlation coefficient, using $1/\sqrt{N}$ as the standard error for a loading, or following a procedure recommended by Harman (1967, page 435). In it the average correlation in the factor matrix, r, is computed and from it the standard error is obtained as follows:

$$\sigma_a = \frac{1}{2}\sqrt{\frac{\frac{3}{r} - 2 - 5r + 4r^2}{N}} \tag{8.4}$$

This can then be treated as any other normal deviate.

107

Table 8.3 does emphasize the superiority of rotations over the principal components solution. With loadings over .50 asterisked in the varimax solution the partitioning of variables into factors is very clear:

		Variables
Factor 1	the three ability measures	20 21 22
Factor 2	personal and social self-concept	9 10 16 17
Factor 3	secondary attitude to school	13 14 15 18 19
Factor 4	motivation	2 11 12 19
Factor 5	attitude to primary school	6 8

Apart from the large first principal component, few of the others in that analysis are readily interpretable. One reservation with the five varimax factors is that the fifth does not meet the criterion of having at least three high loadings. A factor that only has two dominant variables says no more than a simple correlation coefficient. The four-factor solution does not suffer from this fault and indeed comprises more interesting factors:

		Variables
Factor 1	ability	20 21 22
Factor 2	self-concept	9 10 11 16 17
Factor 3	academic attitude	12 13 14 18 19
Factor 4	anxiety	7 8 15

Being much more clearly-defined dimensions of human behaviour these should be easier to interpret within the context of the research problem. The substantial difference between the four-factor and five-factor varimax solutions emphasizes the value of reanalysis to arrive at the most suitable number of factors.

When an oblique analysis is performed, the factor intercorrelations can produce so many moderately high factor-structure loadings that interpretation becomes difficult. In that case the factor pattern matrix is more suitable for interpretation although the structure matrix can be used as supporting evidence. The matrix of factor intercorrelations is also useful since it indicates which factors are related. In Table 8.4 factors two and three are highly correlated and consequently the structure loadings are similar. It is the pattern matrix that enables the differences between the two factors to be seen and these are in fact quite pronounced.

One valuable interpretative aid stems from the device of *reflection*. Just as high negative correlations are significant, so negative loadings should not be ignored. Indeed, it is frequently constructive to reflect a factor by changing the signs of *all* loadings, particularly when a large number of negative ones exist. This tactic redefines the factor in terms of the negatively loaded variables and the factor must be renamed accordingly.

REFINING A FACTOR STRUCTURE

Difficulties in interpretation may suggest that a factor structure could be refined by appropriate modifications to the sample or the constituent variables. Rimoldi (1948) has proposed the *squared multiple correlation* (SMC) of a variable with the rest as a useful

Table 8.4 Oblique four-factor analysis structure and pattern matrices

	Structure				Pattern				
	1	2	3	4	1	2	3	4	SMC
6 JASS	01	13	23	−20	−08	05	26	−20	.20
7 JAPS	25	26	23	44	03	09	13	40*	.29
8 JAPH	−23	−25	−37	22	−15	−04	−29	29*	.30
9 JSCS	07	16	45	01	−15	−12	58*	03	.31
10 JSCP	33	33	59	09	07	−07	60*	04	.41
11 JSCA	37	48	58	20	03	15	47*	13	.44
12 JMOT	38	52	38	42	04	37*	12	33*	.45
13 SASS	21	56	30	04	−08	63*	−04	−05	.39
14 SAPS	−04	−28	−01	18	02	−49*	26	25*	.25
15 SANX	−22	−37	−31	24	−10	−32	−09	33*	.28
16 SSCS	03	16	37	−15	−13	−02	46*	−14	.29
17 SSCP	20	31	43	−09	01	10	38*	−14	.28
18 SSCA	41	62	47	10	10	51*	12	−03	.46
19 SMOT	32	64	35	22	−04	67*	−05	11	.48
20 JNVR	69	32	29	21	71*	−03	−03	02	.53
21 JRED	63	34	32	20	60*	00	04	03	.46
22 JMAT	75	39	35	19	76*	00	00	−02	.63

RELATIVE CONTRIBUTIONS	36%	29%	25%	10%					

FACTOR	1	1.00			
CORRELATION	2	0.52	1.00		
MATRIX	3	0.47	0.61	1.00	
	4	0.28	0.18	0.07	1.00

SMC is the squared multiple correlation with remaining variables. Salient coefficients in the factor pattern matrix are asterisked. The only difference compared with the four-factor varimax solution is the inclusion of junior motivation and secondary attitude to primary in the anxiety factor.

diagnostic aid suggesting that if a large proportion of the variables had low SMC values then very few common factors would arise. A level of .30 was offered as a possible criterion. The low values for variables 6 and 14 make these possible candidates for exclusion. A common failing in factor analysis is to use too few cases. From the correlation basis of the method, and recalling that even a sample of 100 requires a correlation of .2 for significance, it is unwise to use fewer than 100 cases. A more acceptable minimum is 200 cases.

FACTOR SCORES

Having generated a factor structure for a set of variables it is often useful to be able to estimate these factors from the variables. Applying this relationship to individual scores produces factor scores which can then be treated as variables just like any other measures. Their advantage is that they are fewer in number than the original variables. Most programs can compute factor scores but simpler forms can easily be computed by hand if the facility is not available. Horn (1965) and Horn and Miller (1966) assess a range of methods and conclude that certain of these more elementary methods are adequate for many applications.

COMPARISON OF FACTORS

Occasionally it may be necessary to compare the results of separate factor analyses. Two distinct possibilities exist since either the variables or the samples may be different, but not both.

Same sample: different variables

Here the procedure is straightforward. The factor scores for all cases are obtained for both sets of factors and standard product-moment correlations between all factor scores are computed. Similar factors correlate highly.

Same variables: different samples

The above procedure cannot be applied in this instance since the two samples cannot be related. Harman (1967) discusses this situation in detail and offers two methods. The *root mean square method* is unsatisfactory in that it does not identify equivalent but reflected factors (those with similar loadings but opposite signs). Since this is a highly likely outcome for two different analyses the procedure is not recommended. His alternative, the *coefficient of congruence*, does not suffer from this limitation. Although its computation resembles a correlation coefficient the two are not equivalent because the values used are loadings and not deviations:

$$C_{pq} = \frac{\Sigma a_{jp} \times b_{jq}}{\sqrt{\Sigma(a_{jp})^2 \times \Sigma(b_{jq})^2}} \qquad (j = 1, NV) \qquad (8.5)$$

where a_{jp} is the loading of variable j on factor p
$\quad b_{jq}$ is the loading of variable j on factor q

Values of the coefficient of congruence range from $+1$ for complete agreement through 0 for no relationship to -1 for complete disagreement (that is, reflection).

A RECOMMENDED PROCEDURE

For many researchers applying factor analysis is their first experience of using a statistical method whose outcome seems to demand something akin to blind faith. Although this is an undesirable reaction, without spending considerable time studying texts such as Rummel (1970) or Harman (1967), a degree of superficiality in one's understanding must be accepted. Nevertheless, it is possible to protect against serious misunderstanding by following a series of relatively simple precautions.

Data checking: Examine the means and standard deviations of the input variables to ensure that they are correct, and that very small or very high variances are not distorting the analysis.
Correlations: Examine the correlation matrix since even a cursory inspection should allow some of the more obvious patterns to be seen. If highly intercorrelated variables do not appear within the same factors, then something may be amiss. Also any very high

correlations (in excess of .95) should be noted as these may produce a suspect solution.
Variance proportions: The analysis will extract factors according to your initial specification. However, inspection of the variances associated with successive factors might suggest that more or fewer factors could improve the analysis. This is particularly so if an eigenvalue very close to 1.0 is involved.

Factor plots: The factor plots enable the dominant measures on a factor to be identified quickly, and so simplify the task of characterizing and naming factors. Any factors with fewer than three dominant measures are no more than restated correlation coefficients.

Pattern and structure matrices: For an orthogonal analysis such as varimax a single factor loading matrix is produced since the pattern and structure are the same. Interpretation of an oblique analysis (for example, promax or Kaiser's Little Jiffy) is best performed via the pattern matrix. The structure matrix serves to indicate the strength of association between a variable and a factor.

Factor intercorrelations: Relationships between oblique factors as indicated by the factor intercorrelation matrix should confirm your interpretation of individual factors. Negative correlations in particular should be checked to ensure that the factors concerned have been defined in the appropriate direction. Orthogonal factors are uncorrelated and therefore this check cannot be made.

Reflection of factors: Negative constructs such as lack of commitment or school dislike can confuse statistical interpretation. Where such a factor arises it may be preferable to reflect that factor by changing the signs of all loadings on it.

Factor measurement: Frequently, factor analysis is used to derive summary measures for subsequent analysis. The two forms most often used are factor scores, which incorporate weighted variable combinations, and scales which usually combine disjoint sets of variables by simple addition. The former are more appropriate for the investigation of factor structures, the latter being easier to interpret tend to fulfil psychometric needs better, especially in individual assessment or subgroup analysis.

Factor refinement: It is rare for a first trial factor analysis to provide the best solution. Usually reanalysis with a different number of factors extracted, or with a modified selection of variables, will improve the first attempt.

8.3   Multiple regression analysis and its uses

No special emphasis is placed on any of the individual variables in a factor analysis although the generated structure may highlight the dominant role of particular measures. Where researches specifically identify important variables it is likely that some form of multiple regression analysis will offer a more appropriate analytical approach. Typically, one variable is considered the dependent variable, usually called the criterion, and its relationships with one or more other independent variables is to be investigated. Factor analysis had a variety of possible applications and the basic multiple regression model can similarly be applied to a number of different types of relationship. Probably the commonest of these is the prediction of one attribute from others. Also the method is used to examine the relationship between composite scores and a criterion, for example in item analysis, or in constructing test batteries. In some circumstances it can even be used to assess causality. McNeil *et al.* (1975, level C) offer a detailed account of the applications of multiple regression models. A good introduction to the method is provided by Kerlinger (1973, level B) while a considerably extended version is given by Kerlinger and Pedhazur (1973, level C). Two long articles (Cohen, 1968, level C; Darlington, 1968, level B) together cover a wide range of the more general considerations in multiple regression analysis, emphasizing its breadth of applicability.

A multiple linear regression model is defined in terms of a criterion variable V_c and a set of k predictor variables $V_{p1} \ldots V_{pk}$. The method attempts to construct a linear relationship of the form:

$$V_{pc} = B_o + B_1 V_{p1} \ldots + B_k V_{pk} \tag{8.6}$$

so that V_{pc}, the predicted measure, is as close as possible to V_c the criterion. The product moment correlation between V_c and V_{pc} is the multiple correlation R. The coefficients B_j in Eq. (8.6) are weightings that have to be applied to the k predictor variables to maximize this multiple correlation. Generally the method can only approximate to the actual criterion, but should the prediction be perfect the multiple correlation would be 1.0. This would imply that for each person his criterion score, say achievement in some skill, could be calculated from his scores on the predictor variables using Eq. (8.6).

Once more a knowledge of the mathematical details of the method is less important than an understanding of its correct usage. The main considerations involved will be demonstrated within the transfer research.

Predicting secondary school adjustment

One measure of a successful transfer from primary to secondary school can be obtained from the secondary attitude to school scale, variable 13. Although some value might be gained from assessing this attribute in the secondary school, far more benefit would arise if it could be predicted beforehand. Given that a wide range of personal data was collected at the primary stage, multiple regression analysis offers a method whereby the predictive data for this sample can be used to estimate the level of adjustment. The derived relationship could then be applied to any other sample.

SPECIFYING A MODEL

A basic multiple regression model comprises a criterion variable and a set of predictors. Normally, no relative importance is accorded to these predictors but on occasions it can be preferable to specify an order of priority beforehand. Another variation is known as stepwise regression. In it more predictor variables than are considered relevant are entered so that the method itself can identify the significant predictors, much as principal components analysis extracts decreasingly important factors. The method works from correlation coefficients and therefore similar conditions apply as for factor analysis. Sample size is even more important here because the method capitalizes on chance variation to such an extent that results from small samples have little general applicability. Ideally, samples should exceed 200, or at worst 100 members. The number of variables should be kept low for the same reason. Darlington (1968) suggests a maximum of between 50 and 100 predictors. On no account must the number of predictors be greater than the number of cases.

The linear form of Eq. (8.6) does not imply that the variables themselves must be linear. Christal's (1968) classic article on selecting a harem succinctly demonstrates how a variety of variable transformations can be incorporated within multiple linear regression models. Even categoric data can be used so long as they are converted into dichotomous variables first (see later).

In the transfer analysis variable 13, secondary attitude to secondary school, becomes the criterion. Since temporal prediction is the aim only primary school variables can be used as predictors. The two categoric school codes are best analysed separately and social class records an excessive amount of missing data. This leaves the 12 variables 3–4, 6–12, and 20–22 as the predictor set.

THE COMPUTATIONAL METHOD

The majority of regression programs use matrix inversion techniques making them difficult to follow. The method is most easily understood from Veldman's (1967) program which uses Greenberger and Ward's (1956) iterative multiple regression approach. The process of constructing the best regression equation commences by identifying the predictor variable that has the highest correlation with the criterion. From Table 8.1 (page 98) for criterion variable 13 this is variable 11 with a correlation of .25. The next step is to find the variable which *together with variable 11* produces the greatest increase in the multiple correlation with variable 13. Table 8.5 gives the complete iteration cycle showing that variable 12 is taken next. Since its correlation with the criterion is only marginally lower (.24) than that of variable 11 this is reasonable. On the next iteration, however, preference is given to variable 4 (sex) with a criterion correlation of –0.11 rather than to variable 7 with one of .18. This happens because the latter variable has relatively high correlations with variables already in the prediction equation (i.e., .40 with variable 12, .29 with 11) and therefore has much of its contribution accounted for. Figure 8.4 represents this idea of variance. The degree of correlation between a predictor (circle) and the criterion (square) can be shown as an appropriate amount of overlap. By the time the two high overlap predictors 12 and 11 have been included, only a small proportion of the criterion variance of variable 7 remains (the black area).

And so the process repeats. Each time either a new variable from the predictor set is included, or the weighting of one already present is adjusted, so as to increase maximally the criterion variance explained. Gradually this improvement diminishes until it becomes less than some arbitrarily defined limit and there the process terminates.

SIGNIFICANCE OF A MODEL

The overall process is automatic and will produce a solution regardless of the levels of correlation in the initial matrix. Its significance is assessed from the final multiple correla-

113

Table 8.5 Regression model predicting secondary school attitude from primary school characteristics

CRITERION	Variable 13	SECONDARY ATTITUDE TO SECONDARY SCHOOL
PREDICTORS	Variable 3	AGE
	Variable 4	SEX
	Variable 6	JUNIOR ATTITUDE TO SECONDARY SCHOOL
	Variable 7	JUNIOR ATTITUDE TO PRIMARY SCHOOL
	Variable 8	APPREHENSION OVER TRANSFER
	Variable 9	JUNIOR SELF-CONCEPT SOCIAL
	Variable 10	JUNIOR SELF-CONCEPT PERSONAL
	Variable 11	JUNIOR SELF-CONCEPT ACADEMIC
	Variable 12	JUNIOR ACADEMIC MOTIVATION
	Variable 20	NON-VERBAL REASONING
	Variable 21	READING COMPREHENSION
	Variable 22	MATHEMATICS

Iteration	Predictor included	Multiple R	Multiple R squared
1	11	.2468	.0609
2	12	.2914	.0849
3	4	.3035	.0921
4	8	.3195	.1021
5	3	.3265	.1066
6	7	.3324	.1105
7	22	.3367	.1134
8	6	.3391	.1150
9	9	.3409	.1162
10	11	.3422	.1171
11	20	.3428	.1175
12	4	.3434	.1179
13	10	.3437	.1181
14	22	.3438	.1182
15	21	.3442	.1185
16	12	.3444	.1186
17	6	.3445	.1187
18	22	.3446	.1187
19	20	.3447	.1188
20	22	.3447	.1188
21	8	.3447	.1188
22	20	.3447	.1188

FINAL MULTIPLE CORRELATION	0.3447
SQUARED	0.1188
F-RATIO	5.9559
PROBABILITY	0.000**
SHRUNKEN MULTIPLE CORRELATION	0.3080
CROSS-VALIDATION CORRELATION	0.2751
REGRESSION CONSTANT	19.2909

tion R by means of an F-ratio:

$$F = \frac{R^2/k}{(1 - R^2)/(N - k - 1)} \tag{8.7}$$

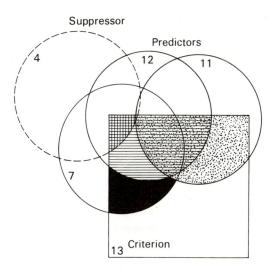

Suppressor

Predictors

Criterion

Variables

13 secondary attitude to secondary school

11 junior academic self-concept
12 junior academic motivation
 7 junior attitude to junior school
 4 sex

Fig. 8.4 *Representation of relative value of predictors. Variables 11 and 12 are substantial predictors, also covering most of the contribution of variable 7. Variable 4 is a suppressor, furthering the overall prediction by suppressing the unwanted effects of variables 12 and 7, rather than through a correlation with the criterion.*

where N is the number of cases
            k is the number of independent predictors
degrees of freedom are k and $(N - k - 1)$.

For the transfer example of Table 8.5 the F-ratio of 4.95 with degrees of freedom 12 and 441 is highly significant ($p < 0.0001$) indicating that the relationship between the primary predictors and secondary school attitude is a definite one. The multiple correlation for a sample will be an overestimate for the population. A standard method for producing a better estimate for a population is to obtain a *shrunken multiple correlation* using the correction:

$$R_s^2 = 1 - \frac{N-1}{N-k-1} (1 - R^2) \qquad (8.8)$$

115

The value obtained is .308, a slight reduction from the original .345. Alternatively, a cross-validation check can be made using half of the sample to generate the regression equation, but deriving the multiple correlation by applying that equation to the other half of the sample. Using an odd-even split on the transfer sample results in a *cross-validation correlation* of .275 a much greater reduction than that given by the shrunken R. In general the cross-correlation underestimates the population value (Ferguson, 1976).

RELATIVE IMPORTANCE OF PREDICTORS

A model represents a complete interdependent structure and as such it is inappropriate to overemphasize the importance of individual predictors within it. Nevertheless, given suitable interpretation, certain measures of relative power have been suggested and Darlington (1968) provides a detailed discussion of them. Table 8.6 lists these for the attitude model. The raw weights, B, are the coefficients of Eq. (8.7) and together with the regression constant B_0 they enable the predicted scores V_{pc} to be calculated. However, they are unreliable indications of relative importance since their magnitude depends on the scale of the variable to which they refer. The standard weights (*beta weights*) apply to standardized forms of the predictors and therefore avoid this distortion. Even so they have limited value in determining relative merit since low beta weights do not necessarily correspond to lack of importance. If two predictors are highly correlated with each other, one will necessarily attract a low beta weight simply because its effect has already been included in the other. Variable 10 offers a good example here; in spite

Table 8.6 Relative importance measures for predictors

	CRITERION VARIABLE 13 SECONDARY ATTITUDE TO SECONDARY SCHOOL						
Predictor	Raw weight B	Standard weight b	Criterion correlation RC	RCxb Rb	Structure correlation RS	Terminal variance (%) TV	Entry order
3 AGE	.08	.06	.07	.004	.20	0.4	5
4 SEX	−.86	−.09	−.11	.011	−.33	0.8*	3
6 JASS	.07	.04	.09	.003	.27	0.1	8
7 JAPS	.12	.07	.18	.013	.53	0.4	6
8 JAPH	−.13	−.09	−.14	.013	.41	0.6	4
9 JSCS	.08	.04	.11	.005	.32	0.1	9
10 JSCP	.03	.02	.17	.003	.50	0.0	11
11 JSCA	.20	.10	.25	.026	.72	0.7	1
12 JMOT	.17	.13	.24	.033	.71	1.2*	2
20 JNVR	−.01	−.03	.11	−.004	.30	0.1	10
21 JRED	−.01	−.02	.14	−.003	.42	0.0	12
22 JMAT	.03	.09	.17	.016	.50	0.4	7

Regression
constant B_0 19.29

A range of different indicators of predictive importance is included here. The asterisks against two of the terminal variances indicate that each of those variables contributes significantly ($P < 0.05$) when added to the rest.

of a relatively high correlation of .17 with the criterion it receives a low beta weight because of its high correlation with predictors entered earlier into the regression equation (for example, 9, 11, and 12). Darlington does cite one situation where the beta weights validly indicate relative importance. Basically the condition is that all determinants of criterion variation must either be contained in the model, or be uncorrelated with any of the included predictors, a relatively rare occurrence.

The criterion correlation RC gives a misleading indication of importance when predictors are correlated, as they usually are. By multiplying the criterion correlation and the beta weight a better estimate of strength is obtained (Cooley and Lohnes, 1971). This statistic also enables a special type of predictor known as a *suppressor variable* to be identified. It is one which has a low correlation with the criterion but which nevertheless acquires a high beta weight because of its ability to suppress the unwanted effects of other predictors. Figure 8.4 shows the situation diagrammatically. Variable 4, sex, offers an example since its beta weight of .09 is quite high in spite of a low correlation of –0.11 with the criterion. Its contribution towards the overall prediction derives from its high correlation of .25 with primary school liking, variable 7. One property of the Rb measure that should not be overrated is the fact that the sum of the Rb values equals the squared multiple correlation. The interdependence of correlated predictors prevents these values being taken separately as indicators of individual variance contributions.

Cooley and Lohnes actually recommend use of the *structure correlation*, obtained by dividing the criterion correlation RC by the multiple correlation R. This measure is analogous to the loadings in factor analysis as it gives the correlation between a predictor and the regression equation, that is the predicted score V_{pc}. Interpretation is straightforward since it indicates the degree to which a predictor approximates to the overall prediction model.

Few programs output the *terminal variance* although it can usually be determined by specifying a suitable sequence of models. Having obtained a full model analysis including all predictors, another multiple correlation is computed by specifying a complementary model including all the predictors *except* the one under consideration. Since squared multiple correlations correspond to variances, the difference between the squared multiple correlations for the full and complementary models gives the variance contributed by that predictor when all the others have been used. This is the terminal variance and its significance can be tested by applying an F-test for the comparison of models (see below).

One final indication can quickly be seen from iterative or stepwise programs and that is the *order of entry* of the predictors. Again, it has the drawback of masking the importance of late entries arising from intercorrelations with other predictors. Where it does have valuable applications is in the generation of predictive batteries. If it were felt that only a limited number of the predictors could be applied in normal practice, then those entered first would constitute the more efficient subset. From Table 8.5, taking only the first 4 variables, 11, 12, 4, and 8, would produce a multiple correlation only .025 lower than the eventual .345.

So once again no definite choice exists. Preference for the structure correlation could be waived if the aim was to produce a reduced battery. Certainly beta weights are very susceptible to sample changes and should be cross-validated if used at all.

117

COMPARISON OF MODELS

Just as the terminal contribution of an individual predictor can be assessed by comparing full and complementary models, so the effect of any subset of predictors can be tested for significance. The important stipulation is that the larger set must include all those in the subset. The two multiple correlations are then compared using a more general version of Eq. (8.8):

$$F = \frac{(R_L^2 - R_R^2)/(K_L - K_R)}{(1 - R_L^2)/(N - K_1)} \qquad (8.9)$$

where R_L and R_R are larger and reduced multiple correlations
K_L and K_R are the number of independent predictors per model

Table 8.7 shows an application of the model comparison method to assess the effects of subsets of the 12 predictors in determining attitude to secondary school, variable 13, and secondary school anxiety, variable 15. In each case a full model is specified, including all 12 predictors (models 1 and 6). Then suitable blocks of predictors are dropped from the

Table 8.7   Comparison of various models for predicting secondary attitude

Predictors and structure correlations

CRITERION	MODEL	AGE 3	SEX 4	JASS 6	JAPS 7	JAPH 8	JSCS 9	JSCP 10	JSCA 11	JMOT 12	JNVR 20	JRED 21	JMAT 22	R	R²	F-test
13	1	20	−33	27	53	−41	32	50	72	71	30	42	50	.345	.119	FULL
Attitude	2	—	−33	27	54	−41	33	51	73	72	31	42	51	.340	.115	NS
to	3	21	—	28	55	−42	33	52	74	73	32	43	52	.333	.111	*
secondary	4	33	−53								49	67	80	.215	.046	**
school	5	21	−33	27	54	−41	33	51	73	72				.339	.115	NS
CRITERION CORRELATION	RC	07	−11	09	18	−14	11	17	25	24	11	14	17			
15	6	−21	−36	−35	21	85	−22	−42	−43	−19	−31	−39	−48	.398	.158	FULL
Secondary	7	—	−36	−36	21	86	−22	−42	−43	−19	−32	−40	−49	.393	.154	NS
school	8	−22	—	−36	21	87	−22	−43	−44	−20	−32	−40	−49	.389	.151	NS
anxiety	9	−32	−53								−46	−58	−70	.271	.074	**
	10	−23	−38	−37	22	89	−23	−44	−45	−20				.378	.143	*
CRITERION CORRELATION	RC	−09	−14	−14	08	34	−09	−17	−17	−08	−12	−16	−19			

Decimal points are omitted from structure and criterion correlations.
Successive models show the effect of dropping one block of predictors from the full models 1 and 6.

full model and the multiple correlation decreases. By testing the significance of the difference between the squared multiple correlations for the full and reduced models the effect of the corresponding block of predictors is assessed. The *F*-test results for variable 13 show that age and ability have little effect but the sex of the child does determine attitude. One would expect primary school attitude to be related to secondary school attitude and this is strongly confirmed by the highly significant *F*-test result. Anxiety variable 15, manifests similar effects except that ability becomes important in place of sex of the child.

At first sight this might seem an elaborate way of looking at the effect of certain predictors. Why not simply obtain the multiple correlation for, say, ability regardless of other measures? If this *is* done, the multiple correlation of .180 is significant ($P < 0.01$). The drawback is that because of intercorrelations between the measures, any interpretation of the finding must include the reservation that the effect may be due to other measures. By using the reduction approach, this possibility is discounted. It is effectively an analysis of covariance.

ANALYSIS OF COVARIANCE

If it is suspected that certain characteristics of a sample are influencing scores on a dependent measure, but that these extraneous factors cannot easily be controlled experimentally, then the normal analysis of variance would be replaced by an analysis of covariance.

Programs for analysis of covariance are few and far between and frequently limited in their scope. By using the regression method demonstrated in Table 8.7 many of these difficulties can be overcome. Even complex designs can be handled so long as the initial coding of data is suitable. Cohen (1968), Kerlinger (1973), and McNeil *et al.* (1975) all give details of the application of multiple regression analysis to analysis of covariance designs. One feature they incorporate is variously called dummy variable or dichotomous coding. Since this technique has a number of applications it is worthy of study. Chapter 10 contains a more detailed account of its use.

DICHOTOMOUS DATA

It is equally valid to use continuous or dichotomous predictors in regression analysis although Veldman (1967) and McNeil *et al.* (1975) disagree on whether this generalization extends to the criterion as well. Regression analysis offers a valuable method for the item analysis of scales comprising dichotomous responses. Its ability to handle dichotomous data also enables multiple regression to be used on categoric data. This is particularly effective in carrying out analyses that would normally require analysis of variance or covariance. Chapter 7 reported an analysis of variance to test differences in secondary school attitude between the three secondary schools (Table 7.1, page 85). Variable 2, secondary school, is nominal but it can easily be made dichotomous by specifying three new variables:

VARIABLE 23   1 if variable 2 = 1, otherwise 0
VARIABLE 24   1 if variable 2 = 2, otherwise 0
VARIABLE 25   1 if variable 2 = 3, otherwise 0

However, as they stand these do not meet the requirements for regression analysis since they are *not* linearly independent. Having specified variables 23 and 24, the value of variable 25 is known, making them linearly dependent. To overcome this one of the three variables has to be omitted from the prediction model. Table 8.8 gives the results for an analysis predicting secondary school attitude from the dichotomous secondary school variables. The multiple R of .147 has an F-ratio of 5.006, identical to the analysis of variance result of Table 7.1. Consequently, the same interpretation applies; secondary school attitude is significantly related to school membership. Regression analysis is equally capable of providing the other statistics arising out of analysis of variance. Group means are obtained directly from the regression constant and the raw weights. The regression constant gives the mean of the excluded group (School 3). Means for the other groups are calculated by adding the raw weights to the regression constant:

SCHOOL 1   (variable 23) mean = 29.01 + 1.28 = 30.29
SCHOOL 2   (variable 24) mean = 29.01 + (–0.23) = 28.78
SCHOOL 3   (variable 25) mean = 29.01

If required, the structure correlation for the excluded category can be calculated from its criterion correlation and the multiple correlation. The same basic method can be extended to produce multiple classification analyses of variance as well as analyses of covariance (McNeil *et al*., 1975; Kerlinger, 1973).

Table 8.8   Predictory secondary attitude using dichotomous secondary school coding

CRITERION	VARIABLE 13	SECONDARY ATTITUDE TO SCHOOL		
PREDICTORS	VARIABLE 23	SCHOOL 1		
	VARIABLE 24	SCHOOL 2		
MULTIPLE R	0.1474			
MULTIPLE R^2	0.0217			
F-RATIO	5.0055			
PROBABILITY	0.0073**			
PREDICTOR	RAW WEIGHT	STANDARD WEIGHT	CRITERION CORRELATION	STRUCTURE CORRELATION
23	1.28	0.13	0.15	0.99
24	–0.23	–0.02	–0.09	–0.60
Excluded variable 25			–0.06	–0.38
REGRESSION CONSTANT			29.01	

RESIDUALS

An individual's residual score is the difference between his actual criterion variable score and that predicted by a particular regression model. Its scale is that of the criterion score. A residual can be used as any other continuous score although its most valuable application is in the measurement of change (see Chapter 11).

EXTENSIONS

Cohen (1968) puts a strong case for using multiple regression techniques to solve many data analytic problems. His enthusiasm has been justified since more recently further support has appeared for the method's application to a variety of situations (see, for example, Kerlinger and Pedhazur, 1973; Woodward and Overall, 1975; McNeil *et al.*, 1975). There is a strong likelihood that any analyst seeking a ready-made solution to his statistical problems might be able to achieve that by a suitable application of some multiple regression procedure.

8.4 Other multivariate relationships

Apart from the classification and discrimination methods described in Chapter 9, few other multivariate approaches to assessing relationships have achieved much popularity.

Table 8.9 Concordance coefficients for academic attitude and ability

Variables included	13 SASS Secondary attitude to secondary school
	18 SSCA Secondary self-concept academic
	19 SMOT Secondary academic motivation
	20 JNVR Junior non-verbal reasoning
	21 JRED Junior reading comprehension

Variables included					Coefficient of concordance	Probability	
13 SASS	18 SSCA	19 SMOT	20 JNVR	21 JRED	.361	.000	**
SASS	SSCA		JNVR	JRED	.357	.005	**
SASS		SMOT	JNVR	JRED	.373	.002	**
SASS	SSCA	SMOT		JRED	.396	.001	**
SASS	SSCA	SMOT	JNVR		.430	.000	**
	SSCA	SMOT	JNVR	JRED	.450	.000	*
SASS	SSCH			JRED	.371	.220	
SASS			JNVR	JRED	.397	.109	
SASS		SMOT		JRED	.423	.045	*
SASS	SSCA		JNVR		.424	.044	*
SASS		SMOT	JNVR		.432	.032	*
	SSCA	SMOT		JRED	.472	.007	**
		SMOT	JNVR	JRED	.518	.001	**
	SSCA		JNVR	JRED	.524	.001	**
	SSCA	SMOT	JNVR		.529	.001	**
SASS	SSCA	SMOT			.587	.000	**

121

The *partial correlation*, for example, becomes difficult to interpret when more than three or four variables are involved. Its function of eliminating the effect of certain variables is generally performed much better by analysis of covariance. One area where the partial correlation has been more widely used is in sociological applications, particularly where economic measures are introduced. The specific method in question is *causal*

PROGRAM AVAILABILITY
see Section 3.6

	PMMD	SPSS	BMDP	OSIRIS	VELDMAN	COOLEY
FACTOR ANALYSIS						
principal components analysis	P	S	B	O	V	C
varimax rotation	P	S	B	O	V	C
oblique rotation	P	S	B	O		
cumulative variance	P	S	B	O	V	C
significance of loadings	P					
factor plots	P	S	B			
factor intercorrelation	P	S	B	O		
factor scores	P	S	B	O	V	C
factorial simplicity	P		B			
squared multiple correlation	P	S	B	O	V	C
comparison of factors				O	V	
MULTIPLE REGRESSION						
multiple correlation	P	S	B	O	V	C
significance of multiple correlation	P	S	B	O	V	C
regression weights	P	S	B	O	V	C
significance of regression weights		S	B	O		
structure correlations	P					C
stepwise inclusion	P	S	B	O	V	
residuals	P	S	B	O		
predicted scores	P	S	B		V	
corrected multiple correlation	P	S				
cross-validation	P	S	B	O	V	C
model-comparison	P	S	B	O	V	
analysis of covariance	P	S	B	O	V	C
dummy variables	P	S	B	O	V	
OTHER METHODS						
partial correlation		S	B	O		C
causal path analysis		S		O		
Kendall's coefficient of concordance	P					

path analysis and descriptions of it appear in a number of articles (for example, Duncan, 1966, level B; Christopher and Elliott, 1970, level B; Nygreen, 1971, level B). A good introductory account is provided by Silvey (1975, level A).

A multivariate method which has been surprisingly ignored is *Kendall's coefficient of concordance, W.* In some ways it resembles a multiple correlation since it also measures the degree of association between a group of variables. It differs in that none of them is considered special as the criterion variable is in regression. The method is rather cumbersome when more than about 100 cases or 5 variables are involved and that probably explains its low usage. Siegel (1956) describes the procedure. It can often be used to examine the relationships between a range of variables, very much as one would apply factor analysis to larger datasets. In Table 8.9 three academic measures and two ability measures are analysed. All combinations of five or four of them are significant indicating a generally high level of association between these measures. Taken three at a time the concordances are higher for the attitude measures, a partial restatement of the results of the factor analysis.

References

Bennett, S. and D. Bowers (1976) *An Introduction to Multivariate Techniques for Social and Behavioural Sciences*, London, Macmillan.

Christal, R. E. (1968) 'Selecting a harem—and other applications of the policy capturing model', *J. Expt. Educ.*, **36**, 24–27.

Christopher, M. G. and C. K. Elliott (1970) 'Causal path analysis in market research', *J. Market Research Society*, **12**, (2), 111–123.

Cliff, N. and C. Hamburger (1967) 'The study of sampling errors in factor analysis by means of artificial experiments', *Psychological Bulletin*, **58**, 430–445.

Cohen, J. (1968) 'Multiple regression as a general data–analytic system', *Psychological Bulletin*, **70** (6), 426–443.

Cooley, W. W. and P. R. Lohnes (1971) *Multivariate Data Analysis*, New York, John Wiley.

Crawford, C. B. (1975) 'Determining the number of interpretable factors', *Psychological Bulletin*, **82**, 226–237.

Darlington, R. B. (1968) 'Multiple regression in psychological research and practice', *Psychological Bulletin*, **69** (3), 161–182.

Duncan, O. D. (1966) 'Path analysis: sociological examples', *American J. Sociology*, **72**, 1–16.

Ferguson, G. A. (1976) *Statistical Analysis in Psychology and Education*, Fourth edition, New York, McGraw-Hill.

Greenberger, M. H. and J. H. Ward (1956) 'An iterative technique for multiple correlation analysis', *IBM Technical Newsletter*, **12**, 85–97.

Harman, H. H. (1967) *Modern Factor Analysis*, Second edition, Chicago, Chicago University Press.

Horn, J. L. (1965) 'An empirical comparison of methods for estimating factor scores', *Educ. and Psychol. Meas.*, **25**, 313–322.

Horn, J. L. and W. C. Miller (1966) 'Evidence on some problems in estimating common factor scores', *Educ. and Psychol. Meas.*, **26**, 617–622.

Horst, P. (1965) *Factor Analysis of Data Matrices*, New York, Holt, Rinehart and Winston.

Kaiser, H. F. (1958) 'The varimax criterion for analytic rotation in factor analysis', *Psychometrika*, **23** (3), 187–200.

Kaiser, H. F. (1970) 'A second generation Little Jiffy', *Psychometrika*, **35**, 401–415.

Kaiser, H. F. (1974) 'An index of factorial simplicity'. *Psychometrika*, **39**, 31–36.

Kaiser, H. F. and J. Rice (1974) 'Little Jiffy Mark IV', *Educ. and Psychol. Meas.*, **34**(1), 111–117.

Kerlinger, F. N. (1973) *Foundations of Behavioral Research*, Second edition, New York, Holt, Rinehart and Winston.

Kerlinger, F. N. and E. J. Pedhazur (1973) *Multiple Regression in Behavioral Research*, New York, Holt, Rinehart and Winston.

McNeil, K. A., F. J. Kelly and J. T. McNeil (1975) *Testing Research Hypotheses Using Multiple Linear Regression*, Carbondale and Edwardsville, USA, Southern Illinois University Press.

Nygreen, G. T. (1971) 'Interactive path analysis', *American Sociologist*, **6**, 37–43.

Rimoldi, H. J. A. (1948) 'A study of some factors related to intelligence', *Psychometrika*, **13**, 27–47.

Rummel, R. J. (1967) Understanding factor analysis, *Conflict Resolution*, **11**, 444–480.

Rummel, R. J. (1970) *Applied Factor Analysis*. Evanston, Northwestern University Press.

Siegel, S. (1956) *Nonparametric Statistics for the Behavioral Sciences*, New York, McGraw-Hill.

Silvey, J. (1975) *Deciphering Data*, London, Longmans.

Veldman, D. J. (1967) *FORTRAN Programming for the Behavioral Sciences*, New York, Holt, Rinehart and Winston.

Woodward, J. A. and J. E. Overall (1975) 'Multivariate analysis of variance by multiple regression methods', *Psychological Bulletin*, **82**, 21–32.

9. Classification and Discrimination within Data

The process of classification is so fundamental to human behaviour that it is perhaps surprising that a similar interest has not been apparent in statistical methodology until quite recently. At the personal level we categorize people on the basis of a whole range of characteristics, largely to simplify our interactions with them. Analytically, a comparable result can be achieved by means of individual measures, or even using groups of attributes. Classifications based on single characteristics such as social class or ability level are of limited value in most social research. However, when more measures are introduced the number of possible combinations can be so large that any analysis becomes extremely cumbersome, and often statistically invalid. The advent of large, high-speed computers has led to a reappraisal of this problem and as a result a range of automatic classification procedures has been developed. Also called numerical taxonomy or cluster analysis, the procedures enable entities to be classified on the basis of a large number of measures. Early applications tended to be limited to biological problems where taxonomy has always featured prominently. More recently, the methods have achieved greater popularity, particularly in social research where the complexity of the domain of relevant variables is ideally suited to cluster analysis.

Bailey (1974, level B) gives an excellent introduction to the methods while Brennan (1972, level B) offers a more extended account, demonstrating their use in educational research. Everitt (1974, level B) also provides a good summary of many of the considerations involved. Anderberg (1973, level B) goes into greater detail and his text is recommended as an essential source for serious students of the methods. The relative novelty of cluster analysis means that the statistical and research journals still provide important discussions of unresolved problems. Blashfield (1976) presents a comparative analysis of four common methods. Gower (1967), Lance and Williams (1967a, b), Johnson (1967) and Wishart (1972) also provide important comparisons, but of a rather more mathematical nature. A detailed description of two popular classification methods is given in Appendix 3. The following section discusses the application of clustering techniques.

9.1 Applying cluster analysis: a comparative demonstration

The wealth of classification techniques available (see for example, Lance and Williams, 1967a, b) together with the various elaborations of them might suggest that arriving at a correct analysis is something of a hit-and-miss affair. Practice is more optimistic since

Table 9.1   The ten comparative transfer sample cluster analyses

		Analyses									
Specifications	A1	A2	A3	A4	A5	A6	A7	A8	A9	A10
1 relocation method	+	+	+	+	+	+	+	+	+	A
2 use all 17 measures	+	+	B	+	B	+	+	+	+	+
3 standardize data	+	+	+	+	C	+	+	+	+	+
4 start from 15 random clusters	+	+	+	D	+	+	+	+	+	+
5 proceed down to one cluster	+	E	+	+	+	+	+	+	+	+
6 use error-sum similarity	+	+	+	+	+	+	+	F	+	+
7 no threshold applied	+	+	+	+	+	G	H	+	+	+
8 use all 454 cases	+	+	+	+	+	+	+	+	I	I

Comparisons with A1

	A1	A2	A3	A4	A5	A6	A7	A8	A9	A10
proportionate agreement	–	.95	.62	.95	.52	.78	.69	.70	.65	.71
kappa coefficient of agreement	–	.94	.54	.94	.40	.72	.62	.62	.56	.62

Other selected comparisons	A4	A5						A10	
proportionate agreement	.95	.67						.73	
kappa coefficient of agreement	.94	.58						.66	

A1 A2 A3 A4 A5 A6 A7 A8 A9 A10

Notes
+   all specifications apply unless otherwise indicated.
A   Ward's method starting from individuals.
B   the three ability measures are excluded.
C   raw data used.
D   start with 14 random clusters.
E   restarted using the 13-cluster solution of A3.
F   correlation coefficient similarity measure used.
G   threshold of 2.0 applied (excludes 86 cases).
H   threshold of 2.5 applied (excludes 39 cases).
I   sampling using every fourth case ($N = 100$).

some indication of the most appropriate methods can usually be obtained from the research literature. Also the differences between many procedures often have little effect on the final results and interpretation. Given the limited scope of this text the most useful way of demonstrating some of the considerations involved is to carry out a relatively large number of analyses incorporating a range of facilities. In all 10 different cluster analyses of the transfer sample have been performed as outlined in Table 9.1. The basic analysis A1 includes the same 17 attitude and ability measures as were used in the factor analysis demonstration. In applying cluster analysis to these variables the aim would be to identify types of children with similar patterns of attitude and ability. This in turn might enable the characteristics of groups showing poor adjustment to be seen, and hopefully treated. The remaining analyses of Table 9.1 comprise modifications to the basic specifications. To enable comparisons of these analyses to be made some measure of agreement is needed. The simplest is the *proportionate agreement*, specifically

Table 9.2   Correspondence between classifications A1 and A2

		1	2	3	4	5	TOTALS
				5 clusters of analysis A2			
5 clusters of analysis A1	1	96	2	0	1	4	103
	2	0	51	0	2	5	58
	3	6	0	127	0	2	135
	4	0	0	0	84	0	84
	5	0	1	0	0	73	74
TOTALS		102	54	127	87	84	454

the proportion of the sample that is similarly classified by the two analyses being compared. Table 9.2 shows the correspondence between the five-cluster solutions of analyses A1 and A2. Clearly cluster 1 of A1 is equivalent to cluster 1 of A2, but even here there are disagreements. Totalling the frequencies in comparable clusters (that is, the diagonal) gives the number of cases similarly classified by the two analyses. Dividing this total (i.e., 431) by the sample size of 454 gives .949 proportionate agreement; in other words 95 per cent are allocated to equivalent groups. In this instance the cluster numbering was the same for the two analyses and therefore matches were in the diagonal. This is not always the case. Usually, equivalent clusters are identified by the highest frequency for a cluster. Then either the table can be rearranged so that rows and columns correspond, or the appropriate joint cell values can be totalled directly.

An alternative measure of agreement proposed by Cohen (1960) is *kappa, the coefficient of agreement*. It incorporates a correction for chance agreements and is defined as:

$$K = \frac{P_o - P_c}{1 - P_c} \tag{9.1}$$

where: P_o is the proportionate agreement (as defined above)
   P_c is the chance agreement

P_c is calculated using the standard chi-square procedure for finding expected frequencies in any joint cell, that is $f_r \times f_c/N$. In the above table,

$$P_c = \left(\frac{103 \times 102}{454} + \frac{58 \times 54}{454} + \frac{135 \times 127}{454} + \frac{84 \times 87}{454} + \frac{74 \times 84}{454} \right) \bigg/ 454$$

$$P_c = .2150$$

$$K = \frac{.949 - .215}{1.0 - .215} = \frac{.734}{.785} = .935$$

Both measures range foom 0 to 1 but in general kappa tends to be lower than the proportionate agreement. This difference increases as the values decrease. In Table 9.2 all values relate to the five-cluster solutions since it is not generally possible to use these measures to compare different numbers of clusters.

The application of cluster analysis involves the following considerations:

Choice of method.
Choice of similarity measure.
Selection of variables.
Transformation of variables.
Producing a starting point.
Deciding how many clusters.
Diagnosis of clusters.
Refining a classification.
Validation.

CHOICE OF METHOD

The diversity of methods available is readily seen in the summary offered by Bailey (1974). He categorizes the methods under various criteria. For example, methods may be *agglomerative* or *divisive*. In the former, classification starts with individuals and gradually forms clusters by a process of accumulation. Divisive methods split the complete sample. Then again, a method is *hierarchical* if it generates a series of classifications comprising different numbers of clusters, rather than producing a single solution. Another consideration is whether the condition for cluster membership is *monothetic* (all members have identical scores) or *polythetic* (groups are based on approximations to similarity). Further categorizations make the number of possibilities even larger.

In choosing from this range of options it will be necessary to take both research objectives and statistical criteria into account. Probably the first consideration is sample size since large samples (over 200) can usually only be analysed using centroid or divisive methods. Complete agglomerative methods (such as Ward's) require excessive computer time and space. Since this choice is inevitable, how far is the final result affected by it? The large size of the complete transfer sample (454 cases) precludes using Ward's method. Instead, the comparative analyses of Table 9.1 include two quarter sample analyses, A9 and A10, using the relocation centroid and Ward's method respectively. As the lower section of the table shows, the proportionate agreement for the two analyses is .73 (kappa is .66) which implies that 27 per cent of the cases are differently classified. These two methods are relatively extreme, but the implication is that any final classification is likely to be method dependent to a degree.

SIMILARITY MEASURE

The method determines the overall procedure used to generate a classification. Within a method it is necessary to assess degrees of similarity, either between individuals or between groups. Even more choice exists here than for the method (Wishart, 1972) although the range is somewhat artificially broad since many are minor modifications of the basic distance measure (Appendix 3). One popular alternative is the *Q correlation coefficient* calculated from the paired scores of two individuals, or from the centroids of two groups. There are, however, certain reservations about its use (Fleiss and Zubin, 1969). The most serious objection is that a high correlation coefficient (even $+1.0$) does not necessarily imply that two individuals have the same score patterns. This value could arise if one person scored systematically higher by a fixed amount, or by a constant multiple. Clearly, this contradicts the natural definition of similarity.

In Table 9.1 analyses A1 and A8 differ only in respect of choice of similarity measure. A1 uses the *error sum of squares* distance measure while A8 uses the *Q* correlation coefficient. The level of agreement between the two analyses is .70, marginally worse than for the two different methods. Unless the research specifically demands certain properties of a similarity measure (for example, ignoring disagreements in binary data) the error sum of squares distance measure is generally a reliable choice (Wishart, 1972; Blashfield, 1976).

SELECTION OF VARIABLES

Any classification depends heavily upon the classificatory measures, even though it may occasionally be possible to generate some more general structure, as in plant taxonomy for example. Consequently, the choice of variables is crucial. Apart from rather obvious constraints such as the need for the measures to be at least ordinal, most of the justification for including or excluding variables should be in terms of the research hypotheses. Ignoring the biographic data the transfer sample has been analysed on the basis of the 17 measures covering attitude and ability. Some indication of the powerful effect of a small subset of the constituent variables can be seen by dropping the three ability measures, analysis A3 of Table 9.1. The proportionate agreement of .62 is even lower than for different methods or similarity measures. That so few measures can have such a large effect on a classification does emphasize the need for extreme care in variable selection.

TRANSFORMATION OF VARIABLES

Bearing in mind the important qualification concerning the interpretability of a cluster analysis there are surprisingly few restrictions regarding the nature of clustering variables. Even the requirement that variables should be ordinal need not be prohibitive since *nominal data* can easily be converted to dichotomous form as was shown in Chapter 8. *Missing data,* however, do present a problem since similarity computations are based on the complete score profile. Wishart (1972) has proposed a rather elaborate solution which requires special programs. A more practicable solution with binary data involves introducing a secondary attribute for each attribute with missing values. This secondary attribute is coded 0 or 1 to indicate whether the response is absent or present. At the extreme this tactic could double the number of attributes (variables) but with relatively few misses the effect is less drastic. Frane (1976) offers various solutions for continuous data, most of them based on regression procedures.

Most similarity coefficients operate on all variables together and this can result in serious distortions in a classification through the dominance of high variance measures. In the transfer data the non-verbal reasoning and mathematics scores are standardized to a mean of 100. Any distance calculation based on squaring score differences will clearly be strongly influenced by these two measures since most of the other scores fall around 20. If this variation is felt to be incidental then the solution is to *standardize* all variables. Occasionally, for example with semantic differential or percentage data, it may be important to preserve this variation and then standardization would not be required. Analyses A3 and A5 of Table 9.1 examine the effects of standardization, even excluding

129

the high variance ability measures. The proportionate agreement of .67 is very low considering the apparent equivalence of the two analyses. Standardization is probably the most important consideration after choice of method and similarity measure. Other transformations with more specific applications are described in detail in the specialist texts already mentioned.

STARTING POINT

Ward's method, like all fully hierarchical methods, starts with individual cases and therefore no decision is required from the analyst. Centroid methods such as the relocation one outlined above demand an initial classification. Wishart (1972) shows that different starting points can result in severe disagreements in final classifications. Anderberg (1973) describes several starting strategies; mostly they involve generating a part-optimal approximation. A simpler alternative is to begin with a random classification. This can be produced using random numbers between 1 and K where K is the number of initial groups, or even by sequentially allocating cases to the K groups. Anderberg does not favour this latter method. Nevertheless the evidence of Table 9.1 is encouraging where real data are concerned.

Analyses A1 and A4 differ only in their number of initial clusters, 15 and 14 respectively. Moreover, since both constitute sequential allocations it follows that the starting configurations are quite different. Yet at the five-cluster level their percentage agreement is 95 per cent, as high as with any of the other analysis modifications applied. Even more encouraging is the comparison of analyses A1 and A2. The latter was restarted at 13 clusters using the 13-cluster solution of analysis A3, attitude only. This restart represents a part-optimal classification as recommended by Anderberg, yet there is no improvement in the final level of agreement with A1 (.95 again). It suggests that random starting points are acceptable *so long as the data are classifiable*. This in turn implies that resulting classifications must be validated, a process dealt with later.

HOW MANY CLUSTERS?

The problem of determining the number of clusters within a dataset depends very much on the definition of cluster implicit in the research. When a study sets out to confirm the existence of a certain classification, natural or constructed, then the number of clusters is predetermined. More often the method is applied as a descriptive analysis and then the choice of final classification is not so obvious. But that should not be taken to mean that the analysis becomes the automatic determinant of the correct or natural number of groups present. It will always be necessary to diagnose and validate any derived classification and that process may itself influence the choice of a final solution. Surprisingly, this is one area where the otherwise excellent reference texts (for example, Anderberg, 1973; Bailey, 1974) are rather uninformative. Everitt (1974) offers some guidance, albeit largely of a statistical nature.

It is suggested in Appendix 3 that plotting a graph of the error or similarity associated with successive fusions enables undesirable fusions to be spotted. Any sudden jump in the criterion measure indicates that relatively dissimilar groups have been combined and therefore that the grouping *before* that fusion is more valid. Thorndike (1953) points out the limitation of this guide, namely that although such a jump does tend to be informative, the absence of one is not necessarily an indication of a bad classification. So long as more than one of these discontinuities are examined and provided other considerations are also borne in mind, the error plot does offer a convenient starting point for selecting a solution.

Rather more detail of the analysis structure is given in the *dendrogram* showing the successive fusions forming the complete analysis. The length of each horizontal branch is proportional to the increase in error associated with the subsequent fusion and therefore long branches again suggest that classifications before that increase are worthy of study. Figure 9.1 shows the dendrogram for analysis A7. The initial fusions (up to the eighth) do tend to have low errors. There then follows a relatively large gap before clusters 4 and 15 are fused to form 6 clusters. The next two fusions occur soon afterwards while the remaining ones have increasingly long branches. Visual inspection suggests that seven-cluster solution and either the five- or four-cluster groupings could be of interest.

The principle of parsimony favours a relatively small number of clusters and it is rarely advantageous to consider more than 20 unless the sample is exceptionally large. The actual size of clusters may be a useful guide since the presence of many small clusters within a classification tends to reduce the subsequent value of that solution. Fragmentation of this kind is particularly common in the divisive methods; it can also occur with Ward's method. Once the set of candidate solutions has been reduced to a practicable

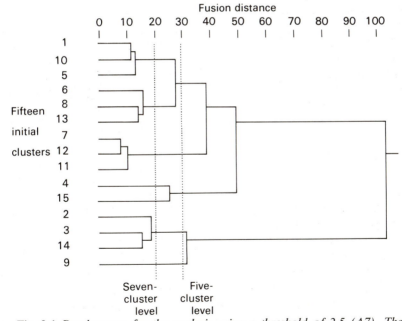

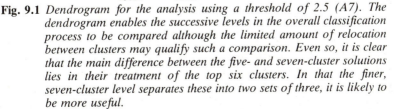

Fig. 9.1 *Dendrogram for the analysis using a threshold of 2.5 (A7). The dendrogram enables the successive levels in the overall classification process to be compared although the limited amount of relocation between clusters may qualify such a comparison. Even so, it is clear that the main difference between the five- and seven-cluster solutions lies in their treatment of the top six clusters. In that the finer, seven-cluster level separates these into two sets of three, it is likely to be more useful.*

131

number it is preferable to use more detailed criteria. For example, the actual member-ship of the clusters comprising two classifications can be compared using the same cross-tabulation procedure as was presented earlier. Table 9.3 shows the correspondence between the five- and seven-cluster solutions of analysis A7. This is the basic analysis with a threshold of 2.5 applied (see later). It is immediately clear that clusters 3, 4, 5, and 6 of the seven-level are essentially the same as clusters 2, 3, 4, and 5 respectively of the five-level solution. On the other hand the large cluster 1 of the five-group solution is split into two similar sized groups, 1 and 2, at the seven-level. If it were felt that cluster 5.1 was sufficiently important *within the context of the research problem* to warrant further elaboration then the seven-cluster classification provides this extra detail. The seven-cluster solution also displays another possible benefit in that it contains a cluster not present in the five-cluster solution. Cluster 7.7 comprises individuals who appear in a range of clusters at the five-group level. Again, if further investigation of cluster 7.7 shows it to be pertinent to the research, then the seven-cluster solution would be prefer-able.

A final decision regarding the number of clusters may need to be left until the more detailed cluster diagnoses and even the final classification validation have been per-formed. In a sense cluster analysis is a wholly iterative method with many opportunities for refinement available to the persistent analyst.

DIAGNOSIS OF CLUSTERS

A cluster is merely a collection of individuals. Before it can assume any research signifi-cance it must be characterized in terms of the classificatory variables, and possibly using other information as well. Where further information is available, it can often provide a very quick outline of a group's character. Table 9.4 shows that although the two bio-graphic features sex and secondary school are similarly represented throughout the whole sample, this is not so for the seven clusters of analysis A7. Cluster 6, for instance, is predominantly male; cluster 7 has a disproportionately high number of pupils from secondary school 1.

Mostly though, information of this kind is incidental to the main purpose of the analysis. The discrimination and therefore the fundamental character of the clusters

Table 9.3 Comparison of five- and seven-cluster solutions of analysis A7

				Seven-cluster solution					
		1	2	3	4	5	6	7	RESIDUE TOTALS
	1	55	52	0	0	0	0	0	0	107
	2	1	0	80	0	2	0	5	1	89
Five-	3	6	5	1	58	0	0	13	0	83
cluster	4	13	0	2	0	57	1	1	0	74
solution	5	0	3	0	3	0	53	2	1	62
RESIDUE		2	5	0	0	0	1	8	23	39
TOTALS		77	65	83	61	59	55	29	25	454

The cross-comparison shows that the seven-cluster solution agrees closely with the five-cluster solution in the composition of clusters, 3, 4, 5 and 6. On the other hand cluster 5.1 is split into two similar sized clusters at the seven-cluster level, clusters 7.1 and 7.2, while cluster 7.7 has no corresponding group at the five-cluster level.

Table 9.4 Sex and secondary school characteristics for the seven clusters of A7

| | PERCENTAGE OF EACH CLUSTER PER CATEGORY | | | | | |
| | | | Secondary school | | | |
	Boys	Girls	1	2	3	TOTALS
cluster 1	48	52	25	31	44	77
cluster 2	40	60	37	35	28	65
cluster 3	49	51	27	35	39	83
cluster 4	31	69	21	49	30	61
cluster 5	54	46	36	32	32	59
cluster 6	89	11	40	20	40	55
cluster 7	48	52	55	17	28	29
RESIDUE GROUP	56	44	44	24	32	25
TOTALS	232	222	148	147	159	454

Cells give the percentage of each cluster falling in the specified category. The residue group would not normally be analysed with the clusters, but is included here for comparison purposes.

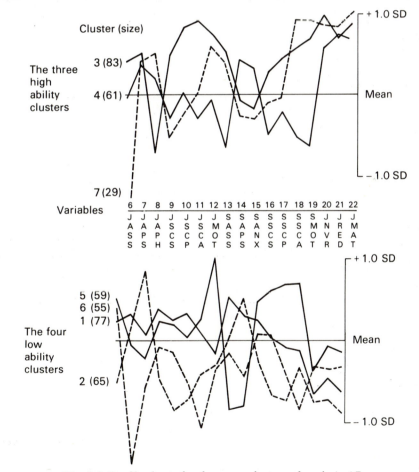

Fig. 9.2 *Profile charts for the seven clusters of analysis A7.*

133

derives from the measures included in the cluster analysis. The clusters themselves are subgroups as defined in Chapter 7 and can be analysed by any of the methods described there. Since it was suggested that the seven-cluster solution of analysis A7 might be more revealing than the five-group classification, these seven clusters will be examined. Profile charts usually provide a useful comparison of clusters but to include as many as seven groups could obscure details. Fortunately, the seven clusters fall neatly into two types on the basis of ability level. Figure 9.2 plots the three high and four low ability clusters separately. Earlier it was suggested that the splitting of cluster 1 of the five-cluster solution might be important. The profile chart confirms this as the two clusters concerned, 1 and 2, are patently different. The high apprehension (V8) and anxiety (V15)

Table 9.5   Atypicality profiles of the seven A7 clusters

CLASSIFICATORY VARIABLES	CLUSTERS high ability			low ability			
	3	4	7	5	6	1	2
6 J:attitude to secondary	+		−	+	+		−
7 J:attitude to primary	+	+			−	+	
8 J:apprehension	−		+		−		+
9 J:self-concept social	+	−				+	−
10 J:self-concept personal	+						−
11 J:self-concept academic	+	−			−	+	−
12 J:academic motivation	+		+		−		−
13 S:attitude to secondary	+	−		+	−		−
14 S:attitude to primary		+		−		+	
15 S:anxiety		+		−	−	+	+
16 S:self-concept social		−		+			−
17 S:self-concept personal	+			+			−
18 S:self-concept academic	+	−	+	+	−		−
19 S:academic motivation	+	−	+	+	−		−
20 J:non-verbal reasoning	+	+	+	−	−	−	−
21 J:reading comprehension	+	+	+	−	−	−	−
22 J:mathematics	+	+	+	−	−	−	−
PERFORMANCE AFTER TWO YEARS							
23 S:reading comprehension	+	+	+		−	−	−
24 S:mathematics	+	+	+		−	−	−
25 S:school adjustment	+				−		
CLUSTER SIZES	83	61	29	59	55	77	65

CLUSTER SUMMARIES

1 unsettled
2 anxious
3 academic
4 disenchanted
5 contented
6 non-academic
7 insecure

+ or − indicates that the cluster is respectively above or below the mean of the remaining clusters as tested by the Scheffé atypicality test.

scores of cluster 2 indicate a worried character. This is accompanied by low self-concept and poor motivation. Cluster 1 is only marginally superior in ability but its overall attitude is far more positive.

Detail of this kind is necessary to develop a complete picture of a group, but having reached that stage some form of summary is needed. One approach is to use the atypicality test results to identify the measures on which group means are significantly higher or lower than the mean of the rest. These patterns can be presented as atypicality plots (see Chapter 7) or more simply as a table. The simplification in Table 9.5 not only exposes the extreme differences, such as between clusters 3 and 2, but it also enables some of the finer discriminations to be seen. Particularly interesting is the fact that cluster 5's low ability does not seem to result in similarly poor performance. The wealth of plus signs beside the secondary attitude measures, and for the primary attitude to secondary, indicates that this positive attitude has to some extent overriden an apparent intellectual disadvantage.

Even at this point the clusters remain somewhat anonymous, always being referred to by number instead of some more identifiable epithet. Discussion of a classification is helped if names or labels can be devised for clusters. The profiles of Table 9.5 provide a starting point. So cluster 3 is very able with a positive attitude and strong motivation, it is *academic*. Cluster 7 is also able and motivated, but rather *insecure*. Cluster 4 is able but lacking motivation, it seems *disenchanted*. Of the lower ability groups cluster 5 has already been shown to be below average ability but highly motivated, *contented*. Cluster 6 could be deemed *non-academic* since it lacks ability and motivation yet is unconcerned. The next cluster, numbered 1, is interesting in that it displays positive feeling for the primary school but not for secondary. For some reason these children have not accepted the new school. They are *unsettled*. The final group, cluster 2, is almost an archetype in its uniformly negative attitude. However, its high apprehension and anxiety suggest more than just dislike of school. A suitable name would be *anxious*.

The many facets of clusters make numerous other formulations possible if the research justifies them. One further approach that is generally appropriate is to apply discriminant function analysis. Given that a cluster is a multivariate construct, then multivariate discrimination is a natural choice of method for identifying the overall pattern of differentiation. Section 9.2 deals with this technique.

REFINING A CLASSIFICATION

During the process of describing a classification it may seem that although the analysis is essentially sound, some further refinement might produce a completely satisfactory result. Some procedures for improving classifications, such as standardizing or excluding variables, have already been discussed. One additional approach attemps to improve the definition of clusters by removing badly classified individuals. Most methods necessarily classify all cases. With centroid methods the need to compute the similarity between individuals and clusters introduces the possibility of not only relocating cases into different clusters, but of removing them altogether. All that is needed to produce this result is a *threshold value*. If an individual is so unlike any of the group centroids that its similarity

135

Table 9.6   Comparison of the five clusters of analyses A1 and A7

		A7 clusters					
		1	2	3	4	5	RES	TOTALS
A1 clusters	1	69	0	2	28	0	4	103
	2	34	0	3	0	1	20	58
	3	0	87	0	36	0	12	135
	4	3	2	78	0	0	1	84
	5	1	0	0	10	61	2	74
TOTALS		107	89	83	74	62	39	454

The difference between the two analyses is such that only four clusters appear in both, accounting for approximately two-thirds of the complete sample.

falls short of this threshold value for all clusters, then that individual is placed in a residue group. If in later cycles cluster centroids have changed to the extent that a residue case passes the threshold criterion, then it can be reclassified. In general, however, the size of the residue group does tend to increase as the relocation analysis proceeds.

There are no simple guidelines for choosing a threshold value. An initial analysis without a threshold will supply information about the level of similarity (or distance) at which switches tend to occur. From these it should be possible to estimate a value which will exclude a suitable proportion of the full sample. Depending on the research topic, between 10 and 25 per cent should be sufficient. Although in most instances the subsequent cluster diagnoses will ignore the residue group, on occasions this set of *outliers* or

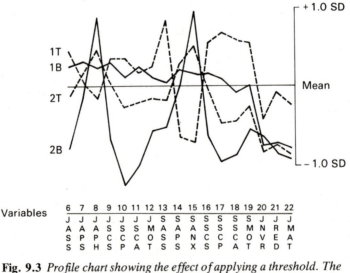

Fig. 9.3 *Profile chart showing the effect of applying a threshold. The two basic clusters 1B and 2B are compared with their equivalents from an analysis incorporating a threshold. The refinement improves the clarity of cluster 1, but slightly reduces the definition of cluster 2.*

136

unclassifiables may be of interest as deviants or exceptions. Since they have no implicit cohesiveness they will have to be examined individually rather than by the more standard diagnostic methods.

Analyses A6 and A7 of Table 9.1 applied threshold values of 2.0 and 2.5 respectively. The former produced a rather large residue group at the five-cluster level and therefore A7 with its less stringent distance threshold becomes more acceptable. The benefit gained from using a threshold can be seen by comparing A7 with the basic analysis A1 (Table 9.6), particularly for cluster 1. Figure 9.3 makes the comparison clearer by plotting the profiles of clusters 1 and 2. The basic analysis produces one extreme cluster, 2B, and one with poor definition. Applying the threshold has the effect of improving the definition of the indistinct cluster at the expense of a slight reduction in clarity of cluster 2T. The increased resolution produced by the threshold is a more satisfactory outcome, largely because discrimination is a prime objective in cluster analysis anyway.

Even though the threshold facility may not be intrinsic to other methods such as Ward's, there is no reason why the procedure should not be applied to the results these methods produce. Field and Schoenfeldt (1975) go so far as to suggest that a threshold check *should* be applied to a Ward classification because of the method's inability to redeem an inappropriate allocation.

THE VALIDATION OF A CLASSIFICATION

The automatic nature of classification procedures generally guarantees that some solution is obtained, but not necessarily a worthwhile one. It is important, therefore, that a final check should be made to ensure that the outcome is plausible, stable, and useful. By the time this validation stage is reached it is unlikely that the clusters will not appear reasonably plausible. Nevertheless, in extreme circumstances the outcome may be unexpected, and therefore possibly an artefact of the method.

Confirming the stability of a classification is analogous to assessing the reliability of research instruments. So, for example, by splitting the sample into two halves, either randomly or using odd-even selection, it is possible to check that both analyses produce similar classifications. A better method is to use two different samples but clearly this may not always be possible. In the transfer research, three rural schools were studied in addition to the three city schools analysed above. This introduces the possibility of performing a cross-validation analysis, although the differences in the two samples limit comparability. Since different individuals are involved in the two analyses the cross-tabulation method of comparison cannot be used. The most appropriate method of comparing clusters from different analyses is to compute distances between clusters using the standard formula.

Table 9.7 gives the distances between all 14 clusters comprising analysis A7 and its counterpart in the rural sample. Distances *within* each analysis appear in the triangular sections of the table. The important distances are those *between* the two analyses, and they are given in the square section. As far as possible the two sets of clusters are numbered so that equivalent clusters bear the same number. Consequently, the diagonal values should be small if the corresponding clusters are alike. For clusters 2, 3, 4, and 5 this is so. Clusters 1 and 7 are also identifiable, but less clearly. However, main analysis cluster 6 is not uniquely represented in the cross-validation analysis since the smallest distance is associated with cluster 1, not cluster 6. Given the known sample differences it seems reasonable to conclude that the main analysis is satisfactorily, but not completely, validated.

Continuing the test reliability analogy, the *internal consistency* of a cluster analysis can also be checked. The two main approaches are to compare the results of different classification methods, and, for centroid methods, to compare different starting points. Both have already been discussed earlier in this chapter. As far as validation is concerned, they comprise two further guides to the generalizability of a final classification.

No matter how intrinsically interesting an analysis might be, responsible research demands that the results should also have some applicability. In test construction the equivalent requirement would be that of *construct validity*. Within the context of school transfer probably the most important additional aspect of child behaviour that one might hope to explain is school progress. How far do the generated clusters predict later success in school? Two achievement measures and one school adjustment measure were obtained after two years in the secondary school. Table 9.5 gives details of these for the seven clusters of A7. As far as achievement is concerned, the secondary school results

Table 9.7 Comparison of cross-validation analysis clusters

	DISTANCE MATRIX *Main analysis clusters*							*Cross-validation analysis clusters*						
	1	2	3	4	5	6	7	1	2	3	4	5	6	7
main analysis														
cluster 1	0													
cluster 2	27	0												
cluster 3	51	111	0											
cluster 4	30	35	45	0										
cluster 5	29	58	29	51	0									
cluster 6	35	36	83	38	41	0								
cluster 7	42	46	26	26	29	56	0							
cross-analysis														
cluster 1	12	9	73	35	31	14	47	0						
cluster 2	29	6	76	24	45	31	39	16	0					
cluster 3	47	100	2	45	23	75	23	67	76	0				
cluster 4	16	30	28	6	33	23	23	24	30	29	0			
cluster 5	11	47	20	35	7	37	30	24	40	19	19	0		
cluster 6	25	13	55	22	45	31	22	20	18	54	20	37	0	
cluster 7	29	36	23	13	23	31	15	34	23	24	18	23	29	0
cluster sizes	77	65	83	61	59	55	29	39	34	55	34	58	15	36

The cross-validation analysis clusters are ordered according to their apparent similarity with the seven main analysis clusters. The square section of the matrix gives the distances *between* these two sets of clusters; the triangular sections contain the distances *within* each set. The boxed values show that four of the main analysis clusters (2, 3, 4, and 5) are replicated, as indicated by the low distances. Clusters 1 and 7 are identifiable, although less clearly. Cluster 6 is not correctly matched since it most closely resembles cross-cluster 1, not 6.

are entirely in accord with those from the junior school. The other measure, school adjustment, shows little discrimination. What differences do arise are entirely consistent with the cluster descriptions. The most positive group, cluster 3, scores significantly highly; poor adjustment is associated with the non-academic group, cluster 6, *not* the anxious cluster numbered 2. When a classification is able to pre-empt such later developments, its value extends beyond the individual clustering measures.

APPLICATIONS

The current research literature contains relatively few instances of the use of cluster analysis compared with other multivariate methods. Blashfield (1976) and Everitt (1974) summarize applications of the method while Brennan (1972) offers a more detailed coverage in educational research. Three examples give some idea of the versatility of the technique. First, Entwistle and Brennan (1971) use cluster analysis to examine the relationship between student achievement and a range of personality and attitude measures, very much in the style of the transfer analysis. This constitutes a common approach, often chosen in preference to factor analysis. Second, a slightly less typical use appears in a study by Bennett and Youngman (1973). Patterns of personality and behaviour were examined by clustering children on 100 items comprising two inventories, rather than by means of the scale scores the inventories usually supply. In the third example, Youngman (1975), attempted to define training objectives for engineers in operational form using a checklist of 434 items. Classifying the engineers produced *worktypes*. Transposing the data matrix enabled the items to be classified to define *activities*. By combining these two analyses it became possible to generate a work structure. This approach could readily be used to characterize numerous social situations where a large number of attributes need to be considered. Indeed, cluster analysis is ideally suited to the current desire for more naturalistic social research.

9.2 Multiple discrimination between groups

In diagnosing the seven clusters of analysis A7 it was clear that the differences were not restricted to one measure, even though ability was a predominant feature of the overall pattern of variation. Motivation, anxiety, and attitude to school also contributed to the characters of individual clusters. Since cluster analysis operates from a similarity definition involving a range of measures, this multiple characterization is hardly surprising. What follows, though, is the need for some method of multiple discrimination between groups, rather than the standard one-way analysis of variance for single measures. Moreover, it seems reasonable to expect that many other groupings used in social research would also benefit from an application of this extension of univariate difference testing.

Multiple discriminant function analysis is the basic method for investigating multiple differences between groups in a set. Variations such as multivariate analysis of variance and multidimensional scaling are discussed later. In discriminant function analysis the overall procedure can be thought of as a combination of analysis of variance

139

and factor analysis. If discrimination were to be tested on one measure alone then the *F*-test of one-way analysis of variance would suffice. Because more than one measure is involved it becomes necessary to find *combinations of these measures that maximally differentiate* the groups. The combinations are linear weightings of the form:

$$D_{jk} = d_{1j}V_{1k} + d_{2j}V_{2k} + \ldots + d_{ij}V_{ik} \ldots + d_{Mj}V_{Mk} \qquad (9.2)$$

where: D_{jk} is the score for individual *k* on function *j*.
   j ranges through all values from 1 to *NF*, the number of functions.
   M is the number of variables defining the functions.
   d_{ij} is the weighting for variable *i* on function *j*.
   V_{ik} is the score of individual *k* on variable *i*.

This should immediately call to mind the definition of a factor as presented earlier. A simple example should help to explain the nature of a function. Figure 9.4 depicts two groups, A and B, measured on the two variables, intelligence and motivation. The artificiality of the example makes the groupings obvious, but its definition is less apparent. Certainly intelligence alone is not sufficient to explain the differences, because some members of B have lower IQ scores than members of A, even though generally B scores higher. Similarly, the motivation scores show some overlap. However, if the *sum of the*

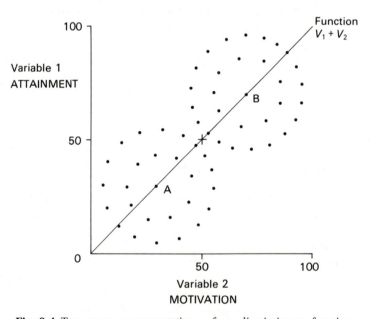

Fig. 9.4 *Two-group representation of a discriminant function. Although neither attainment nor motivation is sufficient in itself to differentiate the two groups A and B, a function defined as the sum of attainment and motivation uniquely differentiates group members. Anyone in group A has a function (total) score less than everyone in B.*

two scores is obtained, every member of B has a total score greater than any member of A. In terms of Eq. (9.2)

$$D = 1.0 \times V_1 + 1.0 \times V_2 \qquad\qquad (9.3)$$

is a perfect discriminating function for these two groups.

In practical applications the number of groups is usually greater than two and invariably more than two measures are used to define the discrimination. Consequently, mathematical procedures are needed to generate the functions, and to test their significance. For an introductory account which avoids all the mathematical aspects, Nunnally (1967, level A) is an excellent source. Veldman (1967, level B), Bennett and Bowers (1976, level B) and Cooley and Lohnes (1971, level C) offer descriptions which cover both general and mathematical considerations. Lachenbruch (1975, level C) gives a highly detailed coverage of the whole area of discriminant analysis and should be consulted for information on specific features. Examples of applications of the method are relatively sparse but Rettig (1964, level B) presents a useful one. Rogers and Linden (1973, level B) use the method to evaluate different cluster analysis procedures. Cacoullos (1973, level B, C) edits a series of papers on discriminant analysis and its applications. As well as giving one of the most complete accounts of the method currently available, Lachenbruch also includes an extensive bibliography which is an excellent source for further information.

Discriminant function analysis differs from factor analysis in that an initial grouping of the sample must be provided. The method attempts to extract orthogonal, unrelated multivariate functions which differentiate these groups. For *NG* groups and *NV* variables, the maximum possible number of functions is $(NG - 1)$ or *NV*, whichever is the smaller. The functions themselves are obtained from the within-groups and between-groups covariance matrices, usually in descending order of size. An overall significance test, Wilk's lambda (Cooley and Lohnes, 1971), is applied to confirm that the set of functions does discriminate between the groups. Each individual function is also tested to see whether that dimension by itself differentiates the groups. The functions are no more than combinations of the constituent variables, but like factors in factor analysis, they need identifying before they can be interpreted within the research. This characterization is obtained from the matrix of correlations between the variables and functions, analogous to the factor structure matrix. Any further interpretation depends on the nature of the research application. Usually, it is worth while to record the average scores for each group on all the significant functions; these are traditionally called the centroids. It can also be revealing to plot the scores of individuals on pairs of functions. This enables the homogeneity of groups to be examined, as well as allowing extreme individuals to be spotted. Scores for individuals on functions are calculated from the weights as given in Eq. (9.2). They are handled like any other variable, so as well as being plotted they can be used to test the significance of differences between the groups, to assess relationships with other measures or in group allocation.

MULTIPLE DISCRIMINATION OF THE SEVEN TRANSFER CLUSTERS

The discriminatory nature of cluster analysis does tend to produce a relatively large number of significant functions and the transfer analysis is no exception. All six possible functions are significant although only the first four contribute substantial proportions of the overall variance. Table 9.8 gives a summary of the discrimination tests. The highly significant Wilk's lambda ($P < 0.001$) indicates that there is overall discrimination among the seven clusters. Similarly the chi-square tests for variation on individual functions also confirm that all functions are significant ($P < 0.001$). The functions are interpreted from the structure matrix of variable-function correlations as given in Table 9.9. Similar criteria are used as apply in factor analysis, correlations of .30 and over traditionally being used to characterize functions. With all the intellectual and motivational variables predominating on the first function this is plainly *academic*. The next function is largely defined by the three primary attitude measures. If the other contributory variables are also considered then the function represents an acceptance of *junior* school and a rejection of secondary schooling. Notice that it tends to show a slight positive association with ability. Function 3 shows a rather stronger relationship with academic ability, but the other main feature is a negative attitude to the current school, and low motivation. It indicates *alienation*. The remaining large function is interesting in that a negative attitude before transfer becomes *acceptance* on arrival in the secondary school. In spite of their statistical significance the last two functions account for only small amounts of the between-cluster variance and have few dominant measures. They hold little research value.

The overall structure suggested by these functions is potentially important within the context of the transfer research. Apart from the first function, the other three large ones do much more than just reiterate standard educational dimensions. Function 2 specifically identifies the basic transfer problem while the alienation and acceptance functions

Table 9.8 Significance tests for the six functions discriminating the seven A7 transfer clusters

The 454 cases were analysed on the 17 measures used for cluster analysis.

(a) *Overall significance test*

WILK'S LAMBDA	0.016
DEGREES OF FREEDOM	102 and 2322
F-RATIO	24.14
PROBABILITY	<0.001**

(b) *Individual function significances*

FUNCTION	PERCENTAGE VARIANCE	CHI-SQUARE	DEGREES OF FREEDOM	PROBABILITY
1	44.9	606.7	22	<0.0001**
2	22.4	404.8	20	<0.0001**
3	16.1	325.0	18	<0.0001**
4	12.7	274.6	16	<0.0001**
5	2.6	73.5	14	<0.0001**
6	1.2	34.2	12	0.0009**

Table 9.9 Discriminant function structure matrix

Discriminatory variables	Correlations with functions					
	1	2	3	4	5	6
6 J:attitude to secondary	11	−**63**	07	−**50**	**33**	−10
7 J:attitude to primary	**44**	**59**	−**37**	−**38**	18	11
8 J:apprehension	−**35**	**50**	−27	06	19	13
9 J:self-concept social	27	−28	−11	−29	−22	10
10 J:self-concept personal	**53**	−25	10	−26	−20	25
11 J:self-concept academic	**59**	−11	−08	−27	−**46**	04
12 J:academic motivation	**62**	20	−26	−08	−03	05
13 S:attitude to secondary	**47**	−26	−**42**	29	18	−17
14 S:attitude to primary	−12	25	18	−**44**	−**40**	**35**
15 S:anxiety	−22	**40**	01	−**40**	−19	−16
16 S:self-concept social	18	−**33**	−24	00	−22	08
17 S:self-concept personal	**36**	−**34**	−05	06	05	**30**
18 S:self-concept academic	**60**	−14	−25	**32**	−16	28
19 S:academic motivation	**60**	02	−**45**	26	−08	−19
20 J:non-verbal reasoning	**66**	25	**50**	12	00	−**27**
21 J:reading comprehension	**59**	25	**42**	12	25	25
22 J:mathematics	**68**	24	**48**	19	14	07
Percentage variance	45	22	16	13	3	1

Values are correlations between variables and functions (decimal points omitted) with those over .30 in heavy type.

isolate aspects of adjustment that could well determine the success or otherwise of secondary schooling. The discriminant analysis provides a basis from which an investigation of subsequent progress could readily be made.

Graphical representations usually give substance to a theoretical structure and this is particularly so with discriminant functions. The normal procedure is to use the discriminant weights (standardized forms of the structure coefficients) to compute scores for each individual on all the discriminant functions. These can then be plotted to show the relative locations of individuals and groups on these functions. Figure 9.5 plots discriminant scores on functions 1 and 2 with the letters indicating cluster membership. Label A corresponds to cluster 1 and so on. The less-than sign (<) is plotted for cases excluded from the clusters under the threshold criterion. To give an indication of the general tendency for each cluster its centroid or average discriminant score is circled. So cluster 7, labelled G, is immediately seen to be relatively high on both functions. This confirms the earlier assessment of cluster 7 as being able, motivated, but insecure. If the groups plotted are sufficiently homogeneous, as clusters tend to be, it may also be possible to draw approximate group boundaries. As well as clarifying the general location of groups, this also makes it easier to see the degree of scatter and the shape of a group. The two extreme clusters 6 (F) and 7 (G) show quite different dispersion characteristics.

Figure 9.6 gives the plotted scores for functions 3 and 4. Although the centroids do show variations between the clusters, the excessive scatter suggests that interpretations based on these two functions should be more reserved than for the previous two. A

143

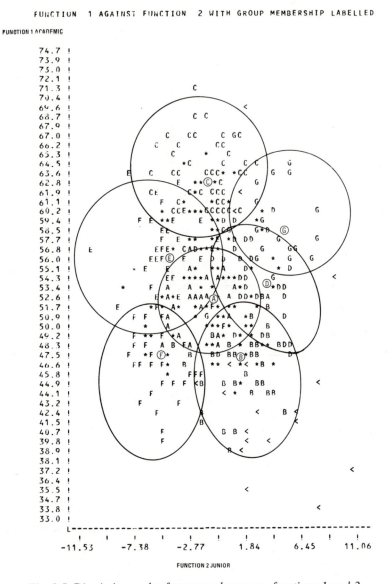

Fig. 9.5 *Discriminant plot for seven clusters on functions 1 and 2.*

sensible use of smaller functions is to qualify findings based on the first two. For example, the academic function tended to separate the high and low ability clusters, yet the high ability cluster 4 achieved only an average score on that function. A possible explanation for this lies in the high level of alienation, function 3, exhibited by cluster 4. Function 4 completes the picture since this same cluster records very low scores on acceptance of secondary schooling.

144

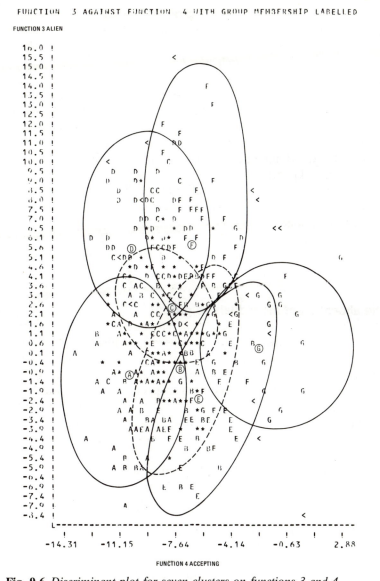

Fig. 9.6 *Discriminant plot for seven clusters on functions 3 and 4.*

The danger of attributing too much importance to the minor functions is neatly demonstrated by the apparently contradictory nature of cluster 7. It has a high centroid value on function 2, acceptance of junior school, yet it also records a similarly high level on function 4, acceptance of secondary school. This almost certainly stems from the fact that both functions are essentially defined by a negative attitude to secondary school *before* transfer together with moderately high ability. They differ in their pattern of

145

secondary attitude. Given that cluster 7 is rather heterogeneous anyway, it is possible for different individuals to display either of these profiles within the cluster. Nevertheless, disparity of this kind is not generally desirable from a research standpoint and it should lead to a sceptical acceptance of cluster 7.

Function 4 displays a further outcome which can be confusing, namely the presence of negative scores. Here the analogy with factor analysis is useful since the direction is immaterial. What does matter both with plotted scores and with centroids is the *order*. A group recording a higher score manifests more of the function characteristic. In practical applications, however, negative concepts are awkward and it may be advisable to change the sign of all the discriminating variable weights to produce a positive function. This is equivalent to reflecting a factor.

Further considerations in the use of multiple discriminant function analysis require more detailed study than is appropriate here and the researcher is referred to the advanced texts mentioned earlier. One problem that may arise, the analysis of correlated samples, is tackled by Lawlis and Sweney (1975), while an extension of the technique enabling individuals to be allocated to known groups is dealt with in the next section.

9.3 The allocation of individuals to groups

Once a classification becomes an established feature of a particular area of application it is quite likely that situations will arise where individuals need to be fitted into that classification. Probably the most familiar use is in vocational placement, the allocation of people to jobs on the basis of aptitudes and abilities (Rulon *et al.*, 1967). Other examples include the diagnosis of illness, selection for special education and the commercial process of market segmentation. In the case of the transfer research a teacher might want to assess whether a child is likely to fall within one of the types showing deterioration on transfer. Prior knowledge of this kind could be used as a screening device for preventative action.

Procedures for performing these allocations are essentially reversals of the classification and discrimination techniques already presented. Taking the *cluster analysis approach*, it is a simple matter to use the basic distance formula of relocation analysis:

$$D(A, B) = \frac{2ab}{M(a + b)} \sum_{i = 1}^{M} (U_{Ai} - U_{Bi})^2 \tag{9.4}$$

where: A is the individual to be classified, and therefore $a = 1$.
B is each cluster to be compared with, b is the cluster size.
M is the number of measures
U_{Ai} represents the score profile of individual A
U_{Bi} is the centroid of the cluster B

By this means the individual is compared with each cluster in turn and finally allocated to the cluster for which this distance value is smallest. An interesting extension of this method is to use it to overcome the problem of *missing data*. Individuals missing only a few measures can be roughly classified using Eq. (9.4) but ignoring those measures for which data are not available. Although the similarity criterion of Eq. (9.4) derives from cluster analysis, it can also be applied to other types of classification so long as the concepts of score profile and group centroid have meaning and can be quantified.

An alternative approach is to construct a *discriminant equation* using discriminant function analysis, and then to use this to compute an individual's function scores. These scores can then be plotted as shown in Figs. 9.5 and 9.6 and the individual allocated to the most appropriate group. Note that this tactic *cannot* be applied if data are missing since function centroids incorporate a component due to the missing variables.

A third but rather cumbersome method is to use *multiple regression procedures.* Membership of each group can be expressed as a dichotomous variable and a prediction equation constructed for it. An individual can be tested against each group in turn by successive applications of these regression equations, and again allocated appropriately. Missing data can be accommodated so long as the variables concerned are omitted from the regression models and the regression equations used for fitting.

9.4 Further developments in multiple discrimination

Just as multiple linear discriminant function analysis is an extension of the familiar one-way analysis of variance, so more elaborate forms of analysis of variance have their multivariate equivalents. Cooley and Lohnes (1971, level C) offer a mathematical outline of *multivariate analysis of variance* but only using a single level classification. It is with multi-way classifications that the method replaces discriminant function analysis. As with many analytical techniques the various multivariate analysis of variance methods can be obtained using multiple regression models. Woodward and Overall (1975, level C) describe the procedures in detail while Kerlinger (1973, level B) gives a good introductory account, particularly of the dummy variable coding needed to apply the method. A computer program is supplied by Woodward and Overall (1974).

An increasingly popular approach to discrimination is *multidimensional scaling.* One of its virtues is its ability to operate on non-metric data, only needing some form of similarity or dissimilarity matrix between cases. However, this does raise problems of interpretation since the discriminating dimensions are not defined in terms of variables, but only with respect to the cases analysed. Thus to facilitate interpretation it is common to include marker cases or other suitable reference points. The most comprehensive text on this method is the two-volume compilation edited by Shepard *et al.* (1972, level B, C). Lingoes and Roskam (1973, level C) offer an extended empirical analysis of two scaling methods. Nunnally (1967, level A) describes the method without giving the mathematical foundations. Bennett and Bowers (1976, level B) also cover this technique.

As a brief demonstration of the method it is possible to use it to cross-validate the seven transfer clusters. Originally this was done by inspecting the distance matrix relating the seven clusters of analysis A7 to seven equivalent clusters generated from a different sample (Table 9.9). This same distance matrix can be subjected directly to multidimensional scaling analysis. Of the many programs available, in this instance the one developed by Roskam and Lingoes (1969) was used. Figure 9.7 plots the 14 clusters in the two-dimensional configuration produced. The clusters are numbered 1 to 7 with the

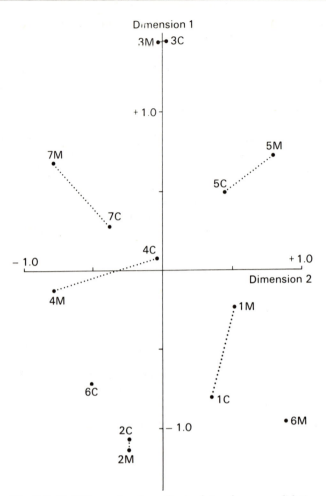

Fig. 9.7 *Multidimensional scaling plot of cross-validation clusters. The 7 main analysis clusters, labelled M, are plotted for comparison with the 7 cross-validation analysis clusters (C). Numbers identify equivalent clusters and in general the distances confirm this equivalence. Only cluster 6 is not replicated.*

suffices M and C referring to the main and cross-analyses respectively. For acceptable cross-validation equivalent clusters should be close together. Indeed the earlier evaluation is upheld. Clusters 2, 3, and 5 are well replicated, with clusters 1, 4, and 7 less satisfactorily so. Again the two clusters numbered 6 have little in common. This example demonstrates one effective use of scaling methods but the difficulty of producing external validation can be a serious drawback in many applications. As a general principle the analyst should never rush into a widespread use of some of the rather elaborate multivariate techniques unless other more accessible methods have been shown to be ineffectual.

148

PROGRAM AVAILABILITY
see Section 3.6

	PMMD	SPSS	BMDP	OSIRIS	VELDMAN	COOLEY
CLUSTER ANALYSIS						
Ward's method					V	
relocation method	P					
other clustering methods			B	O		C
dendrograms	P					
comparison of classifications	P	S	B	O	V	
diagnosis of clusters	P	S	B	O	V	C
MULTIPLE DISCRIMINANT FUNCTION ANALYSIS						
overall significance	P	S	B	O	V	C
function significance	P	S	B		V	C
function structure	P	S	B		V	C
centroids	P	S	B	O	V	C
function plots	P	S	B	O		
OTHER TOPICS						
group allocation	P	S	B	O	V	C
multivariate analysis of variance			B	O		C
multidimensional scaling				O		

References

Anderberg, M. R. (1973) *Cluster Analysis for Applications*, New York, Academic Press.

Bailey, K. D. (1974) 'Cluster analysis.' in: Heise. D (ed.) *Sociological Methodology* 1975, San Francisco, Jossey-Bass.

Bennett, S. and D. Bowers (1976) *An Introduction to Multivariate Techniques for Social and Behavioural Sciences*, London, Macmillan.

Bennett, S. N. and M. B. Youngman (1973) 'Personality and behaviour in school', *Brit. J. Educ. Psychol.*, **43**, 228–233.

Blashfield, R. K. (1976) 'Mixture model tests of cluster analysis: Accuracy of four agglomerative hierarchical methods', *Psychological Bulletin*, **83**, 377–388.

Brennan, T. (1972) *Numerical Taxonomy: Theory and some Applications in Educational Research*, Unpublished Ph.D thesis, University of Lancaster.

Cacoullos, T. (ed.) (1973) *Discriminant Analysis and Applications*, New York, Academic Press.

Cohen, J. (1960) 'A coefficient of agreement for nominal scales', *Educ. and Psychol. Meas.*, **20**, 37–46.

Cooley, W. W. and P. R. Lohnes (1971) *Multivariate Data Analysis*, New York, John Wiley.

Entwistle, N. J. and T. Brennan (1971) 'The academic performance of students: II. Types of successful students', *Brit. J. Educ. Psychol.*, **41**, 268–276.

Everitt, B. (1974) *Cluster Analysis*, London, Heinemann/SSRC.

Field, H. S. and L. F. Schoenfeldt (1975) 'Ward and Hook revisited: A two-part procedure for overcoming a deficiency in the grouping of persons', *Educ. and Psychol. Meas.*, **35**, 171–173.

Fleiss, J. L. and J. Zubin (1969) 'On the methods and theory of clustering', *Multivariate Behavioral Research,* **4**, 235–250.

Frane, J. W. (1976) 'Some simple procedures for treating missing data in multivariate analysis', *Psychometrika,* **41**, 409–415.

Gower, J. C. (1967) 'A comparison of some methods of cluster analysis', *Biometrics,* **23**, 623–637.

Johnson, S. C. (1967) 'Hierarchical clustering schemes', *Psychometrika,* **32**, 241–254.

Kerlinger, F. N. (1973) *Foundations of Behavioral Research*, New York, Holt, Rinehart, and Winston.

Lachenbruch, P. A. (1975) *Discriminant Analysis*, New York, Haffner Press.

Lance, G. N. and W. T. Williams (1967a) 'A general theory of classificatory sorting systems: 1. Hierarchical systems', *Computer Journal*, **9**, 373–380.

Lance, G. N. and W. T. Williams (1967b) 'A general theory of classificatory sorting systems: 2. Clustering systems', *Computer Journal*, **10**, 271–277.

Lawlis, G. F. and A. B. Sweney (1975) 'The application of discriminant function analysis to correlated samples', *Educ. and Psychol. Meas.*, **35**, 313–317.

Lingoes, J. C. and E. E. Roskam (1973) 'A mathematical and empirical analysis of two multidimensional scaling algorithms', *Psychometrika Monograph Supplement* No. 19, **38**, number 4, part 2.

Nunnally, J. C. (1967) *Psychometric Theory*, New York, McGraw-Hill.

Rettig, S. (1964) 'Multiple discriminant analysis: An illustration', *American Sociological Review*, **29**, 398–402.

Rogers, G. and J. D. Linden (1973) 'Use of multiple discriminant function analysis in the evaluation of three multivariate grouping techniques', *Educ. and Psychol. Meas.*, **33**, 787–802.

Roskam, E. and J. Lingoes (1969) 'MINISSA-1, a FORTRAN IV(G) program for smallest space analysis of square symmetric matrices', *Behavioral Science*, **14**.

Rulon, P. J., D. V. Tiedman, and M. M. Tatsuoka (1967) *Multivariate Statistics for Personnel Classification*, New York, John Wiley.

Shepard, R. N., A. K. Romney, and S. B. Nerlove (eds.) (1972) *Multidimensional Scaling: Theory and Applications in the Behavioral Sciences*, New York, Seminar Press.

Thorndike, R. L. (1953) 'Who belongs in a family?' *Psychometrika*, **18**, 267–276.

Veldman, D. J. (1967) *FORTRAN Programming for the Behavioral Sciences*, New York, Holt, Rinehart and Winston.

Wishart, D. (1972) 'A general tripartite clustering method and similarity generating function', London, Civil Service Statistics Division, Report R-31.

Woodward, J. A. and J. E. Overall (1974) 'A general multivariate analysis of variance computer program', *Educ. and Psychol. Meas.*, **34**, 653–662.

Woodward, J. A. and J. E. Overall (1975) 'Multivariate analysis of variance by multiple regression methods', *Psychological Bulletin*, **82**, 21–32.

Youngman, M. B. (1975) 'Structuring work for training purposes', *Vocational Aspect of Education,* **27**, 77–86.

Part 3
Specialized techniques

10.   The Analysis of Questionnaires

10.1   The importance of planning

The relative effort associated with different stages of research analysis depends very much on the type of research being undertaken. Experimental approaches necessarily demand very careful selection of design, samples and measures, but the subsequent analysis then tends to be almost automatic. In questionnaire analysis the balance of effort is often assumed to be reversed. Certainly, to compile and distribute a large number of questionnaires may seem, and indeed sometimes is, a straightforward clerical exercise requiring very little research skill. Unfortunately, this simplicity is too often exaggerated, to the extent of assuming that statistical considerations are irrelevant at this stage. Such an approach will almost inevitably result in the introduction of difficult, and even unsurmountable, problems at the analysis stage. The solution lies in accepting that the initial and concluding stages of a survey are not independent; the questionnaire structure must include all the facilities deemed to be necessary for a successful analysis. For example, the treatment of various types of non-response (questions refused, pages missed, or even whole questionnaires not returned) should be considered from both the coding and analysis standpoints. Similarly, the role of open-ended questions should be decided upon in advance since failure to do so may result in the loss of essential factual information. Probably the simplest safeguard is to plan the questionnaire coding, before distribution, to take into account as many of the analyses as can be anticipated. Inevitably some will depend upon the outcome of preliminary tests, but the majority of analytical requirements can be accommodated with a reasonable amount of prior thought.

10.2   Questionnaire coding

Most of the considerations discussed in Chapter 2 on the preparation of data apply equally well to the coding of questionnaire responses. Some features require closer attention because of the large quantity of information that tends to result from questionnaire research. Others need extra careful preparation because of the difficulty in communicating precisely the intended meaning of a question or response category. But the general principles of producing exclusive and exhaustive categories for answers, of distinguishing between categoric and continuous data, and of recording the data in a form suitable for the anticipated analysis remain.

One problem that does tend to arise more often in questionnaire research than in other types is the need to accommodate a variety of categories of non-response. These may range from missed pages, through refusals (often explained in the margin!) to no incidence of the feature sought (qualification, for example). Should these need to be discriminated, then the coding must incorporate a suitable differentiation. In general, maximum detail should be sought in the initial coding since subsequent recoding can usually produce any refinements or combinations thought desirable. So in the Engineer Training Survey (Youngman *et al.,* 1978) qualification (Question 4, Appendix 10.1) is coded as follows:

0 = non-response	5 = first degree
1 = city and guilds	6 = postgraduate degree
2 = ordinary national (ONC)	7 = degree plus technical qualification
3 = higher national (HNC)	8 = other
4 = higher national diploma (HND)	9 = no qualification

to maintain separation of non-response, other, and no qualification categories. The coding frame (Appendix 10.3) is primarily a record of these decisions for the whole questionnaire. It can later be extended to include comments resulting from the actual response coding (e.g. questions frequently unanswered). A further invaluable use of the coding frame is to record details of the computer coding employed (cf. Chapter 3) and of the inclusion of questions in the different analyses.

10.3 Tabulating the raw data

Although the various stages in questionnaire analysis do tend to be standard, the actual specification of each step depends very much on the outcome of the previous operation. Indeed, this cumulative analysis structure is ideally suited to the interactive program packages currently becoming more widely available. Both the larger packages such as SCSS or MIDAS, and certain mini-computer facilities enable tables to be defined as the analysis proceeds. With the more traditional complete computer runs the equivalent procedure is to submit consecutive jobs, each one being constructed on the basis of information obtained from the previous ones. True, there exist computer programs purporting to carry out the complete analysis of questionnaires, but such blind faith seldom produces the most revealing analyses. The steps themselves do not differ fundamentally from the equivalent basic techniques described earlier, and therefore readers should refer back for detailed accounts of the methods. In the following sections the specific role of the methods will be demonstrated and particular considerations discussed.

An initial inspection of the responses is carried out by obtaining frequency tabulations for all questions. By this means, all actually occurring codes are identified and any illegal ones can be traced and corrected. Even at this early stage minor modifications to the basic coding may be useful. With the age question, for example, to record every occurring code from around 20 to 65 would reveal little. Instead, by taking the first digit only, age is effectively plotted in 10's, producing a clearer picture (Table 10.1).

Apart from supplying basic information on responses, this initial tabulation also can suggest the format for later more detailed analyses. The qualification variable produces both very low and very high frequencies, making some form of combination almost

Table 10.1 Frequency distributions for a selection of the questionnaire variables ($N = 199$)

VARIABLE 1 (6 CODES)   Age in 10's

CODE	FREQ	PCT	CUMPCT	
1	1	1	1	*
2	26	13	13	*************************
3	69	35	48	**
4	68	34	82	**
5	34	17	99	*********************************
6	1	1	100	*

VARIABLE 2 (9 CODES)   Qualification

CODE	FREQ	PCT	CUMPCT	
1	11	6	6	***********
2	26	13	19	*************************
3	71	36	54	***
4	7	4	58	*******
5	35	18	75	************************
6	2	1	76	**
7	3	2	78	***
8	3	2	79	***
9	41	21	100	**

VARIABLE 8 (13 CODES)   Number of jobs held

CODE	FREQ	PCT	CUMPCT	
1	1	1	1	*
2	9	5	5	*********
3	15	8	13	***************
4	21	11	23	*********************
5	29	15	38	*****************************
6	30	15	53	******************************
7	26	13	66	**************************
8	28	14	80	****************************
9	16	8	88	****************
10	12	6	94	************
11	8	4	98	********
12	3	2	99	***
13	1	1	100	*

VARIABLE 23 (5 CODES)   Future value of an extended course

CODE	FREQ	PCT	CUMPCT	
1	29	15	15	*****************************
2	24	12	27	************************
3	36	18	45	************************************
4	38	19	64	**************************************
5	72	36	100	**************************************

inevitable for successful later analysis. The third section of Table 10.1, number of jobs held, results in a much tidier response distribution, albeit with a rather large number of codes. Any concatenation of codes here should be relatively straightforward.

10.4 Recoding variables prior to main analyses

The initial coding system may not meet the requirements of all subsequent analyses. Recoding can enable the researcher to remedy this situation by:

clarifying the definition of important concepts.
producing variables that conform to statistical requirements.
eliminating invalid responses from an analysis.

A good example of clarification is supplied by the qualification variable. As it stands (cf. Table 10.1) the response distribution is unlikely to produce useful findings because of the diversity present. It would be reasonable to hypothesize that the graduate/non-graduate dimension should discriminate; recoding to generate this dichotomy is a simple operation. The small frequencies for some categories would also violate the statistical assumptions for chi-square, an instance of the second situation where recoding can be of help. The third possibility requiring recoding also arises on the qualification question, specifically from the presence of the no-qualification response. By recoding this as zero it becomes possible to eliminate these cases from chi-square and percentage calculations in a graduate/non-graduate analysis.

Recoding is very often effected by specifying a set of new codes to replace the original ones in ascending order. From Table 10.1 it is seen that the qualification variable records codes:

QUALIFICATION   1 2 3 4 5 6 7 8 9
recoding as follows: 1 1 1 1 2 2 2 1 0

transforms the variable into a non-graduate (new code 1)/graduate (new code 2) dichotomy with new code 0 signifying neither.

AGE with the 6 codes   1 2 3 4 5 6
can be recoded: 2 2 3 4 5 5

thereby removing the isolated responses at each end of the range.

NUMBER OF JOBS   1 2 3 4 5 6 7 8 9 10 11 12 13
recoded as: 1 1 1 1 2 2 3 3 4 4 4 4 4

produces four categories with approximately equal frequencies in each.

Any of the questions can be treated in this manner, the actual details of the recoding depending on the limitations and facilities of the programs available. A further type of transformation to produce binary variables (1/0 or YES/NO) will be demonstrated later.

10.5 Obtaining cross-tabulations and statistics

While surveys may be carried out purely to obtain factual information on the occurrence of certain features, more often it is the relationships between responses to different questions that provide deeper insight into the topic under investigation. A number of methods exist for performing this type of analysis (cf. Chapter 6) although with questionnaire data the commonest approach is to generate cross-tabulations (or contingency tables) for selected pairs of questions. The significance of any pattern in such tables can be tested by various statistics of which chi-square is the most popular. Frequently, the raw data will have to be modified to clarify any relationships that might seem to exist.

The possible benefits gained from recoding the qualification variable have already been discussed. Table 10.2 shows a sequence of cross-tabulations involving qualification which demonstrates the gradual process of teasing out a relationship. The most basic table (10.2a) does not produce a significant chi-square, but the assumptions of that statistic (minimum expected frequency of five) are violated anyway. Inserting row percentages in the cells rather than straight frequencies makes the comparison of rows easier (Table 10.2b) and does suggest that there may be variations in attitude to long courses for different types of qualification. Applying the recoding to form a graduate/non-graduate dichotomy (Table 10.2c) produces a table with fairly obvious tendencies; the graduates seem to favour the low value cells. The reason this table is not completely acceptable is that the no-qualification category (coded zero) is confounding the relationship. By computing chi-square *without* this row a genuine graduate/non-graduate difference can be tested (Table 10.2d) and a borderline chi-square value appears (chi-square = 5.803, $P = 0.054$). An important additional benefit from recoding is that clarification of a concept also tends to make the final interpretation that much easier. Here it seems that non-graduates *may* place a higher value on extended future training. Given the borderline result, is it possible to qualify the interpretation to produce a more definite statement?

If the comparison of responses to two questions provides more information than an analysis of one question alone, it seems reasonable to assume that three questions taken together should give even more detail. Three-way contingency tables are used but there are limitations. Even with a two-way table (cf. Table 10.2a) the frequencies for some joint categories can be very small; this drawback is more likely when the data are split even further. However, if care is taken to ensure that expected frequencies do remain sufficiently high three-way cross-tabulations can extend the information gained from two-way tables. In Table 10.3 the comparison of qualification and training value is extended further to take age into account. Age is dichotomized at 40 by recoding the original coding as described earlier producing two similarly sized categories. Any finer coding would almost certainly result in very small expected cell frequencies. This final refinement of the analysis does indeed allow an unequivocal statement; among *young* engineers, the non-graduates place a higher value on the possible benefits of an extended training course. Since graduates already have done such a course, it does seem reasonable that they should not want more.

10.6 Forming scales from sets of related questions

Rating scales, semantic differentials, and YES/NO questions are as much a feature of questionnaires as descriptive questions seeking factual information. Where opinion or attitude items are included they tend to appear in relatively large numbers (30 or more) and to analyse them individually becomes a laborious way of building up their overall

Table 10.2   Sequence of cross-tabulations for qualification against future value of extended educational courses

(a) *No recoding; include all codes; frequencies in cells*

| | | future value of extended courses (V23) | | | | | |
| | | HIGH | | | | LOW | TOTALS |
Qualification (V2)	CODES	1	2	3	4	5	
CITY AND GUILDS	1	4	1	1	0	5	11
ONC	2	3	3	6	5	9	26
HNC	3	10	13	13	11	24	71
HND	4	1	0	3	0	3	7
DEGREE	5	1	3	6	13	12	35
POSTGRADUATE	6	1	0	0	1	0	2
DEGREE + TECHNICAL	7	0	0	0	0	3	3
OTHER	8	1	0	1	0	1	3
NONE	9	8	4	6	8	15	41
TOTALS		29	24	36	38	72	199

CHI-SQUARE = 36.82   PROBABILITY = 0.260 (32 DF)   CONTINGENCY COEFF = 0.395

(b) *No recoding; exclude zero codes; row percentages in cells*

Qualification	CODES	1	2	3	4	5	
CITY AND GUILDS	1	36	9	9	0	45	11
ONC	2	12	12	23	19	35	26
HNC	3	14	18	18	15	34	71
HND	4	14	0	43	0	43	7
DEGREE	5	3	9	17	37	34	35
POSTGRADUATE	6	50	0	0	50	0	2
DEGREE + TECHNICAL	7	0	0	0	0	100	3
OTHER	8	33	0	33	0	33	3
NONE	9	20	10	15	20	37	41
TOTALS		29	24	36	38	72	199

Statistics are the same as for (a) since no zero codes occur

(c) *Recode both variables; complete table statistics; frequencies*

RECODE FOR V2: qualification
    CODE 0 REPLACES 9   (NONE)
    CODE 1 REPLACES 1 2 3 4 8   (NON-GRADUATE)
    CODE 2 REPLACES 5 6 7   (GRADUATE)
RECODE FOR V23: future value of extended course
    CODE 1 REPLACES 1 2   (HIGH VALUE)
    CODE 2 REPLACES 3 4   (MEDIUM)
    CODE 3 REPLACES 5   (LOW VALUE)

| | | future value of extended courses (V23) | | | |
Qualification	CODES	HIGH 1	2	3 LOW	
NONE	0	12	14	15	41
NON-GRADUATE	1	36	40	42	118
GRADUATE	2	5	20	15	40
TOTALS		53	74	72	199

CHI-SQUARE = 6.016   PROBABILITY = 0.198 (4 DF)   CONTINGENCY COEFF = 0.171

Table 10.2 (continued)

(d) *Recode; exclude zero codes; row percentages in cells*

Qualification	CODES	1	2	3	
NON-GRADUATE	1	31	34	36	118
GRADUATE	2	13	50	38	40
	TOTALS	41	60	57	158

CHI-SQUARE = 5.803   PROBABILITY = 0.054 (2 DF)   CONTINGENCY COEFF = 0.188

impression. A more succinct treatment of them is to use factor analysis to generate subscales comprised of groups of related questions. A person's responses to these questions can then be combined to produce a score on that subscale, and similarly for the remaining scales. The analysis of subscale scores then becomes no different from that of any other continuous score.

In the Engineering Training Survey (Youngman *et al.*, 1978) the training questionnaire was supplemented by a 52-item semantic differential scale designed to measure job perceptions (Appendix 10.2). Each semantic differential was rated on a seven-point continuum and since no non-response category was included, the ratings could be assumed to be continuous. This is an important qualification as missing data and 'don't know' responses make factor analysis invalid unless some suitable substitution is made

Table 10.3   Three-way cross-tabulation showing relationship between age, qualification, and value placed on extended training

| | | | | Value placed on extended course (V23) | | | |
| | | | | HIGH | | LOW | |
Age (V1)	*Qualification* (V2)			1	2	3	TOTALS
	YOUNG	NON-GRADUATE	1	20(34%)	23(39%)	16(27%)	59
1	(under 40)	GRADUATE	2	2(8%)	15(58%)	9(35%)	26
		TOTALS		22	38	25	85
	CHI-SQUARE – 6.546 (2 DF) $P = 0.037$ CONTINGENCY = 0.267						
	OLD	NON-GRADUATE	1	16(27%)	17(39%)	26(44%)	59
2	(40 and over)	GRADUATE	2	3(21%)	5(36%)	6(43%)	14
		TOTALS		19	22	32	73
	CHI-SQUARE = 0.323 (2 DF) $P = 0.852$ CONTINGENCY = 0.066						
							158

Age is recoded as shown on page 164; qualification and value of extended courses are recoded as in Table 10.2. All statistics are for the reduced tables (zero codes eliminated) as presented.

Table 10.4   Factor pattern matrix of the MYJOB scales

Scales (right side)	FACTORS AND LOADINGS					
	Inventive 1	Analytical 2	Responsible 3	Varied 4	Demanding 5	Satisfying 6
1 not team work	–41*	09	06	32*	09	25*
2 risky	09	–25	06	00	–08	00
3 satisfying	45*	–07	–01	–22*	06	46*
4 uninventive	–60*	–04	–14	18	21	11
5 experience not needed	–08	–21	06	13	34*	25*
6 participative	00	–02	54*	01	00	29*
7 pleasant	08	06	02	–03	–14	57*
8 vague	–10	–42*	–08	33*	17	06
9 disappointing	–34*	–05	25*	–01	–23*	–21*
10 ill-defined	–03	–42*	11	33*	–14	–14
11 tense	30*	13	–09	–02	00	–34*
12 involves diagnosis	–05	–05	–16	–38*	14	20
13 sociable	–14	00	00	19	–14	51*
14 variable	47*	05	15	36*	02	–03
15 passive	–04	–02	–02	–44*	20	–04
16 no common sense	15	08	04	–07	65*	–08
17 interesting	71*	09	10	00	01	07
18 involves many things	21	19	08	41*	–06	–09
19 cooperative	06	28*	19	17	–12	02
20 undemanding	–16	–15	08	–12	22*	06
21 low status	04	–07	72*	03	–02	–02
22 desirable	14	27*	–02	10	03	32*
23 broad	35*	01	–16	25*	02	–03
24 theoretical	10	–24	–19	–23	–12	14
25 unconventional	46*	–36*	–14	06	00	–10
26 no responsibility	21	–06	52*	–09	29*	–05
27 no education	01	15	07	06	62*	–11
28 stable	–23	18	–14	–24*	10	04
29 individualistic	11	–09	–13	32*	–05	14
30 industrious	01	43*	–06	08	–17	05
31 utilitarian	–12	31*	36*	–05	–11	–22*
32 well paid	15	02	–31*	–24*	32*	18
33 no intelligence	–08	–08	02	05	58*	–01
34 personal	–08	–07	–32*	49*	16	10
35 fascinating	72*	–08	–01	06	06	07
36 manager	05	–23	53*	01	–18	–21*
37 development-orientated	–15	–03	–08	32*	11	–14
38 decisive	–01	39*	–15	12	–11	–05
39 careless	14	–47*	–20	–02	29*	–20*
40 flexible	01	08	02	57*	11	00
41 fast	12	25	–15	30*	19	–11
42 extravagant	02	–50*	–01	–07	–21	13
43 no training	–41*	–02	14	30*	18	19
44 unimportant	05	–36*	28*	–02	04	–02
45 production-minded	08	53*	17	–10	21	–11
46 difficult	38*	17	–06	–07	–10	–20*
47 not very useful	–14	–40*	26*	09	02	–06
48 disciplined	07	47*	–01	–07	10	00
49 inefficient	10	–67*	11	–09	–10	–02
50 unpredictable	05	–21	04	45*	–11	–04
51 materialistic	02	20	26*	–01	–12	–16
52 undirected	–20	–01	–20	07	14	–05
% COMMON VARIANCE	24	20	16	15	14	10

1. Factors 2,3, and 5 have been reflected to form a positive concept.
2. Items printed in bold type are used to define the 6 scales initially.

for these occurrences. Generally, the items to be factor analysed intercorrelate quite highly making oblique factor analysis preferable to an orthogonal one. Applying Kaiser's Little Jiffy transformation (Kaiser and Rice, 1974) to the MYJOB semantic differential scales produced six factors accounting for 40 per cent of the overall variance. This proportion is quite acceptable for scale construction even though a structural factor analysis might require a higher figure (cf. Chapter 8). Interpretation of the factors is taken from the factor pattern matrix (Table 10.4), the asterisks inserted by the Kaiser program assisting in the identification of salient contributory items. In allocating items to scales, the usual factor interpretation has to be extended to meet certain additional criteria, not all of which can be decided upon immediately. One that can is the need for items to be exclusive to one scale. Where this is not clearly so (items 1, 3, 9, and 11, for example) the solution is either to place the item in the candidate scale to which it seems to belong best, or to include it in the smallest associated scale. This latter tactic helps to ensure that all scales have at least the minimum number of items, normally taken as five or six (Oppenheim, 1966). Failing either of these possibilities, the item is excluded altogether, along with items whose low loadings show them to fit no scale (items 2, 24, 28, 52).

However, this screening is not final. Once a provisional scale allocation has been arrived at, an item analysis is performed to assess the reliability of each scale, and to check the suitability of items for inclusion in their respective scales (Chapter 11 deals with this topic in greater detail). Any items whose correlations with their scale total are too low are removed and the scale statistics recomputed. As soon as satisfactory results are obtained, scale scores are derived for each person and further analysis on them can be carried out. Table 10.5 gives the accepted item analysis results for the MYJOB scale, together with alternative allocations. So, for example, initially it seems reasonable to include items 32 and 51 in scales 5 and 3 respectively, working from the factor loadings (Table 10.4). However, the item-scale correlations (Table 10.5) of .38 for both suggest otherwise. Eliminating these two items improves the alpha reliabilities for scales 3 and 5 to .67. The initial reliability figure for scale 6 is low (.604) but although switching items 1 and 11 between scales 1 and 6 results in higher item-scale correlations (Table 10.5) it also further reduces the reliability of scale 6. The original allocation is therefore preferable.

10.7 Recoding into binary form for multivariate analysis

The discussion of two- and three-way tabulations hinted that a greater degree of insight into response patterns was obtained by considering more variables at once. Although, in principle, it is possible to carry out four- and five-way cross-tabulations, in practice any extension beyond three-way tables becomes out of the question. Even if samples are sufficiently large to maintain reasonably high expected cell frequencies other problems such as the difficulty of interpreting the analyses make the development of cross-tabulation analysis impracticable. Nevertheless, there still remains the recurrent but promising task of identifying patterns in questionnaire responses. The analogous problem with continuous data can be tackled using a variety of multivariate statistical methods (cf. Chapters 8 and 9). What is needed is a means of transforming categoric data into a continuous form. The simplest solution is to replace the separate response

161

Table 10.5 Item analysis of MYJOB scales

(a) ITEM STATISTICS				*Accepted scale correlation*	*Alternative scale correlation*
Item	*Scale*	*Mean*	*Sigma*		
1 not team work	−1	5.01	1.83	.37	(.47 with scale 6)
2 risky		4.58	1.57		
3 satisfying	6	4.90	1.50	.69	
4 uninventive	−1	5.33	1.37	.57	
5 experience not needed	−5	6.20	1.38	.58	
6 participative	−3	4.58	1.65	.65	
7 pleasant	6	5.53	1.19	.73	
8 vague	−2	5.39	1.50	.54	
9 disappointing	−1	4.90	1.12	.45	
10 ill-defined	−2	4.25	1.78	.52	
11 tense	−6	3.91	1.30	.37	(.40 with scale 1)
12 involves diagnosis	−4	5.90	1.40	.48	
13 sociable	6	5.36	1.46	.69	
14 variable	1	5.73	1.33	.64	
15 passive	−4	5.47	1.45	.64	
16 no common sense	−5	6.40	1.00	.70	
17 interesting	1	6.11	0.98	.67	
18 involves many things	4	6.61	0.71	.59	
19 cooperative	2	6.08	1.13	.41	
20 undemanding	−5	5.50	1.22	.60	
21 low status	−3	4.71	1.23	.71	
22 desirable	6	5.49	1.18	.63	
23 broad	1	5.64	1.42	.66	
24 theoretical		4.26	1.40		
25 unconventional	1	4.19	1.57	.53	
26 no responsibility	−3	5.49	1.15	.62	
27 no education	−5	5.48	0.99	.60	
28 stable	−4	3.38	1.62		
29 individualistic	4	4.69	1.45	.59	
30 industrious	2	5.69	0.96	.57	
31 utilitarian	−3	3.51	1.43	.50	
32 well paid		4.24	1.19		(.38 with scale 5)
33 no intelligence	−5	5.68	0.98	.70	
34 personal	4	4.91	1.45	.62	
35 fascinating	1	5.08	1.23	.73	
36 manager	3	4.12	1.71	.67	
37 development-orientated	4	4.03	1.50	.42	
38 decisive	2	5.87	1.00	.53	
39 careless	−2	6.40	0.84	.56	
40 flexible	4	5.76	1.16	.64	
41 fast	4	4.76	1.21	.55	
42 extravagant	−2	4.70	1.34	.46	
43 no training	−1	5.36	1.12	.44	
44 unimportant	−2	6.07	0.98	.51	
45 production-minded	2	4.47	1.81	.48	
46 difficult	1	4.80	1.39	.51	
47 not very useful	−2	6.02	1.14	.60	
48 disciplined	2	5.42	1.53	.56	
49 inefficient	−2	5.43	1.33	.71	
50 unpredictable	4	4.70	1.66	.61	
51 materialistic		3.13	1.56		(.38 with scale 3)
52 undirected		4.86	1.61		

162

Table 10.5 (continued)

| (b) SCALE STATISTICS | | ACCEPTED | | | | ALTERNATIVE | | |
Scale	*Items*	*Mean*	*S.d.*	*Alpha*	*Items*	*Mean*	*S.d.*	*Alpha*
1 inventive	10	52.15	7.35	.733	10	51.23	7.30	.762
2 analytical	12	65.78	8.21	.755				
3 responsible	5	22.40	4.76	.668	6	25.53	5.14	.611
4 varied	10	51.46	7.22	.701				
5 demanding	5	29.26	3.67	.665	6	33.02	3.95	.608
6 satisfying	5	25.19	4.15	.604	5	24.27	4.37	.560

The scale column gives the scale allocation of each item. A negative sign indicates that the item is to be reversed before scoring.
The main criterion for final acceptance is to achieve sufficiently high reliabilities for all scales.

categories by a series of YES/NO variables, usually called dummy variables (Kerlinger, 1973) or binary attributes. Once the original data have been transformed into the corresponding binary attributes (normally coded 1/0 for presence or absence of that attribute) the whole range of multivariate statistics becomes available.

Systems for constructing binary attributes feature in most large statistical packages. The particular one used here (Youngman, 1976) allows various types of attribute to be defined ranging from individual categories at the simplest extreme through to joint conditions involving up to 7 measures at the other. With the first form each category for a question defines an attribute. For example, the qualification question (variable 2) records 9 categories and therefore could produce 9 corresponding attributes:

ATTRIBUTE 1   VARIABLE 2   EQUAL TO 1   (i.e., city and guilds)
a person responding in category 1 would be scored YES (1), otherwise 0.
ATTRIBUTE 2   VARIABLE 2   EQUAL TO 2   (ONC)
ATTRIBUTE 3   VARIABLE 2   EQUAL TO 3   (HNC)

and so on for each of the 9 categories. Obviously a person would only record a 1 on one attribute because of the exclusive coding employed on this occasion.

Every question could be treated in a similar manner, each one producing the same number of attributes as it has categories. With questions having only a small number of categories, the system works well; the major drawback is that questions with a large number of categories (such as age or number of years worked) produce an inordinate number of attributes. One solution is to combine categories very much in the way that recoding did (cf. Section 10.4). Again using the qualification question, a graduate attribute can be defined as follows:

   VARIABLE 2   EQUAL TO 5
or VARIABLE 2   EQUAL TO 6
or VARIABLE 2   EQUAL TO 7

If any one of these conditions is satisfied, the graduate attribute is possessed, otherwise a zero would be scored. A complete range of attributes could be defined to cover the whole questionnaire. For YES /NO questions it is simply a matter of direct transfer; many other questions like age or number of jobs held can usually be dichotomized to produce attributes such as 'old' (AGE GREATER THAN 40) or 'many jobs' (NUMBER OF JOBS OVER 6). Occasionally, it may be preferable to define more than one attribute for a question to ease interpretation. So from job level (variable 6, Appendix 10.3) a

Table 10.6 Forty-four attributes formed from the questionnaire

Attribute	Specification	Description
1	V1.GE.40	age 40 or over
2	V2.GT.4 *and* V2.LT.8	graduates
3	V2.EQ.9	no qualification
4	V3.GT.1	substantial study
5	V4.GT.0	professional endorsement
6	V4.EQ.2	professional membership
7	V6.LT.4	senior position
8	V6.EQ.4	middle position
9	V8.GT.6	many jobs held
10	V9.EQ.1	department change likely
11	V10.EQ.1	company change likely
12	V11.EQ.1	promotion likely
13	V12.EQ.1	more administration likely
14	V13.EQ.1	more technology likely
15	V14.EQ.1	redundancy possible
16	V15.EQ.1	changes will require further training
17	V16.LT.3 *and* V16.NE.0	high rating for training (exclude non-responses)
18	V17.LT.3 *and* V17.NE.0	high rating for present experience
19	V18.LT.3 *and* V18.NE.0	high rating for overall experience
20	V19.LT.3 *and* V19.NE.0	value experience in other department
21	V20.LT.3 *and* V20.NE.0	value experience with other problems
22	V21.LT.3 *and* V21.NE.0	value experience in other firm
23	V22.LT.3 *and* V22.NE.0	value short course of training
24	V23.LT.3 *and* V23.NE.0	value extended course of training
25	V24.EQ.1	possible to reorganize work
26	V25.GT.1	long time needed to reorganize
27	V26.EQ.1	unfamiliar tasks occur often
28	V27.EQ.1	consult books
29	V31.EQ.1	consult past records
30	V32.EQ.1	consult superior
31	V34.EQ.1	consult other departments
32	V37.EQ.1	responsible for people
33	V38.EQ.1	responsible for training people
34	V39.EQ.1	trained by someone
35	V40.EQ.1	apprenticeship with firm
36	V41.EQ.1	first job with firm
37	V42.GT.13	long time with firm (over 13 years)
38	V43.LT.2	only 1 job not with firm
39	V44.GT.4	long time in current job (over 4 years)
40	V45.GT.2	more than 2 years in services
41	V7.LE.4	job function: administration
42	V7.GE.5 *and* V7.LE.8	job function: design and development
43	V7.GE.9 *and* V7.LE.18	job function: production and manufacture
44	V7.GE.19 *and* V7.LE.24	job function: commercial and services

In the attribute specifications V refers to variables and the abbreviations GE, GT, LE, LT, EQ, and NE are the standard logical relationships greater than or equal to, greater than and so on. In certain instances two conditions are needed to define the attribute.

seniority attribute could be defined (codes 1, 2, and 3) together with one for middle positions (code 4) and another for the remainder (codes 5 to 9), three attributes in all:

ATTRIBUTE 1 (senior) VARIABLE 6 LESS THAN 4, BUT GREATER THAN 0
ATTRIBUTE 2 (middle) VARIABLE 6 EQUAL TO 4
ATTRIBUTE 3 (junior) VARIABLE 6 GREATER THAN 4

Each person could then be scored automatically on all these attributes, the end result being a series of 1's and 0's for every case.

The attributes derived from the Engineering Training Questionnaire are given in Table 10.6. Although not all of the survey questions are involved, the 44 attributes cover the majority of the questionnaire content. Some of the questions generate more than one attribute (qualification and professional membership, for example) but in most cases a single attribute can be defined from each question. Where non-responses occur, such as in variables 16 to 23, the non-response category must be excluded from the attribute definition. Clearly, the attributes cannot be constructed until the initial response tabulation has been obtained. This first tabulation can also suggest that certain questions are of little importance and need not be included in the attribute set. The questions on information sources (Appendix 10.1, Question 9b) were of minor interest and only a selection was considered worthy of inclusion. Once all 44 attributes had been defined and prepared for the computer program, scoring was automatic, the end result being a series of 44 1's and 0's for each case. The recoded data are then added to the basic data file and any further analysis carried out.

10.8 Cluster analysis of attribute data

Many surveys are as much concerned with classifying responses as recording facts. Given that multiple tabulations are cumbersome to compute and difficult to interpret, cluster analysis provides a valuable alternative. Using the standard procedures (cf. Chapter 9) the attribute coding allows all questionnaire responses to be compared, and groups of similar ones to be identified. The members of these groups or clusters can then be examined in greater detail to see how they differ from the rest. Also, any additional information that may be at hand (from attitude or achievement testing, for example) can be used to extend the group characterization.

The 194 engineers in the Engineer Training Survey with complete data were scored on the 44 attributes already described (Table 10.6) and then classified using a centroid relocation method of cluster analysis (Wishart, 1969; Youngman, 1976). This classification only took into account the 44 questionnaire attributes although other data were available. By using this further information for diagnosis only, it became possible to examine, independently, relationships between training attitudes and work, without the danger of introducing patterns implicitly in the clustering process. Seven types were distinguished (cf. Table 10.7) although one contained only five members. Nevertheless that cluster remained stable throughout the analysis and therefore was diagnosed separately. The remaining 6 clusters all comprised approximately 30 members. Apart from the 44 attributes, Table 10.7 contains cluster average scores on 14 activity measures

Table 10.7   Classification of engineers on the basis of their attitudes to training and experience as indicated on the interview questionnaire

		Old seniors 1	Low status 2	Young qual. 3	Unqual. comm. 4	Middle rank 5	Older qual. 6	Rigid loyal 7	
1 A	Quality monitoring	39	42	48	39	44	+ 68	50	1
2 A	Customer liaison	45	29	39	46	27	55	53	2
3 A	Testing	20	38	35	25	30	39	17	3
4 A	Organize materials/methods	26	40	44	26	38	+ 54	35	4
5 A	Contract supervision	35	17	26	30	− 11	30	32	5
6 A	Draughting	− 12	33	33	21	25	25	27	6
7 A	Project supervision	+ 59	− 32	49	42	− 29	+ 59	48	7
8 A	Design	24	31	+ 41	21	21	+ 45	27	8
9 A	Production scheduling	35	26	31	32	21	37	− 17	9
10 A	Facilitate manufacture	46	38	42	34	42	53	60	10
11 A	Organize testing	18	23	28	23	23	+ 39	25	11
12 A	Produce specifications	23	22	32	19	− 12	+ 38	22	12
13 A	Information organization	61	61	73	61	63	+ 83	74	13
14 A	Long-term planning	+ 39	− 15	26	− 17	− 15	32	45	14
15	Age over 40	+ 90	56	− 3	55	38	+ 84	+ 80	15
16	Graduate	10	16	+ 49	− 0	− 7	+ 48	− 0	16
17	No qualification	19	31	− 0	36	24	8	40	17
18	Substantial study	13	22	+ 74	− 6	14	24	− 0	18
19	Endorsement	42	− 6	44	− 6	17	+ 84	− 20	19
20	Profession membership	35	− 3	31	− 0	− 7	+ 80	− 20	20
21	Senior position (SE or above)	+ 87	− 6	21	− 15	− 0	48	60	21
22	Middle position (ENGR)	− 10	34	44	58	62	52	− 20	22
23	Many jobs held (over 6)	+ 74	56	− 10	61	− 21	68	60	23
24	Change to other dept. likely	10	16	+ 46	21	31	40	− 20	24
25	Change to other firm likely	16	− 0	36	24	− 7	32	− 20	25
26	Promotion likely	29	− 3	+ 69	36	31	32	40	26
27	More administration likely	39	− 3	+ 62	18	17	12	40	27
28	More technology likely	− 6	− 3	+ 41	+ 42	28	28	40	28
29	Redundancy possible	19	− 9	33	33	38	28	− 20	29
30	Changes require further training	39	− 0	62	+ 76	45	− 16	40	30
31	Rate education and training highly	45	− 19	+ 79	+ 79	52	+ 80	40	31
32	Rate exp. in present job highly	58	− 19	+ 79	+ 88	69	56	− 20	32
33	Rate overall experience highly	42	− 13	59	+ 85	45	+ 80	40	33
34	Value experience in other department	− 16	34	44	+ 55	28	36	40	34
35	Value experience with diff. problems	− 13	44	44	52	45	56	60	35
36	Value experience diff. firm/same job	+ 71	− 34	56	61	55	40	− 20	36
37	Value short course of training	42	44	36	+ 73	48	44	60	37
38	Value extended course of study	19	19	18	33	+ 45	28	60	38
39	Possible to reorganize work	100	100	100	100	100	100	− 0	39
40	Long time needed to reorganize	34	34	23	27	21	− 4	40	40
41	Unfamiliar tasks occur often	+ 81	50	69	− 36	59	72	+ 80	41
42	Refer to books	− 52	66	79	70	83	+ 96	+ 80	42
43	Refer to past records	71	91	90	85	76	92	80	43
44	Refer to supervisor	− 55	78	77	79	72	80	+ 100	44
45	Refer to other departments	71	78	85	85	86	+ 100	80	45
46	Anyone report to you	+ 84	− 28	64	45	− 7	64	40	46
47	Train anyone	+ 58	− 3	49	36	− 0	32	− 20	47
48	Anyone train you	39	28	+ 64	39	48	52	60	48
49	EE Apprenticeship	− 19	− 9	+ 82	− 12	+ 69	− 4	− 20	49
50	First job EE	− 19	− 6	+ 87	− 12	+ 79	− 4	− 20	50
51	Long time with EE (over 13 years)	+ 94	41	− 8	30	48	36	+ 80	51
52	Only a job not EE	+ 71	34	+ 100	36	+ 100	− 20	+ 100	52

Rows 24–52 are labelled CLASSIFICATION VARIABLES (vertical label).

Table 10.7 (continued)

		Old seniors 1	Low status 2	Young qual. 3	Unqual. comm. 4	Middle rank 5	Older qual. 6	Rigid loyal 7	
53	Long time in current job (over 4 years)	32	+ 53	− 15	39	− 14	46	20	53
54	More than 2 years' services	55	34	− 0	+ 61	− 7	28	40	54
55	Function: Administration	+ 74	− 0	− 15	− 9	− 0	28	20	55
56	Function: Engineering	− 6	+ 63	51	15	17	40	60	56
57	Function: Production	− 10	25	− 10	18	+ 76	24	− 0	57
58	Function: Commercial	10	13	18	+ 55	7	8	20	58
59 J	Inventive	+ 56	− 48	52	52	50	53	+ 58	59
60 J	Analytical	68	64	64	66	67	66	67	60
61 J	Responsible	+ 28	− 22	25	27	24	27	26	61
62 J	Varied	+ 45	− 40	42	44	43	42	44	62
63 J	Demanding	34	− 31	33	33	32	34	34	63
64 J	Satisfying	27	24	25	26	26	24	27	64
65 S	Efficient	+ 63	59	59	63	61	61	+ 64	65
66 S	Determined	+ 41	− 36	40	40	40	39	38	66
67 S	Sociable	44	− 41	45	44	46	43	46	67
68 S	Dominant	26	24	26	24	25	24	27	68
69 S	Expert	40	− 36	+ 41	39	+ 41	39	37	69
70 S	Conforming	21	21	21	22	+ 24	22	22	70
	NUMBER OF MEMBERS	31	32	39	33	29	25	5	194

Column figures are the percentages of each cluster possessing the corresponding row attribute. A + or − is inserted if that frequency is significantly higher or lower than the mean of the rest (Scheffé's method). Only the middle block of variables was used to generate the classification. The outer blocks provide additional diagnostic information.

(assessing the degree to which a person is involved in a particular activity) and 12 job perception scales derived from semantic differentials. The first 6 of these (variables 59 to 64) are the 6 MYJOB scales already described (Section 10.6); they assess an engineer's perception of his job. Self-perceptions were considered of equal importance and therefore a comparable inventory of MYSELF items was administered. Variables 65 to 70 are the 6 scales resulting from an analysis of it. The +'s and −'s for each cluster indicate measures on which a group scores significantly higher or lower than the remaining engineers, as tested by Scheffé's method (Chapter 7).

Some idea of the nature of each cluster is gained from the labels used in Table 10.7 but a more accurate description demands further details from that table.

TYPE 1   OLD SENIORS ($N = 31$)
Relatively old and senior, these engineers are mostly in administration. Consequently, they show little enthusiasm for further training, except possibly for a change of company. They do have a positive view of their job, and a high rating of themselves.

TYPE 2   LOW STATUS ($N = 32$)
Sixty per cent are assistant engineers or lower, and mostly work in engineering. They see little chance of change, and rate all training and experience lowly. Generally they have little responsibility.

TYPE 3 YOUNG QUALIFIED (*N* = 39)

All but one are under 40 and 50 per cent are graduates. Various changes are anticipated, and training and education are rated correspondingly highly. They already carry responsibility.

TYPE 4 UNQUALIFIED, MOSTLY COMMERCIAL (*N* = 33)

There are very few senior personnel in this group but they do rate their experience highly even though their job is seen as routine. Short courses are valued. This is the only group with any significant service experience.

TYPE 5 MIDDLE RANK (*N* = 29)

These are non-graduates, mostly of engineer status, with little expectation of change. Nevertheless, they do value short courses. The majority of the men are in the production area, and they tend to have been with the company for a long time.

TYPE 6 OLDER QUALIFIED (*N* = 25)

This is a more highly qualified version of TYPE 1 and predictably its members have a more involved job. While education is valued, these engineers do not want more. They have had relatively mobile careers.

TYPE 7 RIGID LOYAL (*N* = 5)

A small but strongly characterized group, these engineers have little expectation of change, nor are they prepared to accept any. Their job cannot be reorganized and they have been with the firm a long time.

For training purposes probably the most revealing aspect of this classification is the emergence of TYPE 2. This is a group of lowly qualified workers, with little or no responsibility and no expectation of change. As a result they show no interest in training, and have a very depressed view of work.

TYPES 4 and 5 have similar qualifications and status, but they differ in that they do hold hopes for the future. This optimism manifests itself in a desire for training. In that the analysis has been able to elicit a differentiation of this kind, it has provided a valuable extension to the simple tabulation analysis. Although one cannot guarantee the outcome of a questionnaire classification, it is likely that the more involved comparison it affords will enable some of the underlying patterns in responses to be seen.

10.9 Further analysis of questionnaires

The classification analysis just described offers one example of a deeper analysis of questionnaires than is normally performed. In that surveys are frequently designed to discover discriminating attitudes within a population it is likely that cluster analysis will meet many of these needs. Where other aims obtain, for example the structuring of questionnaires or even the prediction of some criterion measure, then factor or regression analysis would be more suitable. Indeed, the attribute coding system is ideally suited to multiple regression analysis (Cohen, 1968; Kerlinger, 1973) so long as the appropriate constraints are satisfied (cf. Chapter 8). Throughout the analysis of any questionnaire it is essential that all such possibilities are borne in mind so that the maximum benefit can be gained from this increasingly costly method of data collection.

PROGRAM AVAILABILITY
see Section 3.6

	PMMD	SPSS	BMDP	OSIRIS	VELDMAN	COOLEY
The analysis of questionnaires						
tabulation	P	S	B	O	V	
recoding	P	S	B	O		
cross-tabulation	P	S	B	O	V	
three-way tables	P	S	B	O		
forming scales by factor analysis	P	S	B	O	V	C
binary coding	P	S	B	O		
cluster analysis of binary data	P			O	V	
multivariate analysis	P	S	B	O	V	C

References

Cohen, J. (1968) 'Multiple regression as a general data-analytic system', *Psychological Bulletin*, **70**, 426–443.

Kaiser, H. F. and J. Rice (1974) 'Little Jiffy Mark IV', *Educ. and Psychol. Meas.*, **34** (1), 111–117.

Kerlinger, F. N. (1973) *Foundations of Behavioral Research*, Second edition; New York, Holt, Rinehart, and Winston.

Oppenheim, A. N. (1966) *Questionnaire Design and Attitude Measurement*, London, Heinemann.

Wishart, D. (1969) *CLUSTAN 14: User Manual*, St. Andrews, Scotland, University of St. Andrews Computing Laboratory.

Youngman, M. B. (1976) *Programmed Methods for Multivariate Data*, Version 5, School of Education, University of Nottingham.

Youngman, M. B., R. Oxtoby., J. D. Monk, and J. Heywood (1978) *Analysing Jobs*, Farnborough, Gower Press/Teakfield.

Appendix 10.1 Engineer Training Survey Questionnaire

	Computer Coding

Biographic information — C1,2,3,

1. JOB TITLE	2. DEPARTMENT	3. AGE	C4,5,6 7,8

4.
(a) QUALIFICATION

No-answer	0	Degree	5
City and guilds	1	Postgraduate	6
ONC	2	Academic + technical	7
HNC	3	Other	8
HND	4	NONE	9

C9,10
C11
C12
C13
C14,15

(b) METHOD | Part-time | 1 | Block | 2 | Sandwich | 3 | Full-time | 4 |

C16
C17,18
C19,20

(c) PROFESSIONAL STATUS | Endorsement | 1 | Membership | 2 |

5. EXPERIENCE

Start	End	Job	Department/Firm	
				1
				2
				3
				4
				5
				6
				7
				8
				9
				10
				11
				12
				13
				14

In the interviews already carried out in your firm, reference was made to training needs which relate to the firm's objectives.
We are asking you to complete the following questionnaire to help identify some of these problems of training.
PLEASE TICK (√) the word, or phrase, or rank as appropriate.

6. CHANGES AND TRAINING
(a) Are any of these changes likely to occur in your job?

i	Transfer to another department in the firm	YES	1	NO	0		C50
ii	Transfer to another firm	YES	1	NO	0		C51
iii	A change to a more senior position	YES	1	NO	0		C52
iv	A change involving more administration	YES	1	NO	0		C53
v	A change involving more technology	YES	1	NO	0		C54

(b) OTHERS — C55

(c) In order to make these changes will you require training | YES | 1 | — C56
| NO | 0 |

(d) Rate the importance of these factors in helping to change.
(1 = very useful —— 5 = of little or no help).

1 2 3 4 5

			C57
i	Your previous training and education		C57
ii	Your experience in the present job		C58
iii	Your overall experience in industry (excluding *training*)		C59

Appendix 10.1 (continued)

7. IMPROVEMENTS

Which of the following suggestions do you believe would help to improve your performance in your present job?
(Rate 1 to 5 where 1 = extremely useful and 5 = little or no use)

		1	2	3	4	5	Coding
i	Experience in another type of department						C60
ii	Experience in same department with different problems						C61
iii	Experience in another firm with same type of job						C62
iv	A short course of training suitably designed						C63
v	An extended educational course						C64

8. REORGANIZATION

(a) If the company decided to sponsor a short training course (say 2 weeks) would it be possible for your work to be organized in the department so that you could attend such a course?

YES	1	C65
NO	0	

(b) Would the time needed for a reorganization be:

Less than a fortnight	1	C66
Between 2 weeks and 3 months	2	
More than 3 months	3	

9. UNFAMILIARITY

(a) How often are you faced with unfamiliar problems?

Frequently	1	C67
Not very often	2	
Never	3	

(b) Which, if any, of these sources do you use to seek information or guidance in solving novel problems?

Technical books	1	C68
Technical periodicals	2	C69
Trade or industrial associations	3	C70
Professional institutions	4	C71
Past records or designs in the firm	5	C72
Your supervisor	6	C73
Your colleagues	7	C74
Other departments with specialized knowledge	8	C75
Other firm's products	9	C76
Other firms' expertise	10	C77

Other sources (please specify)

10. APPRENTICESHIP

What improvements would you suggest in the firm's graduate/other apprenticeship?

11. Do you have any prople reporting or responsible to you?	YES	1	C78
	NO	0	

12. Are you responsible for the training of these people?	YES	1	C79
	NO	0	

13. Is anyone in the firm responsible for your training needs?	YES	1	C80
	NO	0	

Appendix 10.2   The MYJOB semantic differential scales

MY JOB

#	Left	1	2	3	4	5	6	7	Right
1	involves working as a member of a team	1	2	3	4	5	6	7	does not involve working as a member of a team
2	safe	1	2	3	4	5	6	7	risky
3	frustrating	1	2	3	4	5	6	7	satisfying
4	inventive	1	2	3	4	5	6	7	uninventive
5	requires experience	1	2	3	4	5	6	7	does not require experience
6	authoritative	1	2	3	4	5	6	7	participative
7	unpleasant	1	2	3	4	5	6	7	pleasant
8	precise	1	2	3	4	5	6	7	vague
9	exciting	1	2	3	4	5	6	7	disappointing
10	well-defined	1	2	3	4	5	6	7	ill-defined
11	relaxed	1	2	3	4	5	6	7	tense
12	involves diagnosing trouble	1	2	3	4	5	6	7	does not involve diagnosing trouble
13	unsociable	1	2	3	4	5	6	7	sociable
14	routine	1	2	3	4	5	6	7	variable
15	active	1	2	3	4	5	6	7	passive
16	requires a great deal of common sense	1	2	3	4	5	6	7	does not require common sense
17	uninteresting	1	2	3	4	5	6	7	interesting
18	involves one thing	1	2	3	4	5	6	7	involves many things
19	uncooperative	1	2	3	4	5	6	7	cooperative
20	demanding	1	2	3	4	5	6	7	undemanding
21	high status	1	2	3	4	5	6	7	low status
22	undesirable	1	2	3	4	5	6	7	desirable
23	narrow	1	2	3	4	5	6	7	broad
24	practical	1	2	3	4	5	6	7	theoretical
25	conventional	1	2	3	4	5	6	7	unconventional
26	involves much responsibility	1	2	3	4	5	6	7	involves no responsibility
27	requires much education	1	2	3	4	5	6	7	requires no education
28	changeable	1	2	3	4	5	6	7	stable
29	conforming	1	2	3	4	5	6	7	individualistic
30	lethargic	1	2	3	4	5	6	7	industrious
31	glamorous	1	2	3	4	5	6	7	utilitarian
32	badly paid	1	2	3	4	5	6	7	well paid
33	requires very much intelligence	1	2	3	4	5	6	7	does not require intelligence
34	impersonal	1	2	3	4	5	6	7	personal
35	tedious	1	2	3	4	5	6	7	fascinating
36	worker	1	2	3	4	5	6	7	manager
37	design-oriented	1	2	3	4	5	6	7	development-oriented
38	indecisive	1	2	3	4	5	6	7	decisive
39	careful	1	2	3	4	5	6	7	careless
40	rigid	1	2	3	4	5	6	7	flexible
41	slow	1	2	3	4	5	6	7	fast
42	economical	1	2	3	4	5	6	7	extravagant
43	requires very extensive training	1	2	3	4	5	6	7	does not require training
44	important	1	2	3	4	5	6	7	unimportant
45	sales-minded	1	2	3	4	5	6	7	production-minded
46	easy	1	2	3	4	5	6	7	difficult
47	very useful	1	2	3	4	5	6	7	not very useful
48	undisciplined	1	2	3	4	5	6	7	disciplined
49	efficient	1	2	3	4	5	6	7	inefficient
50	predictable	1	2	3	4	5	6	7	unpredictable
51	idealistic	1	2	3	4	5	6	7	materialistic
52	motivated	1	2	3	4	5	6	7	undirected

Appendix 10.3 Coding frame

Card column	Variable	Description		Question
1– 3	ID	Identification number (001–284)		
4– 8				(blank)
9–10	1	Exact age		3
11	2	Qualification	[0–9/see separate coding]	4a
12	3	Method	[0 = not given/1 = P/T/2 = BLOCK/3 = SANDWICH/4 = FULL]	4b
13	4	Profession	[0 = no/1 = ENDORSEMENT/2 = MEMBERSHIP]	4c
14–15	5	Job area	[01–09 = ENGINEERING/10–21 = COMMERCIAL]	2
16	6	Job level	[0–9/see separate coding]	1
17–18	7	Job function	[1–4=ADMIN/5–8=ENG*9–18= PROD/19–24=SALES]	2
19–20				(blank)
21–22	8	No. of jobs		5
23–39		No. of years in each job	[1 column per job]	5
40–49		Related jobs (not used)	[0= NO/1 = YES]	5
50	9	Department charge likely?	[0 = NO/1 = YES]	6a(i)
51	10	Company charge likely?	[0 = NO/1 – YES]	6a(ii)
52	11	More seniority?	[0 = NO/1 = YES]	6a(iii)
53	12	More administration?	[0 = NO/1 = YES]	6a(iv)
54	13	More technology?	[0 = NO/1 = YES]	6a(v)
55	14	Redundancy possible?	[0 = NO/1 = YES]	6b
56	15	Changes require training?		6c
57	16	Importance of previous training?	[1 = HIGH/5 = LOW]	6d(i)
58	17	Importance of present experience?	[1 = HIGH/5 = LOW]	6d(ii)
59	18	Importance of overall experience?	[1 = HIGH/5 = LOW]	6d(iii)
60	19	Value of another department?	[1 = HIGH/5 = LOW]	7(i)
61	20	Value of different problems?	[1 = HIGH/5 = LOW]	7(ii)
62	21	Value of another firm?	[1 = HIGH/5 = LOW]	7(iii)
63	22	Value of short course?	[1 = HIGH/5 = LOW]	7(iv)
64	23	Value of extended course?	[1 = HIGH/5 = LOW]	7(v)
65	24	Possible to attend 2 week course?	[0 = NO/1 = YES]	8a
66	25	Time needed to reorganize work?	[1 = <2 WEEKS/2 = 2W–3M/3 = >3m]	8b
67	26	Frequency of unfamiliar tasks	[1 = FREQ/2 = SELDOM/3 = NEVER]	9a
68	27	Consult technical books	[0 = NO/1 = YES]	9b(i)
69	28	Consult technical periodicals	[0 = NO/1 = YES]	9b(ii)
70	29	Consult trade associations	[0 = NO/1 = YES]	9b(iii)
71	30	Consult professional institutions	[0 = NO/1 = YES]	9b(iv)
72	31	Consult past records or designs	[0 = NO/1 = YES]	9b(v)
73	32	Consult supervisor	[0 = NO/1 = YES]	9b(vi)
74	33	Consult colleagues	[0 = NO/1 = YES]	9b(vii)
75	34	Consult other departments	[0 = NO/1 = YES]	9b(viii)
76	35	Consult other firms' products	[0 = NO/1 = YES]	9b(ix)
77	36	Consult other firms' expertise	[0 = NO/1 = YES]	9b(x)
78	37	Anyone report to you?	[0 = NO/1 = YES]	11
79	38	Responsible for training?	[0 = NO/1 = YES]	12
80	39	Anyone train you?	[0 = NO/1 = YES]	13
1– 3		Identification number on card 2		
4	40	Apprenticeship with firm	[0 = NO/1 = YES]	5
5	41	First job with firm	[0 = NO/1 = YES]	5

Appendix 10.3 (continued)

Card column	Variable	Description	Question
6– 7	42	Years with firm	5
8– 9	43	Number of jobs outside firm	5
10–11	44	Years in current job	5
12–13	45	Years in services	5

Qualification and job level coding

QUALIFICATION (Q2)	JOB LEVEL (Q6)
0 = no answer	0 = no answer
1 = City and guilds	1 = manager
2 = ONC	2 = principal engineer
3 = HNC	3 = senior engineer
4 = HND	4 = engineer
5 = Degree	5 = assistant engineer
6 = Higher degree	6 = draughtsman
7 = Degree plus technical	7 = senior technician
8 = Other	8 = technician
9 = None	9 = technical assistant

11. The Construction of Scales and Tests

Whenever research requires the assessment of some attribute for which no suitable measuring instrument exists it becomes necessary to construct such a device. Moreover, there may also be situations where it is possible to generate some means of comparative assessment even though quantification was not originally intended. Regardless of the intention, any measurement used in the investigation of a research problem must first be shown to be sound. Various criteria exist to assess the soundness of instruments. For published scales and tests the accompanying instructions usually include the information needed to make this judgement. Using self-constructed instruments it will be necessary to construct the scale or test with these criteria in mind, and then to confirm that the finished product actually meets them.

The criteria for evaluating research instruments cover a wide range of applicability but they are traditionally classified under the two headings of reliability and validity. Any standard text on research design will consider these concepts in detail. Briefly, *reliability* is an indication of the degree to which an instrument performs consistently, both for the subjects being assessed and in the differing situations under which the measurement is made. The *validity* of an instrument indicates how far it actually measures what it is intended to measure. Both definitions specify *degree* rather than perfection and consequently the researcher further needs to decide what levels are desirable or satisfactory for the attribute under consideration.

Typically, the steps involved in the production of an acceptable research instrument are as follows:

1. Compile a pool of relevant items.
2. Assemble these into the form of an instrument.
3. Apply the instrument to one or more samples.
4. Perform an item analysis of the responses obtained.
5. Remove any unsuitable items.
6. Assess the reliability and validity of the modified instrument.
7. Repeat steps 5 and 6 if necessary.

This procedure assumes that the scale or test is *unidimensional*, that is it measures one attribute only. Should a *multidimensional* instrument be required the same steps apply except that an extra stage (after step 3) is needed to identify the subscales within the overall instrument. Chapter 10, Section 10.6, contains an extended discussion of the special problems of generating subscales. The following account of the techniques employed in constructing scales and tests is offered largely as an example. Detailed discussions of the principles involved are available from numerous texts on assessment and measurement (e.g., Cronbach, 1970; Stanley and Hopkins, 1972; Lewis, 1976, all level A). Statistical presentations are a feature of most texts on quantitative methods (e.g., DuBois, 1965; Nunnally, 1967; Ferguson, 1976, all level B).

11.1   Item analysis

Although variations in the overall method do exist, the main aim in item analysis is to assess the response level and discrimination of each item, and to compare these with standard levels of acceptability. An excellent account of the simplest of these variations is given by Stanley and Hopkins (1972, Chapter 11). The following demonstration takes a sample of 100 cases from the transfer dataset and examines their responses to the first 13 items of the Brighty Reading Comprehension Test (Lunzer and Gardner, 1977). Normally, an item analysis would involve a larger sample and more items. Nevertheless, the underlying principles are readily seen.

In the traditional approach to item analysis the first step is to extract high-scoring and low-scoring groups from the complete sample. Following the recommendation of Kelley (1939) it is usual to define high and low groups as those cases whose total test scores fall within the top and bottom 27 per cent respectively. Kelley showed that these cut-off levels produced maximum discrimination. Recently, however, D'Agostino and Cureton (1975) have questioned this assertion, pointing out that Kelley's assumption that the two groups are independent is incorrect. Without this assumption they show that maximum discrimination is achieved with a cut-off point of 21 per cent. Nevertheless they also accept that the improvement is only marginal; they suggest that if convenience dictates, then any point around 25 per cent will suffice.

RESPONSE LEVEL OR FACILITY

The *response level* is the proportion agreeing with or ticking an item. For ability or achievement tests it is customary to refer to the *facility* or easiness of the item. Occasionally the opposite concept, *difficulty*, is used but all three carry the same information about an item. In terms of the high and low groups:

N = number in each of the high and low groups.
N_H = number in the high group responding to the item.
N_L = number in the low group responding to the item.
P_H = proportion in the high group responding (i.e., N_H/N).
P_L = proportion in the low group responding.

Consequently the response level for an item is defined as:

$$R = \frac{P_H + P_L}{2} \qquad (11.1)$$

It is important to appreciate that this is only a *definition* of response level. The *actual* response level would have to take into account the responses of cases in the middle group excluded by the high-low group method. In fact for data coded 1/0 the true response level is simply the mean score for an item.

A scale should contain items showing a range of response levels otherwise cases at the extremes cannot be assessed. Traditionally response levels should be between 20 and 80 per cent, with values 5 per cent below and above these levels, respectively, being considered borderline. Table 11.1 summarizes a number of item statistics for the test data. Both the 27 per cent and 21 per cent groups are considered. If the above criteria are applied to the response levels for the 27 per cent analysis, R_1, then item 2 fails through having too low a level, while item 3 exceeds the accepted level. The same items are rejected by the 21 per cent analysis. The actual response levels are given to the right of the table. Here although items 2 and 3 are again rejected, items 5, 6, and 7 also have borderline response levels. The conclusion must be that response levels alone are rather unreliable estimates of an item's worth, and this applies equally to the 27 per cent and 21 per cent approaches.

DISCRIMINATION

Once the response proportions P_H and P_L have been computed, the discrimination is obtained from their difference:

$$D = P_H - P_L \qquad (11.2)$$

Table 11.1 Item statistics for various item analysis methods

| | 27% Groups | | | | | | 21% Groups | | | | | | Point biserial | | | Rasch method | |
Item	N_H	N_L	P_H	P_L	R_1	D_1	N_H	N_L	P_H	P_L	R_2	D_2	M	S	RT	DIFF	PROB
1	23	7	.85	.26	.56	.59	19	6	.91	.29	.62	.62	.59	.49	.53	49.6	.57
2	7	0	.26	.00	**.13**	.26	6	0	.29	.00	**.14**	.29	**.08**	.27	.35	64.8	.87
3	27	21	1.0	.78	**.89**	.22	21	15	1.0	.71	**.86**	.29	**.93**	.26	.40	37.3	.89
4	25	10	.93	.37	.65	.56	21	6	1.0	.29	.64	.71	.66	.47	.53	47.9	.88
5	27	13	1.0	.48	.74	.52	21	9	1.0	.43	.72	.57	.84	.37	.56	42.4	.44
6	27	13	1.0	.48	.74	.52	21	9	1.0	.43	.72	.57	.80	.40	.58	43.9	.78
7	27	14	1.0	.52	.76	.48	21	10	1.0	.48	.74	.52	.85	.36	.58	41.9	.67
8	25	2	.93	.07	.50	.85	19	2	.91	.10	.50	.81	.46	.50	.62	52.6	.32
9	14	1	.52	.04	.28	.48	11	0	.52	.00	.26	.52	.25	.43	.48	57.8	.88
10	16	6	.59	.22	.41	.37	14	4	.67	.19	.43	.48	.43	.50	.33	53.3	.20
11	20	10	.74	.37	.56	.37	16	7	.76	.33	.55	.43	.54	.50	.33	50.8	.10
12	17	4	.63	.15	.39	.48	13	4	.62	.19	.41	.43	.36	.48	**.30**	55.0	**.02**
13	21	4	.78	.15	.46	.63	17	2	.81	.10	.45	.72	.46	.50	.54	52.6	.83

Figures in heavy type are statistics which do not meet the criteria for that particular method of item analysis.

N_H	number in high group	M	mean score for total group
N_L	number in low group	S	standard deviation
P_H	proportion in high group	RT	correlation between item and total
P_L	proportion in low group	DIFF	difficulty value
R	response level	PROB	fit probability
D	discrimination		

Again its value in percentage form ranges from 0 to 100 but since high discrimination is desirable, no upper limit exists. At the lower end typically D values of below 20 per cent are considered unsuitable. None of the items fails on this criterion for either the 27 per cent or the 21 per cent analysis.

Part of the justification for using the extreme-groups approach to item analysis is its simplicity. With ready access to computers now commonplace it is reasonable to consider more elaborate methods. For discrimination one such method is the counterpart of the actual response level; the *variance* of an item is taken as an indication of its discriminatory power. However, it is not possible to set acceptability levels since variance values depend on the scaling of the item. Indeed for 1/0 data the variance adds nothing to the information contained in the response level as the two are related by the expression:

$$\text{Variance } \sigma^2 = p(1 - p) \tag{11.3}$$

where: p is the proportion passing (i.e., the response level as a decimal)

A better guide to discrimination is offered by the correlation between an item score and the total test score for each individual. The correlation coefficient used is the *point-biserial correlation* but this is only a computational form of the product-moment coefficient. The *RT* column of Table 11.1 gives the point-biserial correlation values. Nunnally (1967) suggests that levels above .2 are acceptable, a criterion that admits all 13 items. Taking a more stringent level would entail rejection of correlations below .3, that is item 12.

THE RASCH METHOD OF ITEM ANALYSIS

One final method of item analysis is sufficiently new to have had little use to date. It is the method first devised by Rasch in 1960. Two recent accounts (Rasch 1966a, b, level C) give extended descriptions of the method, albeit rather mathematical in content. More general outlines are provided by Wright (1967, level A) and Willmott and Fowles (1974, level A). Tinsley and Dawis (1975) present one of the few evaluations of the method currently available.

The Rasch model can only be applied to unidimensional scales, usually those assessing ability or achievement. *The items must be scored dichotomously.* The important feature of the model is that it purports to be *sample-free*, the resultant analysis being independent of the ability level of the sample used. Associated with this contention there is a more specific assumption that an individual's score on an item is a function of the item's easiness and the individual's ability. This assumption enables a probabilistic model to be constructed. The degree of fit for each item can be assessed and item rejection is based on a statistical probability rather than convention. Table 11.1 includes the Rasch model difficulty scores and fit probabilities for the 13 test items. Only item 12 is rejected by the model if a fit probability of .05 is applied.

Choice is by no means an inevitable virtue and this is patently so with item analysis procedures. Depending on which of the above methods is applied, slightly different subsets of the 13 items would be accepted:

Ignoring item analyses accepts all 13 items, rejects	none
Extreme group analysis (27 per cent or 21 per cent) rejects items	2 and 3
Total group analysis rejects items	2, 3, and 12
Rasch sample-free item analysis rejects item	12

Fortunately this apparent contradiction is not necessarily prohibitive since item analysis is only a precursor to the other checks on test soundness.

11.2 Assessing the reliability and validity of tests

Most measures of reliability and validity are expressed as correlation coefficients. Although in general their interpretation does follow the standard rules for correlations, the main emphasis must be on substantial common variance (high correlations) rather than statistical significance which can often be achieved with relatively low values. Negative values should also be treated with caution since these assessments are normally performed so that perfect reliability or validity is associated with a correlation of $+1.0$.

RELIABILITY

Repeated applications

A popular approach is to compare results obtained from applications of a test on two different occasions. If the same version of the test is used a *test-retest reliability* coefficient is produced by correlating the pairs of scores. An improvement on this involves using different but *equivalent forms* of the test to avoid learning or other contaminating effects. Either way the resulting correlation is taken as an estimate of the reliability of the test, $r_{xx'}$. Squared it gives the amount of variance common to the two applications. Alternatively, the *standard error of the measurement SE_m*, can be computed:

$$SE_m = S_x\sqrt{1 - r_{xx'}} \qquad (11.4)$$

where: S_x is the standard deviation of the measure

Internal consistency

Frequently, reliability has to be assessed from a single application of a test and then an internal estimate is required. The most obvious solution is to split the test into two *comparable* halves, and then to correlate scores on these. Unless some good reason prevents it, the odd and even numbered items can be separated and r_{oe}, the correlation between them, becomes the *split-half reliability*. In practice, however, the reduced size of the two halves will result in an underestimate of the true reliability. This can be corrected for using the Spearman-Brown 'prophecy formula':

$$r_{xx'} = \frac{nr_{aa'}}{1 + (n - 1)r_{aa'}} \qquad (11.5)$$

179

where: r_{aa}' is the reduced size reliability estimate
n is the number of times longer the true test is

For split-half reliabilities, $n = 2$, and therefore Eq. (11.5) becomes:

$$r_{xx'} = \frac{2r_{oe}}{1 + r_{oe}} \qquad (11.6)$$

For the transfer test data the first 13 items of the Brighty Comprehension Test produced a split-half reliability of .566, the corrected value being .728. More items and a larger sample would have resulted in a higher, more acceptable figure.

While the odd-even split is convenient it is also arbitrary. Consequently, the estimate produced may be unstable. Kuder and Richardson (1937) suggested a modification which incorporates all possible splits in a single formula, usually referred to as KR20. Cronbach (1951) generalized this formula to include items scored dichotomously or continuously. In Cronbach's formulation a *coefficient of equivalence, alpha,* is defined as:

$$\alpha = \frac{n}{n-1} \left[1 - \frac{\Sigma V_i}{V_t} \right] \qquad (11.7)$$

where n is the number of items
V_i is the variance of item i
V_t is the variance of the total test scores

Cronbach discusses at length the interpretation of alpha but essentially it is a measure of the degree of consistency within a test. However, it is an estimate and generally only offers a lower bound for the true value. High values are desirable but Cronbach asserts that internal consistency need not be perfect for a test to be interpretable. One consideration that does need to be borne in mind is test size. Lengthening a test tends to increase the associated alpha and this can mask the effect of unsuitable items. Table 11.2 gives the alphas for each set of items accepted by the different item analyses described earlier. The differences between the results for the various methods are so small that none of them can really be considered superior on the basis of this example. The only legitimate conclusion is that reliability alone is not a sufficient guide to test content. Indeed, it is possible to construct a perfectly reliable test which has no validity and therefore no research value. The argument returns to the need for all research analysis to maintain a sound theoretical link with the research objective.

Table 11.2   Alpha coefficients for the results of different item analyses

Item analysis	Number of items	Items excluded	Alpha
NONE	13	–	.6935
RASCH	12	12	.6791
EXTREME GROUPS	11	2,3	.6706
TOTAL SAMPLE	10	2,3,12	.6849

VALIDITY

Names can be very misleading and in test construction the problem is particularly acute. Too often researchers use the terms *face validity* or *content validity* to give unjustified credibility to a procedure involving little more than glancing over a test and deciding that 'Everything looks OK to me'. Although the name of a test, and its content, should be plausible, this kind of tautological reasoning completely misses the essential need to satisfy some *external* criterion before a test can be deemed valid. Cureton (1965) distinguishes between existing and constructed criteria but Nunnally (1967) insists that construct validity should be the overriding concern in test validation. In reality a combination of different comparisons will be made before reaching a final decision regarding the suitability of a test within a particular research area.

Validation against individual criteria

The most direct form of validation is to compare the results obtained using the test instrument with those from another similar device. Unfortunately, more often than not the main reason for constructing a new instrument is that no equivalent alternative exists. Even so there are circumstances where direct comparison is possible, for example in producing a shortened form of some test, or in modifying the language or presentation of an existing version. Failing this, the comparison has to be made with another test which seems as close a match as possible for the new one. In either of these situations the aim is to achieve the highest possible correlation coefficient, or validity coefficient, between the two. Most texts refer to this form of validation as *concurrent validity*.

A more specialized need arises when a test is to be used as a predictive measure. In Britain the best-known example is the procedure applied at the age of eleven to select children deemed most likely to benefit from academic secondary schooling (the 'eleven-plus'). Usually called *predictive validity* this form of validity matches the intended purpose of many measures particularly in the field of job placement. The use of the terms concurrent and predictive emphasizes the temporal difference between the two approaches; the actual assessments are both in terms of correlation coefficients. Levels of acceptability depend very much on the attribute being measured. With intelligence or achievement one would expect validity coefficients of .9 and over. Attitude and personality are less easily quantified and the inevitable lower reliabilities in turn reduce validity levels. Even values as low as .5 may be acceptable in the context of other satisfactory assessments.

No suitable predictive criterion exists for the reading test but it can be evaluated against other concurrent measures. Table 11.3 summarizes the correlations between the different item analyses of the 13 Brighty test items and certain of the transfer measures. As one would expect the highest correlations, around .77, are with the full version of the Brighty test (about three times as long). Somewhat surprisingly, the correlations with the other reading comprehension test, variable 26, are not particularly high. They are in fact lower than those with secondary mathematics. Without doubt the secondary reading measure, variable 23, is the most appropriate concurrent criterion since it comprises a combination of the Brighty and Grieg test scores. Here the correlations obtained suggest a validity of around .75 for the shortened test.

Table 11.3 Comparison of reading test item analyses with other transfer measures

Transfer measures for comparison	ALL ITEMS	VARIOUS Extreme groups	ITEM Point biserial	ANALYSES Rasch method
25 S: Brighty total	.77	.77	.78	.78
26 S: Grieg total	.55	.54	.56	**.57**
23 S: Reading comprehension	.73	.72	.74	**.75**
24 S: Mathematics	.60	.60	.60	.60
20 J: Non-verbal reasoning	.35	.35	**.37**	**.37**
21 J: Reading comprehension	.60	.59	.60	.60
22 J: Mathematics	.49	.49	**.52**	**.51**
18 S: Self-concept academic	.40	.37	.37	.40
19 S: Academic motivation	.38	.36	.35	.37
27 S: Adjustment to school	.22	.18	.19	.23
NUMBER OF ITEMS	13	11	10	12

The correlations between the item analysis results and the selected transfer measures enable the validities of the modified forms to be assessed. To assist interpretation those correlations which improve by .02 or more on no item analysis are in heavy type. This suggests that in this example only the Rasch method performs better than simply taking all items as they stand. Labels S and J refer to Secondary and Junior measures respectively.

In comparing the different forms of the test the correlation differences are too small to be statistically significant. The general patterns suggest that the Rasch method possibly achieves the highest validities, with the traditional extreme-groups method producing results in this instance similar to no item analysis at all.

Construct validation

No matter how novel or specialized a measuring instrument is the mere fact that it is needed in a piece of research implies that certain relationships involving the attribute concerned are already known or suspected. Even when no single comparison is possible, the validity of an instrument can always be tested within the context of a group of related variables. Some relationships will be known from previous research, others might be predictable. By comparing these expectations with the actual pattern of relationships it is possible to assess the *construct validity* of an instrument. It is a particularly relevant and powerful form of validation since it works from a realistic premise and is not dependent on the efficiency of individual criteria.

The measures included in Table 11.3 comprise a suitable domain of variables for assessing the construct validity of the reading comprehension test. Some of the expected relationships, such as high correlations with other comprehension measures, have already been mentioned. One would also predict substantial but lower correlations with different achievement scores together with still lower correlations with the motivation variables. Most of these expectations are confirmed, the important exception being the rather low correlation with the other comprehension test, variable 26. As it stands this finding would throw serious doubt on the validity of the short Brighty test. Fortunately, the complete form does not exhibit this failing (Lunzer and Gardner, 1977). Apart from always being practicable, the great virtue of construct validation is its productivity. If weaknesses are detected, they are done so explicitly, making them relatively easy to correct or remove.

11.3   Alternative approaches to test construction

Two considerable advantages with standard methods of item analysis are the availability of computer programs and substantial experience of their use. Occasionally, social research may favour a slightly modified perspective on human assessment and then different measurement procedures could be needed. Since item analysis is only a procedure for selecting suitable items, it is possible that a combination of the standard methods might succeed in defining the optimum subset even with rather idiosyncratic researches. Alternatively, a different approach altogether could provide the natural model for many kinds of research. An infinite variety of tactics could be devised. This section deals briefly with the following possibilities:

    multiple regression models
    factor analysis
    cluster analysis
    maximizing consistency
    subdomains
    Guttman scales.

MULTIPLE REGRESSION MODELS

The application of multiple regression models to item analysis is a direct analogy of the use of multiple regression in constructing test batteries. All the items are used to predict

Table 11.4   Alternative approaches to item analysis

| | REGRESSION | | FACTOR ANALYSIS | ALPHA MAXIMIZATION |
Item	Entry order	Structure coefficient	Principal component loading	Complementary alpha
1	7	.53	.55	.6685
2	**12**	.35	.31	.6846
3	**13**	.40	.49	.6804
4	10	.53	.54	.6665
5	4	.56	.59	.6613
6	**11**	.58	.67	.6576
7	2	.58	.66	.6584
8	1	.62	.61	.6496
9	3	.48	.45	.6739
10	8	.33	**.22**	**.7035**
11	6	.33	**.23**	**.7040**
12	9	**.30**	**.21**	**.7066**
13	5	.54	.50	.6669

TOTAL ALPHA   .6935

Items in heavy type are those which fail by the criteria for that method:

Regression entry order	95% variance predicted
Regression structure	correlation over .30
Factor analysis	principal loading over .30
Alpha maximization	alpha increases on removal

the test total, or possibly some external criterion, and the best subset of predictors is accepted. An acceptance condition could be the set of items that accounts for 95 per cent of the criterion variance (squared multiple correlation) or those with suitably high structure correlations. The latter procedure is equivalent to using point-biserial correlations between items and totals. Table 11.4 summarizes certain of these alternative methods of item analysis. The regression details include both the variance statistics and structure correlations. If items are accepted until 95 per cent of the total test variance is reached, then items 2, 3, and 6 are rejected. Once more a slightly different subset of items is retained. Using structure correlations as a guide requires a cut-off point. Since the model is relating item scores to totals it is logical to consider the same levels as for point-biserial correlations. Taking the more stringent limit of .30 entails rejecting item 12, the same result as for the Rasch model. As DuBois (1965) points out the danger with multiple regression item analysis is its excessive dependence on sample features. Cross-validation becomes a necessary adjunct.

FACTOR ANALYSIS

Although factor analysis is a standard means of defining subscales, it is less often used in selecting items for a single scale or test. The technique can only legitimately be employed when a single factor contributes a substantial proportion of the overall variance, preferably 50 per cent or more. In factor analysing the 13 Brighty test items the first factor accounts for only 24 per cent of the overall variance, and therefore hardly qualifies as a determinant of item selection. However, all 13 item loadings on the first principal component are included in Table 11.4 so that they can be compared with the other approaches. Traditionally, in factor analysis loadings of over .30 are considered in the interpretation of factors. If the same levels are used to select items then items 10, 11, and 12 are rejected.

CLUSTER ANALYSIS

Here a problem arises because similarity measures do not operate in the same way as correlation coefficients. Items scored in opposite directions might be highly similar in construct, but they could not be classified together because of their extreme quantitative dissimilarity. This drawback effectively restricts the method to unidirectional items such as occur in ability tests. However, the method is valuable in analysing incidence items as might be recorded using checklists for example. Youngman (1975) provides a detailed account of an application of cluster analysis in structuring work. Shield (1974) describes cluster analysis procedures for more traditional areas of psychological evaluation.

MAXIMIZING CONSISTENCY

This method is offered as a suggestion rather than an account of common practice since only van Naerssen's (1969) utility index has any close similarity with it. Internal consistency measures, particularly alpha, are traditionally applied *after* performing one of the standard item analyses. However, if the overall aim is to maximize internal consistency, the effect of individual items can easily be assessed by comparing alpha values *omitting each item in turn* with that for the full test. If alpha *increases* on dropping an item then that item must be disturbing the internal consistency. This criterion is not only objective, obviating the need for conventions, it is also suitably conservative since normally one would expect alpha to drop when the number of items falls. Table 11.4 records the *complementary alphas* for each item. Three items, 10, 11, and 12, show an increase in alpha, the same three items as the factor analysis would have rejected. Further support for their exclusion comes from the regression structure analysis and the Rasch analysis where these are the three worst items.

Table 11.5 provides validation evidence for the two new subsets of items accepted by the alternative methods. The regression variance method results in a rather low alpha of .63, and none of the correlations with the validation measures is better than for the total test without item analysis. Excluding items 10, 11, and 12, as supported by the alpha maximization and factor analysis methods, produces a marked improvement in alpha at .73. Validities obtained from the secondary achievement scores are slightly inferior to the Rasch results (see Table 11.3) but on the whole they tend to be better for the construct validation variables. This does suggest that the alpha maximization approach is worth exploring further.

SUBDOMAINS

In outlining the steps in item analysis it was stated that the construction of subscales only represented an extra stage in the basic procedure. This is largely true, apart from the

Table 11.5 Validation evidence for the alternative item analyses

Comparison measures	ALL ITEMS	ALTERNATIVE ANALYSES	
		Regression variance	Alpha maximization
25 S: Brighty total score	.77	.75	.77
26 S: Grieg total score	.55	.52	.54
23 S: Reading comprehension	.73	.70	.73
24 S: Mathematics	.60	.58	.61
20 J: Non-verbal reasoning	.35	.36	**.38**
21 J: Reading comprehension	.60	.58	.61
22 J: Mathematics	.49	.48	**.52**
18 S: Self-concept academic	.40	.38	.37
19 S: Academic motivation	.38	.37	.34
27 S: Adjustment to school	.22	.17	**.27**
ALPHA	.6935	.6293	.7319
NUMBER OF ITEMS	13	10	10

For the alternative analyses the same comparisons are made as in Table 11.3. The alphas highlight the differences between the regression and alpha methods and the correlations confirm the superiority of alpha maximization. The validities are similar to those for the Rasch method.

special problems associated with questionnaire analysis and attitude measurement (see Chapter 10). In terms of scales and tests the only additional comment necessary concerns instruments which may *appear* to be unidimensional, but which really contain sub-domains within. The best example is the widely used form of intelligence test made up of a series of subskill tests. Often up to 10 separate subskills may be involved, each being assessed by half a dozen or more items. Instances like this contradict the normal assumption of unidimensionality, particularly in the computation of alpha. Cronbach *et al.* (1965) examine this problem at length and recommend the use of special forms of internal consistency measures for scales with subdomains of items.

GUTTMAN SCALES

One method of constructing scales that has diminished somewhat in popularity is Guttman's (1950) procedure. Its early appeal centred on its very high or even perfect reproducibility, the property whereby it is possible to construct an individual's complete score pattern from his total score alone. Various reasons could be offered to explain this change but the most probable is the discrepancy between theory and practice. Guttman scales are not easy to construct, and when they can be formed, other requirements such as validity and discrimination can be lacking. Recent versions of BMD have dropped the Guttman routines through lack of use, although SPSS continues to offer the facility.

11.4   Sources of tests and scales

The whole of this chapter has assumed that no suitable instrument exists for measuring the attribute under consideration. Too often this assumption is accepted without a thorough search for such an instrument. More and more diligent researchers are collating collections of tests and scales for use in social research and reference to these texts will frequently unearth an ideal instrument. The classic reference work of this kind is Buros (1965) which contains detailed reviews of commercially published tests. Johnson (1976) has repeated the exercise for unpublished instruments in the field of child development while Miller (1970) includes a number of social research scales in his handbook. In education the text by Cohen (1976) offers a wide range of measures. To date, the present author's experience with certain of these tests suggests that preliminary checks on reliability and validity may sometimes be necessary. Even so, the wealth of material available from all these sources makes the researcher's task considerably easier. Opportunities of this kind should not be spurned.

				V	
			O	E	C
			S	L	O
PROGRAM AVAILABILITY	P	S	B	I	D	O
see Section 3.6	M	P	M	R	M	L
	M	S	D	I	A	E
	D	S	P	S	N	Y

Item analysis						
extreme groups analysis						
total group analysis	P	S			V	
Rasch method						
internal consistency	P	S			V	
split-half reliability	P	S	B	O	V	C
construct validation	P	S	B	O	V	C
multiple regression item analysis	P	S	B	O	V	C
factor item analysis	P	S	B	O	V	C
alpha maximization	P	S			V	
cluster analysis for items	P			O	V	
subdomains	P	S			V	
Guttman scaling		S		O		

References

Buros, O. K. (ed.) (1965) *Mental Measurements Yearbook,* Sixth edition, New York, Gryphon.

Cohen, L. (1976) *Educational Research in Classrooms and Schools,* London, Harper and Row.

Cronbach, L. J. (1951) 'Coefficient alpha and the internal structure of tests', *Psychometrika,* **16**, 297–334.

Cronbach, L. J. (1970) *Essentials of Psychological Testing,* Third edition, New York, Harper and Row.

Cronbach, L. J., P. Schonemann, and D. McKie (1965) 'Alpha coefficients for stratified-parallel tests', *Educ. and Psychol. Meas.,* **25**, 291–312.

Cureton, E. E. (1965) 'Reliability and validity: basic assumptions and experimental designs', *Educ. and Psychol. Meas.,* **25**, 327–346.

D'Agostino, R. B. and E. E. Cureton (1975) 'The 27 per cent rule revisited', *Educ. and Psychol. Meas.,* **35**, 47–50.

DuBois, P. H. (1965) *An Introduction to Psychological Statistics,* New York, Harper and Row.

Ferguson, G. A (1976) *Statistical Analysis in Psychology and Education,* Fourth edition, New York, McGraw-Hill.

Guttman, L. (1950) in Stouffer, S. A. *et al., Measurement and Prediction,* Chapters 3–6, Princeton, Princeton University Press.

Johnson, O. G. (1976) *Tests and Measurements in Child Development: Handbook II.* (2 volumes), New York, Jossey-Bass.

Kelley, T. L. (1939) 'The selection of upper and lower groups for the validation of test items', *Journal of Educational Psychology,* **30**, 17–24.

Kuder, G. F. and M. W. Richardson (1937) 'The theory of the estimation of test reliability', *Psychometrika,* **2**, 151–160.

Lewis, D. G. (1976) *Assessment in Education,* London, Hodder and Stoughton.

Lunzer, E. A. and W. K. Gardner (1977) *The Effective Use of Reading,* Schools Council Project Report.

Miller, D. C. (1970) *Handbook of Research Design and Social Measurement,* Second edition, New York, McKay.

van Naerssen, R. F. (1969) 'A signal/noise ratio index used for item selection in teacher made tests', *in* Ingenkamp, P. K. (ed.) *Developments in Educational Testing.* Volume 1, London, University of London Press.

Nunnaly, J. C. (1967) *Psychometric Theory,* New York, McGraw-Hill.

Rasch, G. (1966a) 'An individualistic approach to item analysis', *in*: Lazarsfield, P. F. and N. W. Henry *Readings in Mathematical Social Science,* Chicago, Science Research Associated Inc., pp. 89–107.

Rasch, G. (1966b) 'An item analysis which takes individual differences into account', *Brit. Journal Math. Stat. Psychol.,* **19**, 49–57.

Shield, W. S. (1974) 'A clustering model for item analysis of a psychological instrument with missing data', *Educ. and Psychol. Meas.,* **34**, 849–856.

Stanley, J. C. and K. D. Hopkins (1972) *Educational and Psychological Measurement and Evaluation,* Englewood Cliff, Prentice Hall.

Tinsley, H. E. A. and R. V. Dawis (1975) 'An investigation of the Rasch simple logistic model: Sample-free item and test calibration', *Educ. and Psychol. Meas.,* **35**, 325–339.

Willmott, A. S. and D. E. Fowles (1974) *The Objective Interpretation of Test Performance,* Slough, National Foundation for Educational Research.

Wright, B. D. (1967) 'Sample-free test calibration and person measurement', *Proceedings of Invitational Conference on Testing Problems,* Princeton, New Jersey; Educational Testing Service.

Youngman, M. B. (1975) 'Structuring work for training purposes', *Vocational Aspect of Education,* **27**, 77–86.

12. The Measurement of Change

So many researches are concerned with investigating how things change over time that one might expect the associated statistical methodology to have become both standard and automatic. Unfortunately neither hope can be satisfied. Statisticians still show disagreement over how change should be measured, if at all (for example, Harris, 1963; Cronbach and Furby, 1970). And even if any one viewpoint is accepted, particular research problems may require quite different applications of these techniques to satisfy the aims of the investigation. Anyone relying heavily on the assessment of change within a research study must look beyond the following summary for the various qualifications and ramifications that might hold. Apart from introductory statements in some of the statistical textbooks (McNemar, 1969; Ferguson, 1976, both level B) a good background account is given by Bohrnstedt (1969, level B). A detailed discussion of both the statistical and research implications is supplied by Cronbach and Furby (1970, level C). Harris (1963, levels A, B, C) edits a range of papers covering many aspects of measuring change and as such provides an important source for further study. Probably the most up-to-date accounts of the state of change measurement appear in de Gruijter and van der Kamp's (1976, levels B, C) edited series of conference papers.

12.1 The nature of change

Change has various manifestations in social research—progress, growth, alienation for example—and appropriate statistical treatments may differ accordingly. It is therefore important to be clear about the way change is being measured. One generally assumes, for instance, that to assess change the same feature must be measured on different occasions. This is not necessarily so since with suitable sampling techniques it may be possible to record different individuals or events, and even different behaviours. Even the time gap may not be needed given satisfactory controls. Indeed, these variations may be unavoidable. If one wants to examine children's reading standards over a period of 30 years, clearly the same children cannot be used throughout. Different but *equivalent* samples are needed. The attributes being assessed can also vary. In the transfer research academic motivation was tested before and after transfer using the same scale. But it does not follow that the same attitudinal characteristic was being measured. By virtue of their different knowledge and expectations older children will tend to modify their interpretation of the scale questions. Consequently, a twelve-year-old child scoring 15 need not correspond to an eleven-year-old with that score. Bereiter (1963) discusses the interpretation of change scores and any analyst must be aware of the need to decide beforehand exactly what the implications of change analyses are.

Frequently, the analysis of change is simply another way of identifying a standard method. In the simplest instance a before-and-after measurement is made and the research question is 'Are the two overall score levels different?' If the two measurements are made on different samples then this is a simple difference-between-means analysis and any of the standard techniques will do (t-test, chi-square etc.). Where the same sample is retested, the situation becomes that of correlated or dependent groups and a modified test is needed. For the t-test it is the correlated samples form; with chi-square approaches the McNemar test (Siegel, 1956) takes the dependence into account.

Rather more complicated situations arise when more than two groups are involved. For example, the simple before-and-after design can be extended to incorporate extra effects. The research may need to elaborate the original question to discriminate between these additional effects. Most will recognize this as the traditional analysis of variance design, but there could be complications. It may be important to eliminate the influence of some extraneous attribute, such as ability level, in which case an analysis of covariance is needed. The essential point here is that this kind of elaboration *to meet the intention of the research* forces the researcher to be particularly careful over the analysis specification. What at first sight might seem an innocuous design can, when change is involved, require a more complex analysis than was originally intended. The following sections discuss some of these considerations and suggest possible tactics.

12.2 Difference and residualized change scores

The natural definition of change is the difference between the initial and final scores. Regrettably this is an unsatisfactory measure, largely because it is invalid. This deficiency is easily seen at the practical level. Anyone with a low initial score has ample opportunity to improve; a high scorer will be unlikely to better his initial score by more than a small amount. So low scorers tend to have high gain scores while high scorers record low ones. In statistical terms this defines a negative correlation between initial and difference scores. Indeed Table 12.1, which lists the correlations between various change measures and other transfer variables, does show this pattern of negative correlations. Because of this intrinsic negative relationship with initial level, it follows that simple difference scores do not provide a measure of change that is equally applicable for all initial levels.

The reliability of difference scores is also suspect. It is given by:

$$r_{gg'} = \frac{s_y^2 r_{yy'} + s_x^2 r_{xx'} - 2s_y s_x r_{xy}}{s_y^2 + s_x^2 - 2s_y s_x r_{xy}} \tag{12.1}$$

where X and Y are the initial and final measures.

s_x, s_y are the respective standard deviations.

S_{xx}', S_{yy}' are the respective reliabilities.

s_{xy} is the correlation between the two measures.

Clearly this is highly dependent upon variances, themselves relatively unstable. It is easier to see how the reliability of difference scores is determined if the variances of the two measures, and therefore s_x and s_y, are assumed to be equal. In that case Eq. (12.1) becomes:

$$r_{gg'} = \frac{r_{yy'} + r_{xx'} - 2r_{xy}}{2(1 - r_{xy})} \tag{12.2}$$

190

Table 12.1 Correlations between change measures and certain transfer variables

Transfer variables	Differences				Specific residuals					Extended residuals				
	DSCA	DMOT	DMAT	RASS	RSCA	RMOT	RRED	RMAT	EASS	ESCA	EMOT	ERED	EMAT
6 JASS	−12	04	04	[01]	−01	06	02	04	[01]	02	07	04	07
7 JAPS	**−17**	**−21**	10	**17**	04	−03	08	12	**16**	01	−02	06	12
8 JAPH	**20**	−12	−05	09	−01	−12	−06	−07	−08	−01	−12	−04	−08
9 JSCS	**−20**	−02	02	11	03	01	06	03	11	03	01	04	03
10 JSCP	**−29**	**−15**	**17**	13	−02	−03	09	**20**	11	−05	−03	08	**18**
11 JSCA	[**−65**]	−10	08	**23**	[**00**]	09	03	11	**22**	[**00**]	09	01	08
12 JMOT	−17	[**−43**]	08	**28**	14	[**00**]	10	12	**27**	10	[**00**]	08	10
13 SASS	14	**27**	00	**99**	**40**	**44**	07	02	**99**	**41**	**44**	07	03
14 SAPS	**−19**	**−15**	03	**−40**	**−24**	**−19**	01	02	**−40**	**−23**	**−19**	02	02
15 SANX	−13	**−18**	−03	**−22**	**−31**	**−21**	−03	−05	**−22**	**−31**	**−21**	−02	−06
16 SSCS	00	10	−01	13	**15**	09	−11	−01	14	**17**	09	−09	00
17 SSCP	04	01	12	13	**20**	07	−03	**14**	12	**18**	06	−06	12
18 SSCA	**40**	**24**	00	**46**	**90**	**41**	−04	04	**44**	**88**	**40**	−08	00
19 SMOT	12	**53**	09	**52**	**42**	**85**	13	12	**51**	**41**	**84**	13	12
20 JNVR	01	−07	11	07	23	04	**16**	**20**	[01	00	01	00	00]
21 JRED	−06	−02	**16**	10	14	13	[−02]	**24**	07	04	11	[−02]	**23**
22 JMAT	01	−04	[**−12**]	12	**12**	10	**22**	[00]	08	07	07	13	[−01]
23 SRED	−09	02	**31**	12	05	**16**	**72**	**39**	09	−05	**15**	**71**	**39**
24 SMAT	−05	−02	**61**	10	**16**	11	**37**	**70**	06	02	10	**30**	**66**
25 SADJ	−02	12	05	**32**	**22**	**32**	04	08	**31**	**20**	**32**	03	07

Significant correlations ($p < 0.01$) are in heavy type.
Initial variables corresponding to each residual are boxed.

It is not easy to improve $r_{gg'}$, because increasing the test reliabilities $r_{xx'}$ and $r_{yy'}$ also increases r_{xy} the correlation between them. Rather contradictorily, the most efficient way to improve $r_{gg'}$ is to *reduce* r_{xy} but to maintain reliability levels. This effectively means test a different construct!

All in all the use of gain scores defined as simple differences has little merit. Instead a *residualized change score* is generally recommended, although as Cronbach and Furby (1970) emphasize, appropriate interpretation is crucial. Residual scores are not correlated with initial scores (they are with final scores) and they show greater reliability (Bohrnstedt, 1969). Lord (1963) suggests that residuals are particularly useful in examining relationships between change and other variables, a fairly typical research situation. A residual score is the difference between an *expected* final score (predicted from the correlation between the two scores) and the *actual* final score. A positive residual implies that the individual does better than expected. In terms of the two measures X and Y, the residual (R_y) is:

$$R_y = (Y - m_y) - r_{xy} \frac{s_y}{s_x} (X - m_x) \tag{12.3}$$

where X and Y are the individual's scores on the initial and final measures.
s_x and s_y are the standard deviations for these two measures.
m_x and m_y are their means.
r_{xy} is the correlation between them.

191

Since R_y takes only one predictor into account, it can be called a *specific residual*. It is in the scale of the Y measure alone and therefore does not require the X and Y measures to be the same. For reasonably accurate prediction all that is needed is a moderately high correlation. This means that it may be possible to compute a specific residual even if a directly equivalent initial measure is not available; any suitably highly correlated predictor could suffice.

In Table 12.1 the middle block of columns gives the correlations between five specific residual measures (indicated by the prefix R) and a selection of the transfer variables, including the initial and final variables which define these residuals. The left hand correlations are for three difference measures (indicated by D). Since the same measures are needed for difference socres, it is not possible to compute them for attitude to secondary school or for reading where different tests were used at primary and secondary level. For the residuals their correlations with initial scores (RASS with JASS, junior attitude to secondary school, for example) are effectively zero. The slight variations arise from dropping 11, cases absent, on variable 25, secondary adjustment to school. Difference scores show the negative correlation pattern already mentioned. For self-concept academic, DSCA, its correlation with the junior measure, variable 11, is -0.65. The other two show smaller but still negative correlations.

Specific residuals only remove the influence of the initial measure and therefore one would expect them to display positive correlations with final scores. Where the correlation between initial and final score is low (for attitude to secondary school, variables 6 and 13, it is .11) the residual-final correlation is high. In the case of attitude to secondary school, RASS, the figure is .99. As the before-after correlation rises so the residual-after correlation drops:

Measure	Correlations between initial and final score	Correlations between residual and final score
attitude to secondary	.11	.99
academic motivation	.54	.85
mathematics	.72	.70

These last two figures should ring a bell for anyone familiar with the variance explanation of correlation. Since .71 is the magical correlation accounting for 50 per cent of the joint variation (that is .71 squared) then the initial and residual variances for mathematics together add up to 100 per cent. In other words *the residual variance is that portion of the final variance not accounted for by the initial measure*. So in each of the above examples squaring and adding the two correlations should result in 100 per cent.

Returning to Table 12.1, the earlier suggestion that residuals made relationships with other measures more easily examinable can be tested. The specific residuals show a consistent pattern for academic self-concept *vis-à-vis* junior and secondary variables. Effectively, this pattern of significance indicates that junior ability is the main determinant of improvement in academic self-concept at secondary level; junior attitude has little effect. To examine this change using difference scores produces rather implausible conclusions. Ability appears to have no effect while the negative correlations with junior attitude measures imply that children with poor junior attitude improve and those with positive attitudes deteriorate. This is clearly an artefact of the negative correlation between difference scores and initial level. Results for mathematics are more consistent between the two methods.

Although Eq.(12.3) does enable residual scores to be calculated, in practice the simplest and most reliable approach is to use a linear or multiple regression program to compute the new scores. Using multiple regression each residual is obtained by specifying a model with the final score the criterion and the initial score the single predictor. If the program outputs predicted scores rather than residual differences then the final subtraction will have to be performed separately.

12.3 Covariates in determining change

Having already suggested that the predictor for specific residuals need not be the same measure as that used for the final assessment, it seems sensible to question also whether it is only possible to use one predictor measure. The answer is 'No'. If it is thought a more appropriate specification of change can be constructed by taking into account other predictors, then these can be included. Cronbach and Furby (1970, page 75) even go so far as to allow additional *post-test* data to be used if it provides a better estimate of the criterion measure. To differentiate between specific residuals and the extended models, residuals involving more than one predictor will be referred to as *extended residuals*.

Far from being a trivial adjunct to a research design, there may be instances where the use of additional predictor control is necessary to ensure valid interpretation of the results. In the analysis of changes for groups, the use of a single predictor to take into account pre-existing differences among those groups only corrects for variations in that predictor. Since this predictor will usually be the initial score whose change is to be examined, it follows that any other initial group differences continue to operate. It is quite possible that they could be determining the group changes rather than those features of the groups which are *assumed* to relate to any differences arising. If the objective of the research is to examine the effects of these extraneous influences, then it is appropriate to leave them out of the residual predictor set. They are examined via their correlations with the change scores, as in Table 12.1. *However, if any of these extraneous measures are known or suspected to influence the change measure, but at the same time are felt to be incidental to the main determinant understudy, then they should be controlled for by including them in an extended residual predictor set.* A controversial demonstration of this need can be seen in a study by Bennett (1976) in which he examined the relationship between teaching styles and pupil progress. A great deal has been reported about this research (see Wragg, 1976 and Gray and Satterly, 1976, for example) but unfortunately the probing has not clarified certain major issues. The pertinent feature for the present discussion is that, as commonly happens, the three groups whose progress Bennett wanted to examine started off at different levels of achievement. He naturally applied the specific residual correction method to eliminate this difference. He then interpreted the obtained specific residual differences in progress as being *related* to teaching style, but not necessarily *caused* by it. The problem here is that although it is perfectly true that this relationship might exist, it is equally possible that the observed residual changes might be related to other factors not controlled for. These might include ability, motivation, school as well as various teacher characteristics. If the changes are to be interpreted *purely* in terms of teaching characteristics (teaching style) then it is essential that other known determinants of progress should be eliminated. Although initial achievement is clearly the most important, intellectual ability also has an effect, regardless of achievement level, and therefore it should be included in an extended residual predictor set. The effects of other extraneous differences such as motivation and school are less clear. The effects of teacher characteristics fall into the category of pertinent influences and consequently they must *not* be removed, contrary to the assertion of Gray and Satterly.

To summarize, the method of extended residuals enables the features of main concern to be investigated by eliminating all extraneous influences not associated with this main feature. Even with careful preparation it is accepted that the interpretation of

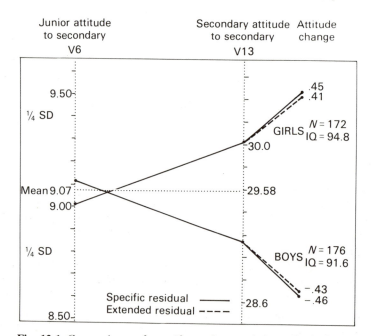

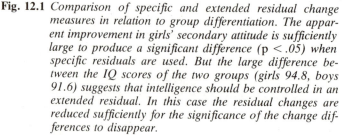

Fig. 12.1 *Comparison of specific and extended residual change measures in relation to group differentiation. The apparent improvement in girls' secondary attitude is sufficiently large to produce a significant difference (p < .05) when specific residuals are used. But the large difference between the IQ scores of the two groups (girls 94.8, boys 91.6) suggests that intelligence should be controlled in an extended residual. In this case the residual changes are reduced sufficiently for the significance of the change differences to disappear.*

194

change scores is dangerous (Lord, 1967); at least one should try to facilitate interpretation as far as is statistically possible.

The transfer research raised a comparable problem to Bennett's in that progress was to be related to a variety of background characteristics of the children. It seemed important therefore to control for differing intelligence by including non-verbal reasoning as well as initial scores to produce change measures. Table 12.1 records the correlations for these extended residuals in the final block. As it happens the results are almost identical with those for the specific residuals, but at least it is now possible to interpret these findings without the complication of uncontrolled ability effects.

How far does this similarity extend to other analyses, particularly group comparisons? Figure 12.1 examines the attitude changes of boys and girls. The fact that the plots cross over indicates that the change is more than simple regression for the mean; the girls apparently improve. Specific residuals reiterate this since the girls change by .45 while the boys deteriorate by a similar amount. The overall change difference of .91 is quite large compared with the secondary attitude standard deviation of 4.36. One-way analysis of variance confirms that the difference is significant ($p < .05$). But secondary attitude to secondary school shows a slight positive correlation with non-verbal reasoning ($r = .05$). With the girls scoring on average three points higher on IQ than the boys, it could be that the ability discrepancy is producing the apparent improvement. When non-verbal reasoning is included in an extended residual, the changes are reduced sufficiently for the significance of the difference to disappear. The marginal nature of this example, and especially the very low correlation involved, makes any practical interpretation tentative. Generally, the effect of using extended residuals will be small, but the main value lies in the assistance given to interpretation rather than in altering patterns of significance.

12.4 The interpretation of change measures

Recalling the earlier comment regarding the need to preserve pertinent features while removing extraneous ones, the researcher alone must decide what measures fall into each category. The problem is not a simple one. Lord (1967) discusses an apparently contradictory situation (Fig. 12.2) where two groups differ initially, but their respective mean scores show no change over time. The natural interpretation here is that no change differences have occurred. But if residuals are computed, the higher group actually records positive change and the other negative. What has happened is that the expected regression to the mean overall has not taken place. An alternative interpretation can be formulated by considering *only those cases with comparable initial scores* (that is, the shaded area of overlap). Of these the higher group members do tend to record higher final scores. So residuals enable the progress of individuals with equivalent starting scores to be compared. But one might ask whether it is legitimate to compare members of different types having the same initial scores. For these individuals to even record similar scores they must somehow be exceptional relative to their own type (social class, sex, treatment group, for example). On an optimistic note Cronbach and Furby (1970) point out that 'learning or growth is multidimensional; many measures could be taken at each point in time' (page 77). They add that to be unduly restrictive in the choice of

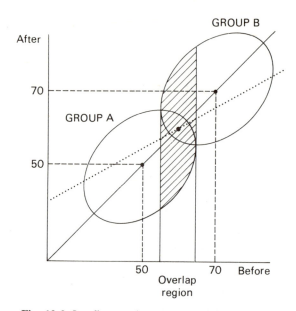

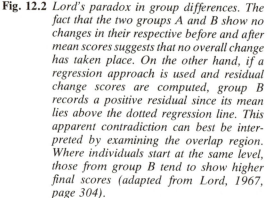

Fig. 12.2 *Lord's paradox in group differences. The fact that the two groups A and B show no changes in their respective before and after mean scores suggests that no overall change has taken place. On the other hand, if a regression approach is used and residual change scores are computed, group B records a positive residual since its mean lies above the dotted regression line. This apparent contradiction can best be interpreted by examining the overlap region. Where individuals start at the same level, those from group B tend to show higher final scores (adapted from Lord, 1967, page 304).*

predictors can only 'sacrifice information and insight'. Empirical social research has never been the domain of the faint-hearted and if there is one ideal to be sought in social research it must be insight.

PROGRAM AVAILABILITY
see Section 3.6

P	S	B	I	D	O
M	P	M	R	M	L
M	S	D	I	A	E
D	S	P	S	N	Y

V
O E C
S L O
D O
M L
A E
N Y

The measurement of change						
difference scores	P	S	B	O		
specific residuals	P	S	B	O	V	
extended residuals	P	S	B	O	V	
correlation validation	P	S	B	O	V	C
change differentiation	P	S	B	O	V	

References

Bennett, S. N. (1976) *Teaching Styles and Pupil Progress*, London, Open Books.

Bereiter, C. (1963) 'Some persisting dilemmas in the measurement of change', in: Harris C. W. (1963)

Bohrnstedt, G. W. (1969) 'Observations on the measurement of change', in: Borgatta, E. F. (ed.) (1969) *Sociological Methodology 1969*, San Francisco, Jossey-Bass.

Cronbach, L. J., and L. Furby (1970) 'How should we measure "change" — or should we?' *Psychological Bulletin*, **74**, 68–80.

Ferguson, G. A. (1976) *Statistical Analysis in Psychology and Education,* Fourth edition, New York, McGraw-Hill.

Gray, J. and D. Satterly (1976) 'A chapter of errors: Teaching styles and pupil progress in retrospect', *Educational Research*, **19**, 45–56.

Gruijter, D. N. M. De and L. J. Th. van der Kamp (eds.) (1976) *Advances in Psychological and Educational Measurement*, New York, John Wiley.

Harris, C. W. (ed.) (1963) *Problems in Measuring Change*, Madison, Milwaukee; University of Wisconsin Press.

Lord, F. M. (1963) 'Elementary models for measuring change', in: Harris, C. W. (ed.) (1963)

Lord, F. M. (1967) 'A paradox in the interpretation of group comparisons', *Psychological Bulletin*, **68**, 304–305.

McNemar, Q. (1969) *Psychological Statistics,* Fourth edition, New York, John Wiley.

Siegel, S. (1956) *Nonparametric Statistics for the Behavioral Sciences*, New York, McGraw-Hill.

Wragg, E. C. (1976) 'The Lancaster study: its implications for teacher training', *Brit. J. Teacher Educ.*, **2**, 281–290.

Appendices

Appendix 1. PMMD: Programmed Methods for Multivariate Data

A1.1 Outline

PMMD has been designed to serve the analysis needs of both research workers and students in the social sciences. Its ease of handling makes it particularly useful for single analyses. The original package (Youngman, 1976) comprises 15 programs which run independently although linking facilities do exist. A further five data manipulation programs (Youngman, 1977) have been added to extend the facilities offered. The modular structure makes it possible for the programs to be made available on relatively small computer installations. Table A1.1 summarizes the range of facilities included. Where the same statistics are offered by different programs (means and standard deviations, for example) the choice of program would depend on the nature of the data and any other analyses required. Each program is documented separately to simplify running procedures and to limit costs. Output is comprehensive, one particularly valuable feature being the insertion of conventional significance markers where appropriate.

A1.2 Documentation

Details on individual programs are contained in a single document, normally of around 10 pages, which does not refer to any operating system instructions. The latter are described separately in guides produced by the local computing services. A number of background documents covering topics such as FORTRAN format statements, error tracking and data analysis procedures are also associated with the package.

The main documents are the program descriptions. These give outlines of the methods with further references where necessary. Program facilities and running instructions are described in detail and any limitations indicated. A test dataset and analysis is shown to demonstrate the construction of specifications and the output produced. Where the methods require more detailed explanation (between-groups testing and cluster analysis are good examples) additional information, including guides to interpretation, is also supplied.

A1.3 Structure

All programs require a parameter card giving basic information such as the number of variables and cases together with certain analysis details and a title. Since data are coded

Table A1.1 Summary of the facilities available on PMMD programs

FACILITIES	BACH 1	DRAX 2	IATS 3	PLOT 4	AVAR 5	BSET 6	CATT 7	CATM 8	CARM 9	DSFN 10	FTAN 11	SMLR 12	KEN5 13	MWUT 14	RTAU 15	CHEK 16	REDY 17	ELAB 18	ALTA 19	MERG 20
DATA HANDLING																				
large samples (1000+)	*	*	*	*	*	*	*	*	*	*	*	*				*	*	*	*	*
missing data	*	*	*	*	*			*			*				*	*	*	*	*	*
unequal-sized groups					*	*	*	*		*		*		*		*	*	*	*	*
binary data	*	*	*		*	*	*	*	*		*	*				*	*	*	*	*
nominal (categoric) data	*	*	*	*												*	*	*	*	*
group extraction						*				*										
reordering						*														
data addition		*				*				*							*	*		*
correlation matrix input											*	*								
RECODING																				
standardization									*								*			
supplied recodes		*																	*	
partitioning variables		*																	*	
binary attribute scoring	*																		*	
factor scores											*						*			
discriminant scores										*							*			
residual scores												*								
scale scoring			*														*			
ranking														*						
BASIC STATISTICS																				
maxima/minima		*		*	*															
frequency distributions		*	*																	
frequency charts		*																		
scatter plots				*						*										
means		*	*		*	*	*	*	*	*	*	*		*						
standard deviations		*	*			*	*	*			*	*								
percentages		*	*																	
two-way tables		*																		
three-way tables		*																		
product-moment correlations						*	*	*			*	*								
Kendall's tau correlation															*					
contingency coefficient		*																		
MULTIVARIATE STATISTICS																				
analysis of covariance												*								
cluster analysis									*											
coefficient of concordance													*							
discriminant function										*										
principal components											*									
oblique rotation											*									
varimax rotation											*									
multiple regression												*								

Table A1.1 (continued)

FACILITIES	BACH 1	DRAX 2	IATS 3	PLOT 4	AVAR 5	BSET 6	CATT 7	CATM 8	CARM 9	DSFN 10	FTAN 11	SMLR 12	KEN5 13	MWUT 14	RTAU 15	CHEK 16	REDY 17	ELAB 18	ALTA 19	MERG 20
STATISTICAL TESTING																				
chi-square analysis		*				*														
Fisher's exact probability		*				*														
one-way analysis of variance					*	*	*	*	*											
two-way analysis of variance					*															
three-way analysis of variance					*															
t-test uncorrelated groups						*	*	*												
Tukey multiple comparisons test					*	*	*	*												
Scheffé multiple comparisons test						*	*	*												
Scheffé group atypicality test						*	*	*												
Bartlett homogeneity of variance						*	*	*												
linear trend test						*	*	*												
non-linear trend test						*	*	*												
Mann-Whitney U-test														*						
correlation significance						*	*	*												
SPECIAL FACILITIES																				
significance level marking					*	*	*	*							*					
probability values		*			*	*	*	*		*		*								
variable labelling											*									
cross-validation												*								
item analysis			*																	

according to the user's specification, an appropriate FORTRAN data format statement must be supplied. All case data *must* start with an integer identification number. Further specification cards may be needed for programs which allow a variety of analyses of the same data. Most of the programs can be recycled to analyse further datasets.

A1.4 Program facilities

The facilities available are summarized in Table A1.1. Details of individual programs are as follows:

BACH: Binary attribute characterization
Original numeric or categoric data can be recoded as binary attributes (scored 1/0 or in list form) suitable for multivariate analysis. The facility is particularly useful to enable questionnaire data to be cluster analysed (program CARM) or subjected to multiple regression analysis (program SMLR) using dummy variable coding.

DRAX: Data recoding and cross-tabulation

Although primarily a frequency and cross-tabulation program, DRAX also allows the user to recode data either by splitting selected variables into a specified number of partitions, or by supplying new codes. Tabulation takes two forms. Firstly, frequency charts of all measures may be obtained, giving frequencies, percentages and a horizontal plot. Secondly, any number of two- or three-way cross-tabulations may be requested and the resulting tables can be tested by chi-square. Cell contents are frequencies plus one of four forms of percentage if required. Zero-coded rows and columns can be excluded enabling missing data to be handled. Fisher's exact probability is calculated for small 2 × 2 tables.

IATS: Item analysis and test scoring

Successive datasets can be item analysed on scales of up to 500 items. As well as providing basic distribution statistics for each item, one or more scales can be defined and the same measures obtained for them. Scale reliability is assessed by Cronbach's alpha and the point-biserial correlation between each item and its scale is also given. Every case is scored on all scales and these scales may be output if required. Missing data can be substituted by a specified code.

PLOT: A4 size scatter plots with labels

Any number of two-way scatter plots may be obtained for successive datasets. A third variable can be allocated to label the points A, B, etc. Alternatively, a simple scatter plot using asterisks may be obtained. Although both axis intervals are normally fiftieth sub-divisions of the scale range, if preferred whole number intervals can be specified. It is also possible to supply limits for both axes rather than accept the existing maxima and minima.

AVAR: One, two, or three-way analysis of variance

The program carries out an analysis of variance for data classified by one, two or three ways without the requirement of equal numbers per cell. Up to 12 levels may be used for each way and a maximum of 70 dependent variables may be analysed. Missing data are acceptable so long as a consistent missing data code has been inserted. Differences between cell means are tested by Tukey's confounded or unconfounded method as appropriate.

BSET: Subset extraction with significance testing

The examination of various subgroups within a single dataset is a common but awkward analysis requirement in social research. BSET enables a user to define a series of subsets and the analyses required. Various statistics including product-moment correlations are computed for the population and each subset in turn. Differences between subsets can be tested by Scheffé's test, student's t, Tukey's q or chi-square, following a one-way analysis of variance. Bartlett's homogeneity of variance test is applied as are linear and non-linear trend tests. The atypicality of each subset is tested by means of Scheffé's test comparing it with the mean of the remaining groups.

204

CATT: Correlational analysis and between-groups testing
Means, standard deviations and product-moment correlations are computed for up to 100 measures. Successive datasets may be input and, if required, up to 20 of these may be tested for significant differences between their means. Between-groups testing, including analysis of variance and trend analysis, follows the same pattern as for BSET.

CATM: Correlational analysis and testing for missing data
This replicates the previous program, CATT, except that missing data are permissible. This reduces the size (60 variables) and speed of the program and therefore complete datasets should always be analysed using CATT. The missing data code must be the same for *all* measures and must not occur naturally within the data. Usually 0 or -1 is acceptable.

CARM: Cluster analysis by relocation methods
Cluster analysis consists of a large number of classification techniques rather than a single analytical method. Program CARM encompasses certain related clustering methods which attempt to improve or modify an existing classification. In practice, the initial grouping is usually random and any modification requested will most often require the analysis to gradually reduce the number of groups in order to achieve a more parsimonious solution to the classification problem. This procedure is quite different from the hierarchical grouping methods (cf. Veldman, 1967, page 308) since individual cases are repeatedly compared with existing clusters only, *not* with every other case. Computationally the process is much faster, and as a result it is possible to analyse larger samples. This particular version will handle up to 2000 cases assessed on a maximum of 200 numeric measures or 600 binary attributes. Thirteen different inter-cluster similarity measures are available, and it is also possible to reanalyse the same dataset more than once by redefining the analysis parameters, or by selecting a different subset of the input variables. The basic program is essentially the RELOC program of Wishart's CLUSTAN 1A package (Wishart, 1969) with modifications to enable the analysis to be done in a single computer run. There are also supplements to the original printout to facilitate the choice of suitable classifications for more detailed analysis (e.g., on programs BSET or DSFN).

DSFN: Discriminant function analysis
It is frequently useful in behavioural research to know in what manner certain groups are differentiated from one another. This program (Veldman, 1967) allows an ordered set of groups, or a series of user-defined groups (cf. BSET) to be analysed on the basis of multivariate functions which maximally discriminate between the groups, the functions being similar to the factors obtained from a factor analysis. Each function is defined in terms of the specified variables and is tested for significance. Individual cases are scored on the functions, and finally scatter plots are produced showing the location of every case on all pairings of the significant functions. The program incorporates a number of facilities not included in the original Veldman version; particularly useful are the ability

to extract groups from a full sample, the opportunity to use a selection of variables to define the functions, the plotting output, and arrangements for repeated analysis of the same or extra datasets.

FTAN: Factor analysis with varimax or oblique rotations

Program FTAN allows orthogonal or oblique methods of factor analysis to be performed using raw data as input, or a correlation matrix. Missing values can be replaced by the variable mean if required. The basis of any analysis is a principal components extraction which may be followed by an orthogonal rotation (Kaiser's Varimax) or by an oblique one (Harris's orthoblique as refined into Little Jiffy Mark IV by Kaiser), or both these methods. Various statistics are output to assess the validity of the analysis. The maximum number of variables allowed is approximately 70, the exact figure depending on whether both types of rotation are requested. A number of variable transformations is incorporated and variable labels may be supplied. Factor scores are computed if specifically requested.

SMLR: Iterative multiple linear regression

A standard correlational analysis (means, standard deviations, and product-moment correlations) is followed by up to 50 multiple linear regression analyses, each model being defined by a single criterion and groups of predictor variables. Output includes the multiple correlation and its significance, the shrunken multiple R and the iteration sequence. Both raw and normalized forms of the regression equation are given together with the structure correlations for each predictor. A covariance analysis can be performed by testing the significance of the difference in R^2 between models. Residual scores can be obtained. A split-half cross-validation analysis is achieved by coding NV negative.

KEN5: Kendall's coefficient of concordance

Kendall's coefficient of concordance measures the degree of association between three or more raters. KEN5 computes W for a maximum of 100 cases each having up to 5 scores or judgements. All possible combinations of 3, 4, or 5 raters are assessed and the relevant statistics, including significance levels, are output.

MWUT: Mann-Whitney U-tests

MWUT computes Mann-Whitney U-tests for two independent samples measured on up to 70 variables. The two groups are limited to 125 in total size. For groups of over 20 members the significance of U is tested by means of an associated Z- value. Individual rankings and group means are also output although the input data need not be already ranked.

RTAU: Kendall's rank order correlation coefficient

Kendall's rank order correlation coefficient (tau) is computed for all pairs of up to 50 input measures for a maximum of 100 cases. The input data need not be ranked and missing data are permissible so long as an appropriate fixed code signals omissions. Significance levels for the coefficients are indicated as are the numbers of joint occurrences. Successive datasets may be analysed.

The remaining five programs comprise Version 5A: CREAM of PMMD. They are designed to perform various data checking and editing operations.

CHEK: Data checking program
Any unintended non-numeric codes can be identified. The program also allows the range of codes within each column to be checked and any values falling outside the specified range are indicated. If required selected columns can be omitted from the checking procedure; this is particularly useful where alphabetic coding occurs.

REDY: Repair and edit your data
In addition to correcting errors in specified columns, a further range of editing facilities is offered. The four basic operations are:
1. Correction of a specified column of a particular card.
2. Replacement of a complete card.
3. Removal of one or more cards.
4. Insertion of one or more cards.
The block removal facility available under 3 is especially convenient for extracting a subset of the complete data by removing suitable blocks outside that subset.

ELAB: Data elaboration by transformation and addition
Most of the traditional mathematical transformations of data (excluding trigonometric ones) are available, either via individual elaboration modes, or by combinations of them. The five basic modes are:
1. General linear combination of variables.
2. Simple sum and difference combination.
3. General product (including division).
4. Powers.
5. Logarithms.
Two further modes have more specific intentions:
6. Add a new variable via an input array.
7. Standardize to one of three common distributions.

ALTA: Alter the original data coding
A single-column alphabetic code can be recoded into a one- or two-column numeric code. Alternatively any numeric value (up to a maximum of four columns wide) can be recoded into a specific numeric code. A final facility enables columns to be switched. This may be useful as a means of compacting or reordering the coding arrangement.

MERG: Merge up to three datasets
Up to three datasets can be combined so that all the data cards for each case are together.

If more than three datasets need combining then this can be achieved by successive runs. The program is intended to process filed datasets but, if required, the first dataset may be on cards. If there are missing cases on one or more of the datasets only those cases present on all are retained.

A1.5 Program statistics

The various limitations mentioned in the program outlines depend on the sizes of the existing versions of the programs. Many of these limitations can be increased or reduced by making minor modifications to the programs. For installations with small computers changes of this kind will quite likely be essential. Table A1.2 gives approximate details of the program sizes together with the amount of array storage needed depending on the values of certain program parameters. In all cases the storage units are 24-bit words as available on ICL 1900 series machines, all integers being compressed to occupy single locations. For IBM installations the number of array locations should be halved unless double-precision is used. However, this does not apply to programs DRAX and IATS which mostly involve integer storage.

A1.6 Availability

PMMD is currently available on the following installations:

    University of Nottingham
    University of Lancaster
    University of Liverpool
    University of Manchester Regional Computer Centre
    Queen's University, Belfast
    New University of Ulster
    University of Sheffield
    University of Hull
    Cambridge Test Development Unit
    Dyfed County Council
    City of Birmingham Polytechnic
    Manchester Polytechnic
    City of London Polytechnic
    University of Newcastle, Australia
    Department of Education and Science, Darlington
    University of Cambridge
    Trinity College, Dublin
Further copies are available from the author at cost.

Table A1.2 Program sizes and limitations

PROGRAM NAME	SIZE	ARRAY STORAGE REQUIRED	CURRENT NS	NV	LIMITS OTHERS	ARRAY SIZE	TOTAL SIZE
BACH	6124	$252 + NV + 39 \times NA$	9999	100	$NA = 400$	16 852	22 976
DRAX	9536	$2034 + NS + 5 \times NV + 2 \times NVMAX$		70	$NC = 101$	24 960	34 496
		$+ NC(5 + NV + MAX(NC, NV))$	4000	$\begin{cases}200\\400\end{cases}$	$NC = 40$ $NC = 20$	24 034 24 934	
IATS	5196	$452 + 28 \times NI$	9999	500		14 452	19 648
PLOT	4216	$2736 + 6 \times NV$	9999	200		4936	9152
AVAR	7301	$1227 + 16 \times NV + NL(12 + 12NL + 4NL^2)$	9998	70	$NL = 12$	11 131	18 432
BSET	9770	$1302 + 14 \times NV + NVC(NVC + 2)$	4999	200	$NVC = 70$	14 742	24 512
		$+ 4 \times NVT \times NG$			$NVT = 70, 140$ $NG = 20$		
CATT	6278	$1186 + NV(NV + 5) + NG(4NV + 1)$	9999	100	$NG = 20$	19 706	25 984
CATM	6492	$1170 + NV(NV + 1) \times 11 \div 2 + 5 \times NV \times NG$	9999	60	$NG = 20$	27 300	33 792
CARM	13 101	$423 + 5 \times NS + 17 \times NK + 3 \times MB$	2000	600	$NK = 100$	19 923	33 024
		$+ MAXB$		200	$MAXB = 6000$		
DSFN	9 413	$3003 + NV(8NV + 22) + NG$	4999	50	$NG = 20$	24 131	33 536
FTAN	13 856	$80 + NV(8 + 2NV + NF)$	9999	65	$NF = 25$	21 280	35 136
SMLR	6775	$263 + NV(2NV + 14) + 3 \times NM$	9999	70	$NM = 50$	21 193	27 968
		$+ 2 \times NMAX$			$NMAX = 5000$		
KEN5	6036	$1460 + NS(10 + 20NV)$	100	5		12 460	18 496
MWUT	6876	$232 + 4 \times NS + NV(10 + 2NS)$	125	70		16 932	23 808
RTAU	6478	$238 + 6 \times NS + 2NV(NS + NV + 1)$	100	50		15 938	20 416
CHEK	3653	$583 + 160 \times NR + 2 \times NV + NR$	9999	400	$NR = 20$	4603	8256
REDY	3646	130	—	—	—	130	
ELAB	6455	$445 + 305 \times NE + 2 \times NS + 9 \times NV$	5000	400		20 745	27 200
ALTA	4462	$38 + 160 \times NR + 7 \times NT + 2 \times NT \times NH$	—	—	$NR = 10$ $NT = 20$ $NH = 100$	5778	10 240
MERG	3954	$286 + 240 \times NRF$	9999	—	$NRF = 25$	6286	10 240

All sizes refer to 24-bit words on ICL 1900 series computers

KEY

NA	Number of attributes.	*NF*	Number of factors.
NC	Number of categories.	*NM*	Number of models.
NVMAX	Maximum number of variables.	*NMAX*	Number of cases × number of residuals output.
NI	Number of items.	*NR*	Number of cards per case.
NL	Number of levels.	*NRF*	Number of cards per case per file.
NVC	Number of correlate variables.	*NE*	Number of elaborations.
NVT	Number of test variables.	*NT*	Number of alterations.
NG	Number of groups.	*NH*	Number of characters to change.
NK	Number of clusters.		
MAXB	Number of binary measures input x number of initial clusters.		

References

Veldman, D. J. (1967) *FORTRAN Programming for the Behavioral Sciences*, New York, Holt, Rinehart and Winston.

Wishart, D. (1969) *CLUSTAN 1A: User Manual*, St. Andrews, Scotland, University of St. Andrews Computing Laboratory.

Youngman, M. B. (1976) *Programmed Methods for Multivariate Data*, Version 5, School of Education, University of Nottingham.

Youngman, M. B. (1977) *Programmed Methods for Multivariate Data*, Version 5A, School of Education, University of Nottingham.

Appendix 2. The Demonstration Data File

The following listing gives the scores for all 454 cases on the 24 transfer measures described in detail in Chapter 4. The contents of each column are given in Chapter 3, Table 3.1. Since the format printed here is direct computer output the leading zeros punched in column 15 onwards do not appear. They do appear on the data cards (see Chapter 2). The headings specifying card columns, variable numbers, and variable names are not normally listed; they have been added by means of a specially written program.

The organization of the 454 cases on the data file demonstrates a convenient way of coping with missing values. The full sample of 454 cases derives from testing carried out immediately before and soon after transfer. Secondary progress was measured some time later. The inevitable loss of sample members reduced the total with all data except social class to 359. To facilitate later analyses these complete cases are stored first. Cases 360 to 454 are absent on one or other of the secondary attainment measures. This tactic is extended even further to take into account the fact that social class data were missing for many cases right from the start. This omission was not particularly important but to enable any analysis by social class to be performed with minimum fuss, the 189 cases for whom the data were available appear first.

Cases   1–189 have all data.
Cases 190–359 have all data except social class.
Cases 360–454 have all data except social class or secondary attainment.

```
---------------------------------------------------------------------
!                                                                   !
!  PRIMARY/SECONDARY TRANSFER PROJECT - BASIC DATA (N=454)  !
!                                                                   !
---------------------------------------------------------------------

        CARD           11111111112222222222333333333344444444445555555
        COLUMN  12345678901234567890123456789012345678901234567890123456

VARIABLE  ID   1 2 3 4 5 6 7 8 91011121314151617181° 20 21 22 23 24

        NAME   P S A S C J J J J J J J S S S S S S J   J   J   S   S
               R E G E L A A A S S S M A A A S S S M   N   R   M   R   M
               I C E X A S P P C C C O S P N C C C O V   E   A   E   A
               M Y       S S S H S P A T S S X S P A T R   D   T   D   T
```

CASE		ID	PRI	SEG	AGE	SEX	CLAS
CASE	1	INDEX . 8	1 135 1 3 9 9 2 4 81017281517 7 7 720 91 25 80 58 86
CASE	2	INDEX . 17	1 140 2 3 9 9 8 8 8 5142412231110 514104 34 90 70 99
CASE	3	INDEX . 21	1 137 2 31011 0 813101835 818 713 620101 30 92 83102
CASE	4	INDEX . 25	1 136 2 31011 9 6111019321022 611 717 95 26 87 59 97
CASE	5	INDEX . 33	1 141 2 311 4 8 5 8 314331029 810 520 76 24 73 48 74
CASE	6	INDEX . 38	1 141 2 3 8 8 5 7 9 31135 5161010 720 86 37 85 60 86
CASE	7	INDEX . 42	1 134 1 310 9 5 711 915281222 912 714106 33102 81 96
CASE	8	INDEX . 44	1 138 1 31111 3 814 9183310201014 821108 34 93 82 98
CASE	9	INDEX . 46	1 134 1 3 71112 710 614341329 810 714 92 15 72 33 86
CASE	10	INDEX . 47	1 131 1 310 6 9 712 41134 629 8 6 416 78 14 72 44 79
CASE	11	INDEX . 50	1 136 1 310 3 31112 9 926 817 712 410 94 30 96 70 99
CASE	12	INDEX . 51	1 139 1 311 6 2 7 9 6 93211201014 721 88 24 89 55 89
CASE	13	INDEX . 59	1 136 2 31110 3 513 615291625 9 9 717 99 38 92 66103
CASE	14	INDEX . 69	1 135 2 3 8 6 8 712 8152915261111 913 83 25 85 61 92
CASE	15	INDEX . 76	2 136 1 310 6 2 7 9 8143411151012 814 92 19 93 46 87
CASE	16	INDEX . 93	2 132 1 21010 2 610 81734 824 411 823109 20103 71106
CASE	17	INDEX .101	2 133 1 310 8 1 913 8153511161011 716 92 21 97 55 96
CASE	18	INDEX .102	2 130 1 3 8 1 8 6 9 2 92811261011 5 9 84 15 78 58 96
CASE	19	INDEX .106	2 140 1 310 4 6 610 41131 8211010 7 9 97 15 89 61 94
CASE	20	INDEX .108	2 132 2 3 81011 310 317321018 611 513100 26 96 68 97
CASE	21	INDEX .111	2 133 2 311 2 3 1 7 71520 927 2 6 311104 27100 76 93
CASE	22	INDEX .115	2 135 2 3 9 7 6 811 717331019 812 822107 32118 73124
CASE	23	INDEX .116	2 132 2 31110 5 914102033 814 911 917104 25 92 65101
CASE	24	INDEX .118	2 138 2 3 8 810 411 419301523 5 6 513 90 28 94 67100
CASE	25	INDEX .119	2 135 2 3 710 8 8 9 619291226 5 6 617100 22 99 53 99
CASE	26	INDEX .120	2 133 2 311 7 5 810 6193210191113023122 33120 28 78
CASE	27	INDEX .121	2 133 2 3 410 7 7 7 515301423 5 8 215 71 10 78 28 78
CASE	28	INDEX .128	2 130 2 1 7 9 7 8 7 7233712201112112 3110 33114 77114
CASE	29	INDEX .129	2 134 2 311 9 3 7 8 518301625 512 719104 29105 90111
CASE	30	INDEX .133	2 131 2 3111112 811 818311021 513 819120 31109 67115
CASE	31	INDEX .138	2 132 2 3 9 7 6 912 81430 921 5 9 612 91 27106 63 96
CASE	32	INDEX .268	5 231 2 210 6 6 810 914281025 2 5 714 89 27 92 61 93
CASE	33	INDEX .269	5 238 2 3 8 611 5 8 31826 721 6 7 213 79 14 85 36 71
CASE	34	INDEX .271	5 239 2 311 811 0 6 314261330 7 9 514 98 21 93 60 90
CASE	35	INDEX .279	5 237 2 31010 51113 818271621 811 721118 34 95 81121
CASE	36	INDEX .280	5 239 2 3 91111 6 8 415291427 911 516 88 7 70 30 71
CASE	37	INDEX .281	5 239 2 2 811 7 710 514301323 810 619 88 37 85 93112
CASE	38	INDEX .283	5 233 2 3 810 6 3 6 5 825 92010 8 710 94 16 84 28 79
CASE	39	INDEX .286	5 237 2 3 710 9 8 9 619301327 910 619 98 18100 73100
CASE	40	INDEX .290	5 235 2 31011 5 6 8 419281223 610 319 73 33 94 71 88
CASE	41	INDEX .297	5 238 2 3 910 5 3 6 318291422 4 2 515 96 20 91 66 90
CASE	42	INDEX .301	5 234 2 3 611 7 412 315281022 6 6 621100 29100 84101
CASE	43	INDEX .303	5 233 2 2 8 8 5 613 514251424 411 615105 30 92 82119
CASE	44	INDEX .304	5 232 2 211 9 61013 61627 83110 9 817105 31 98 65102
CASE	45	INDEX .305	5 240 2 3101012 6 4 214341823 5 6 616113 33105 83112
CASE	46	INDEX .318	5 230 2 3 8 9 61113 6172913181110 919 92 17 90 55 90
CASE	47	INDEX .329	5 232 2 311 8 3 712 82131 924 410 616103 33104 78120
CASE	48	INDEX .332	5 237 2 410 911 9 5 317291121 7 8 713108 29111 84110
CASE	49	INDEX .340	5 233 2 41010 6 6 7 513211118 511 511 92 14 84 32 77
CASE	50	INDEX .345	5 234 1 3 710 91212 9172518251213 715 82 16 83 26 87

211

```
                CARD            1111111111222222222233333333334444444444455555555
              COLUMN  123456789012345678901234567890123456789012345678901234567

         VARIABLE   ID   1 2 3 4 5 6 7 8 910111213141516171819 20 21 22 23 24

              NAME       P S A S C J J J J J J J S S S S S S S J  J  J  S  S
                         R E G E L A A A S S M A A A S S M N  R  M  R  M
                         I C E X A P P C C C O S P N C C O V  E  A  E  A
                         M Y       S S S H S P A T S S X S P A T R  D  T  D  T

CASE  51   INDEX .346   5 241 1  310  9  5  9  8 61133 914  8141018 81  24 87 59 97
CASE  52   INDEX .347   5 231 1  3  8  9  7 713  813291121 711  711 98  17 83 21 90
CASE  53   INDEX .349   5 231 1  31110  6  512  81623205C  8  9 715 88  11 76 27 84
CASE  54   INDEX .350   5 234 1  3 710 91113  515291530 710  6  6 93  15 90 15 86
CASE  55   INDEX .351   5 235 1  21011  31114  9173013191113  818102  30 94 79100
CASE  56   INDEX .354   5 237 1  3  9  9  4 912  814331230 814  715105  23102 82124
CASE  57   INDEX .360   5 241 1  310  9  21113  8153010131112  712100  28103 73116
CASE  58   INDEX .364   5 231 1  3 810  8 610  513251418 612  813108  19 93 23101
CASE  59   INDEX .370   5 238 1  311  7  8 510  714291432  5  8  616106  27100 83127
CASE  60   INDEX .376   5 238 1  2  3 9101110  51126172710  8  612 91  29102 58 81
CASE  61   INDEX .380   5 236 1  31011  3 712  817351121  7  9  618 95  33102 65102
CASE  62   INDEX .382   5 230 1  211  3  6 811  61526 624  6  8  813103  26 90 62 85
CASE  63   INDEX .390   2 234 1  3  9  6  5  4  7 112241121 712  715112  13 82 27 84
CASE  64   INDEX .393   5 239 1  310  8 61014  918271320 814  715 92  18 88 56106
CASE  65   INDEX .394   5 238 1  410  9  4  9  7 815311421 610  715 96  19 90 61 86
CASE  66   INDEX .407   7 337 1  211  2  6 911  611321220  6  7  716104  21 92 66 82
CASE  67   INDEX .408   7 331 1  2  9  31010  8 312121626 610  411113  13 85 53101
CASE  68   INDEX .409   7 330 1  311  611  712  51638 821  9111020 87  22 96 76100
CASE  69   INDEX .411   7 341 1  511  711  810  51536 919  912  616 88   6 85 56 76
CASE  70   INDEX .415   7 340 1  311  5  3  3  9 51738 616  912  916 77  10 77 55 84
CASE  71   INDEX .416   7 331 1  411  2  2  6  9 1 6251216  5  6  511102  32 94 76107
CASE  72   INDEX .417   7 331 1  310  2  5  2  7 3 728  9231012  713 74  24 80 55 88
CASE  73   INDEX .418   7 330 1  411  6  2  7  7 72036 622  8  6  417102  28100 74111
CASE  74   INDEX .419   7 333 1  111  8  3 613  521321321  8  8  822 97  30 97 81104
CASE  75   INDEX .420   7 340 1  210  2  3 512  313241128  5  9  314 77  22 83 72 95
CASE  76   INDEX .421   7 333 1  311  3  2 511  515301123  8  9  615 71   9 87 68 95
CASE  77   INDEX .423   7 330 1  211  7  5  3  6 517301119  3  7  519 74  21 87 64 93
CASE  78   INDEX .426   7 330 2 11110  5 713  921331017  7  9  719104 31  94 68105
CASE  79   INDEX .427   7 341 2  2  7  8  7 912  51627132111  9  517102  33 91 80 95
CASE  80   INDEX .428   7 340 2  4  7  5  9  9  9 517251221  7  8  314 97  28 90 61104
CASE  81   INDEX .429   7 341 2  2  91010  6  5 81520  8141010  611 74  29 86 65 82
CASE  82   INDEX .430   7 333 2  1  811  5 612  918301819 611  815137  28110 73112
CASE  83   INDEX .431   7 331 2 11011  2  1 91219281320  6111222100  25 99 68 96
CASE  84   INDEX .434   7 328 2  31911  7 913  820361019  4  5  821 78  27 88 53 82
CASE  85   INDEX .437   7 335 2 11110  9 713  816321019 611  819 97  25 87 65 93
CASE  86   INDEX .441   7 336 2  21011  9 913  921241824  7  7  316 95  33105 77102
CASE  87   INDEX .443   7 337 1  2  9  9 61011  91235 921  9  91021113  23107 74105
CASE  88   INDEX .444   7 335 1  1  8  8  3 613  515261016 510  714 91  20 80 67108
CASE  89   INDEX .447   7 337 1  2  5  9  0 911  610271217 810  612 98  18 88 57101
CASE  90   INDEX .448   7 340 1  3  6 8111012  916301126  9  8  918107  27109 84123
CASE  91   INDEX .449   7 340 1  2  5 7101011  917271220  9  7  618 93  24 87 74104
CASE  92   INDEX .450   7 335 1  1  7 810  4 6102129 816  5 61122106  31100 85109
CASE  93   INDEX .451   7 334 1  410 910  7  8 82232 822 610  618 73  26 83 64 86
CASE  94   INDEX .453   7 337 1  3 711  5  9  9 711311724  8  9  720 86  10 89 55 94
CASE  95   INDEX .454   7 337 1  310  9 41110  614311018 811  513 86  10 89 47 94
CASE  96   INDEX .455   7 340 1  310  9 41012  7142712171011  711100  27 94 78103
CASE  97   INDEX .458   7 339 1  2  8  9 5121310202610191012  720105  28 91 86 99
CASE  98   INDEX .462   7 337 2  2  910  3 612  81938 916  911  922123  33106 71111
CASE  99   INDEX .463   7 331 2  3 810  7  7  9 71939 8161011  821107  21 99 64110
CASE 100   INDEX .465   7 334 2  3  9  9  5  6  9 413201419 610  413101  23 92 76 99
```

212

```
                  CARD              11111111112222222222233333333334444444444455555555
                COLUMN    1234567890123456789012345678901234567890123456789012345 67

      VARIABLE    ID      1 2 3  4  5  6  7  8  91011121314151617181920 21 22 23 24

      NAME                P S A  S  C  J  J  J  J  J  J  J  S  S  S  S  S  J  J  J  S  S
                          R E G  E  L  A  A  A  S  S  M  A  A  A  S  S  M  N  R  M  R  M
                          I C F  X  A  S  P  P  C  C  O  S  P  N  C  C  O  V  E  A  E  A
                          M Y           S  S  S  H  S  P  A  T  S  S  X  S  P  A  T  R  D  T  D  T
```

```
CASE 101   INDEX .466    7 334 2  1  7  9  3 410 518221722  7  7 611114 31113 75109
CASE 102   INDEX .468    7 340 2  2  5  9  9  6  9 518321626  6  9 518 73 18 78 47 85
CASE 103   INDEX .470    7 333 2  1  9  8  1 91412233312171012 923120 36112 85119
CASE 104   INDEX .471    7 341 2 31010  5 914 820311223  7  8 721 89 27 87 68 93
CASE 105   INDEX .473    7 333 2 310 812  3  9 617181532  5  7 511 99 28 94 65 87
CASE 106   INDEX .561    9 138 1 210  2 41014  9 8301623 610 820 88 33 88 75105
CASE 107   INDEX .562    9 139 1 311  5 21113 9122912171010 813 81 22100 81104
CASE 108   INDEX .564    9 133 1 21010  4 713112335 621 612 722 99 32102 81129
CASE 109   INDEX .565    9 133 1  3 110  5 813 7133311171010 817108 36 96 81108
CASE 110   INDEX .567    9 137 1 311  1  4  7  7 411281217 812 515104 24 88 66 95
CASE 111   INDEX .568    9 131 1  3  8  2  3  8  7  3 927182610  7  4  6 82  7 79 34 78
CASE 112   INDEX .570    9 135 1 411  1  2 812 511261427  6  9 511 88 23 85 25 70
CASE 113   INDEX .575    9 140 1 11010  6 410 620281125 710 615 75 21 78 65 88
CASE 114   INDEX .581    9 138 1  3  9  9  9 510 613261223  6  9 614 90 24 95 72 96
CASE 115   INDEX .584    9 140 1  4  4  2  5  7  8  5 531 72012 8 613 88 23 85 25 70
CASE 116   INDEX .587    9 131 1  3  1  3  4 210  5 9261630  7  9  4  9 81 16 82 50 80
CASE 117   INDEX .588    9 136 1 310  3  6 812 5113010181010 714 84 18 80 41 94
CASE 118   INDEX .590    9 140 2  3  9  9 91013 417301318 713 719 86 19 85 72 80
CASE 119   INDEX .591    9 135 2  3 911  7  2  6 716331128  6  6 416 80 19 79 77 86
CASE 120   INDEX .593    9 137 2  4 91010 512 52032 923 911 619 86 19 78 47 80
CASE 121   INDEX .602    9 157 2 41110  3 813 41029 924 611 612 97 28 86 72100
CASE 122   INDEX .603    9 131 2  4 91010 813 718221127  7  9 410 94 30 91 73108
CASE 123   INDEX .605    9 135 2 41110 411141014341224  9  9 615 89 20 84 60 91
CASE 124   INDEX .606    9 134 2 31010  9 812 81735 818 514 721 92 18 98 76104
CASE 125   INDEX .608    9 130 2 31110  4 911102035 822 610 821 92 25 95 72107
CASE 126   INDEX .610    9 136 2 31110  6 913 713311622 811 713 88 18 89 54 93
CASE 127   INDEX .611    9 132 2 41110  7 913 811341223  8  9 815104 22 84 66 85
CASE 128   INDEX .612    9 139 2  4  9  7  9  8 911271021  9  9 615 88 19 85 50 70
CASE 129   INDEX .613    9 140 2  3 71012  7  7 615341228  8  6 821 97 31 90 67 97
CASE 130   INDEX .614    9 131 2  3 71012  8  7 615321023  7  8 816 85 19 84 65 95
CASE 131   INDEX .621    9 136 2  3  3  7  6  4  7 81833 8201112 824100 27 99 65114
CASE 132   INDEX .713   11 131 1  3 61110 913 815161826  6  9  5  8 85 26 87 52 83
CASE 133   INDEX .714   11 132 1  3 510  9 511 314281524  9  8 416 79 10 75 76 88
CASE 134   INDEX .718   11 138 1  1  9  4  3  2  6 514241417  8  7 711 83 29 85 56 85
CASE 135   INDEX .719   11 133 1  3 610  8 412 614321117 410 719 96 33 99 74108
CASE 136   INDEX .721   11 140 1  3 911 610  9 9163017221110 718 77 34 97 77100
CASE 137   INDEX .723   11 139 1 310  8 81010 419341018 713 821 73 17 72 52 71
CASE 138   INDEX .724   11 134 1 31011  6 813 82036101710  8 917102 29 90 69110
CASE 139   INDEX .726   11 131 1  3 31010  7  9 817291724  7  7 819107 27 97 73114
CASE 140   INDEX .727   11 141 1 311  8  4 510 616351116 612 919 96 36102 79118
CASE 141   INDEX .729   11 135 2  3 910  4 8121016301221  7  6 517 88 20 82 54 83
CASE 142   INDEX .730   11 140 2  3  8  2  9  7  8 93712291212 712 88  9 85 27 70
CASE 143   INDEX .732   11 136 2  1 210  4  4 910193013131014122 0110 31109 88115
CASE 144   INDEX .733   11 139 2 311  9  2  9  9  8 734142110  6 616 82 10 77 48 75
CASE 145   INDEX .735   11 138 2  3 211  7 613 417321019121 3 818 88 30 93 66111
CASE 146   INDEX .737   11 138 2 310  8 91012 62237 821  8  8 822 91 28 91 86 99
CASE 147   INDEX .738   11 140 2 31011 51111 71738 919101 3 818 97 31 96 79116
CASE 148   INDEX .739   11 137 2 310  8  6 514 51734 815 813 717102 27 94 74106
CASE 149   INDEX .740   11 140 2 310  8 21013 716321219 912 914101 29 98 61112
CASE 150   INDEX .743   11 138 2 311  9  6 614 5173610131011 820 81 33 86 81 97
```

213

```
       CARD           1111111111222222222233333333334444444444455555555
     COLUMN  1234567890123456789012345678901234567890123456789012345678901234567

VARIABLE  ID   1 2  3   4 5 6 7 8  91011121314151617181⁹ 20  21  22  23  24

     NAME      P S  A   S C J J J  J J J J S S S S S S J  J   J   S   S
               R E  G   E L A A A  S S S M A A A S S M N  R   M   R   M
               I C  E   X A S P P  C C C O S P N C C O V  E   A   E   A
               M Y          S S S  H S P A T S S X S P A T R  D   T   D   T
```

CASE 151	INDEX	.744	11	134	1	3	0	911	3	8	61932	929	4	6	517	84	12	74	52	74
CASE 152	INDEX	.745	11	131	1	310	9	21112	6	9331326	010	512	80	2	85	44	80
CASE 153	INDEX	.747	11	141	1	410	4	7	6	9	6	725	921	8	8	614	72	23	71	61	78
CASE 154	INDEX	.748	11	133	1	410	4	6	6	7	4	52616201111	3	8	73	9	85	61	83
CASE 155	INDEX	.750	11	137	2	411	6	5	710	715291023	810	613	73	10	79	44	78
CASE 156	INDEX	.754	11	141	2	31010	9	510	613321225	810	614	66	20	79	57	80
CASE 157	INDEX	.755	11	139	2	4	9	9	5	610	614321222	8	6	416	79	17	84	68	88
CASE 158	INDEX	.761	12	333	1	111	4	7	914	915271225	9	9	622	80	21	80	62	92
CASE 159	INDEX	.763	12	339	1	311	9	512	9	91733112410	6	818	70	15	68	46	80
CASE 160	INDEX	.765	12	341	1	31111	11113	918361121111121119	97	30103	81	95
CASE 161	INDEX	.767	12	340	1	11111	2	7121018351215	9	6	923	93	38105	84117
CASE 162	INDEX	.769	12	337	1	31011	3	8111018241817	812	713	88	20	73	46	76
CASE 163	INDEX	.770	12	339	1	41111	7	9111020341929	910	714	75	11	85	45	83
CASE 164	INDEX	.771	12	338	1	21111	3	8121019341117	6	8	919	89	29	90	66102
CASE 165	INDEX	.773	12	332	1	3	4	510	9	8	0	9261421	6	7	612	76	12	77	43	81
CASE 166	INDEX	.776	12	330	1	31011101010	9153414251013	718	94	23	84	55	93
CASE 167	INDEX	.779	12	335	2	211	7	61214101933	51412141219	93	27	91	69	97
CASE 168	INDEX	.781	12	333	2	1	910	1111410152910221012	916	92	26	86	58	91
CASE 169	INDEX	.782	12	338	2	211	8	2	613	811281518	910	816111	36	96	79106
CASE 170	INDEX	.786	12	335	2	2	710	912141018271021	912	915110	20	97	53100
CASE 171	INDEX	.788	13	137	1	411	710	7	7	310171024	8	9	412107	28	99	72112
CASE 172	INDEX	.790	13	130	1	3	7	9	4	914	920251222	910	918119	31101	70101
CASE 173	INDEX	.791	13	135	1	4	9	710	7	7	614301322	810	813	94	18	74	53	85
CASE 174	INDEX	.794	13	134	1	2	41010	710	718281022	8	8	818103	31	91	76108
CASE 175	INDEX	.796	13	140	1	2	9	8	3	6	8	61630	920	911	619	93	27	93	56	90
CASE 176	INDEX	.799	13	135	1	311	7	3	612	61629	917	7	9	817	83	23	90	61	93
CASE 177	INDEX	.802	13	340	1	311	8	2	610	8193314181011	821107	22	87	55	99
CASE 178	INDEX	.805	13	131	1	3	31010	911	612301219	810	714	98	32	95	72104
CASE 179	INDEX	.806	13	133	1	2	5	6	9	8	9	71227	717	910	7	8112	14	97	50	98
CASE 180	INDEX	.807	13	135	1	2	9	9	6	813	919291023	911	817111	28100	72109
CASE 181	INDEX	.808	13	138	1	210	9	6	914	92335	926	712	721	94	31	93	73104
CASE 182	INDEX	.813	13	338	2	2	911	3	511	922361116	712	823113	33106	79110
CASE 183	INDEX	.815	13	139	2	3	8	5	6	7	8	818321224	7	8	818108	32110	80109
CASE 184	INDEX	.817	13	132	2	3	6	9	91011	41030	822	8	7	414	87	22	90	35	79
CASE 185	INDEX	.819	13	138	2	2	311	9	5	6	620301313	511	922109	37115	84105
CASE 186	INDEX	.823	13	133	2	2	6	810	7	8	62436	518	8	7	924114	28101	82109
CASE 187	INDEX	.824	13	139	2	2	41010	610	618321323	6	8	616112	31101	69	99
CASE 188	INDEX	.828	13	332	2	3	411	6	812	821331117	3	61120126	28113	84105
CASE 189	INDEX	.830	13	340	2	21011	3	712	819351426	4	7	922114	33	92	74104
CASE 190	INDEX	. 5	1	139	1	0	8	9	7	4	8	510291018	9	5	615	93	23	86	52101
CASE 191	INDEX	. 11	1	136	1	010	9	2	811	714291322	6	9	212	70	15	85	40	70
CASE 192	INDEX	. 29	1	139	2	011	6	7	811	517261824	7	9	718	79	25	84	67	90
CASE 193	INDEX	. 37	1	138	2	011	7	5	712	513311021	813	3	6	96	29	97	79101
CASE 194	INDEX	. 45	1	130	1	0	5	110	0	6	210241023	0	6	414	99	2	74	51	91
CASE 195	INDEX	. 71	1	133	2	010	9	9	812	618321625	9	7	817	86	28	88	44	87
CASE 196	INDEX	.141	3	335	1	011	4	1	712	4	81916151012	5	7	83	28	97	79104
CASE 197	INDEX	.142	3	239	1	010	7	81212	816261327	9	8	617100	26	96	69104
CASE 198	INDEX	.143	3	337	1	0	9	9	3	714	721281119	713	719	82	25	86	76	92
CASE 199	INDEX	.145	3	234	1	011	9	1	914	81831	9191011	816110	32112	83119
CASE 200	INDEX	.146	3	233	1	0	81010	1	7	817291322	911	817106	24100	51111

```
              CARD              111111111122222222223333333333444444444455555555
            COLUMN  12345678901234567890123456789012345678901234567890123456 7

          VARIABLE   ID   1  2  3  4  5  6  7  8  9101112131415161718 19  20  21  22  23  24

            NAME         P  S  A  S  C  J  J  J  J  J  J  S  S  S  S  S  S  J   J   J   S   S
                         R  E  G  E  L  A  A  A  S  S  S  M  A  A  A  S  S  M   N   R   H   R   M
                         I  C  E  X  A  S  P  P  C  C  C  O  S  P  N  C  C  O   V   E   A   E   A
                         M  Y        S  S  S  H  S  P  A  T  S  S  X  S  P  A   T   R   D   T   D   T
```

```
CASE 201  INDEX .150   3 230 1 0 9 8 3 912 620261324 910 621 89 33107 69113
CASE 202  INDEX .151   3 234 1 011 8 5 9 5 515211417 8 6 615 80  9 81 27 88
CASE 203  INDEX .152   3 240 1 010 9 6 814 717341017 8141019 90 20 84 34 89
CASE 204  INDEX .153   3 233 1 011 9 11014 818341117 9 8 820106 22108 82102
CASE 205  INDEX .156   3 227 1 0 51010 611 317271728 8 7 512 79 28 90 78101
CASE 206  INDEX .161   3 240 1 011 8 51011 71534132111101019 80 29 94 72 83
CASE 207  INDEX .163   3 239 1 011 8 51011 715351322 710 720 86 21 93 67104
CASE 208  INDEX .165   3 338 1 011 3 1 710 3 5241320 8 9 411 87  8 80 46103
CASE 209  INDEX .170   3 236 1 010 8 4 611 4 6301120 811 815 82 31 90 73 93
CASE 210  INDEX .171   3 237 1 0 61111 7 7 414341324 711 717 98 34 92 77 98
CASE 211  INDEX .177   3 231 1 01111 2 911 416261222 7 8 610 93 28 96 68 99
CASE 212  INDEX .181   3 241 1 0 910 5 8 8 41433 9231111 918 89 24 91 66 99
CASE 213  INDEX .185   3 236 1 0 8 9 8 912 81536 82011 6 818 93 22 93 64 92
CASE 214  INDEX .186   3 239 1 0 911 61014111182816221111 915118 32102 78113
CASE 215  INDEX .188   3 234 1 011 0 8 7 8 4 827 919 7 8 410108 27100 72 97
CASE 216  INDEX .190   3 233 1 011 6 6 410 717291226 710 511 86 31 94 67 86
CASE 217  INDEX .192   3 238 1 011 4 11014 91535121711141022 72 20 73 27 82
CASE 218  INDEX .194   3 238 1 011 9 2 811121636131311 8 818 79 21 92 62 97
CASE 219  INDEX .196   3 236 2 010 9 6 811 61731 925 812 618 79 29 90 72 93
CASE 220  INDEX .205   3 240 2 0 81010 4 3 516271023 812 518 94 30 82 72 90
CASE 221  INDEX .207   3 338 2 0101112 2 4 513311320 3 7 916 81 23 94 63 94
CASE 222  INDEX .208   3 239 2 010 9 6 4 7 416301419 611 613 77 29 94 69 95
CASE 223  INDEX .212   3 234 2 010 0 8 9 8 415351020 911 916103 26 95 66 97
CASE 224  INDEX .216   3 237 2 0101112 713 521301324 7 9 714105 34 87 75 99
CASE 225  INDEX .218   3 232 2 010 9101114 9193212271011 923110 36 99 83109
CASE 226  INDEX .219   3 230 2 010 9101014 5173013251011 519117 29101 73108
CASE 227  INDEX .220   3 232 2 01011 5 714 518291122 6 8 414106 31 93 84109
CASE 228  INDEX .222   3 333 2 0 71111 610 916351730 7 8 718 82 28 80 60 92
CASE 229  INDEX .223   3 231 2 0 6 312 8 1 01437 727 9 9 821 80  4 76 26 74
CASE 230  INDEX .224   3 230 2 010 310 9 5 213201725 9 9 515 72 20 76 47 80
CASE 231  INDEX .225   3 223 2 010 8 6 8 91113291220 8 6 818 76 26 81 55 76
CASE 232  INDEX .227   3 241 2 010 910 812 8163114271011 720114 27 91 68102
CASE 233  INDEX .228   3 237 2 010 811 611 716261423 711 514 97 35 96 75103
CASE 234  INDEX .233   3 230 2 01111 6 910 71527152610 9 721103 20100 67105
CASE 235  INDEX .234   3 235 2 01111 1 811 915271525 9 9 722 93 25102 66 95
CASE 236  INDEX .235   3 240 2 0 61011 711 41022122510 8 3 9 93 33 96 89114
CASE 237  INDEX .238   3 231 2 0 9 8 914 71725 822 8 9 612112 34106 91114
CASE 238  INDEX .239   3 239 2 01110 1 813 915241226 810 618 94 32 98 86120
CASE 239  INDEX .241   3 330 2 010 3 7 710 41630 518 710 714 84 22 85 62 95
CASE 240  INDEX .242   3 330 2 011 6 8 611 51837 619 8 9 720 90 25 90 64101
CASE 241  INDEX .244   3 234 2 010 8 3 710 417291223 6 9 717 88 13 83 30 73
CASE 242  INDEX .248   3 233 2 0 910 7 913 5112117251112 717 82 27 95 75 86
CASE 243  INDEX .253   3 333 2 0 810 51114 816311521 812 714127 35105 74104
CASE 244  INDEX .254   3 335 2 01010 5 912 817341319 910 916102 26 92 73 99
CASE 245  INDEX .255   3 238 2 01010 6 5 9 5112619251110 817 83 28 93 41 94
CASE 246  INDEX .257   3 230 2 01010 1 71012153612211111 718 93 28 96 80102
CASE 247  INDEX .258   3 234 2 0 8 9 71012 712261323 810 5 8110 33 99 85109
CASE 248  INDEX .259   3 238 2 0 811 31012 814241124 810 311109 28105 88115
CASE 249  INDEX .275   5 234 2 0 810 8 7 3 613281126 4 7 615 85 19 87 62 96
CASE 250  INDEX .276   5 235 2 01011 6 6 7 51634122311 9 816 81 29 86 73 86
```

215

```
                CARD              1111111111222222222233333333334444444444455555555
                COLUMN   123456789012345678901234567890123456789012345678901234567

          VARIABLE   ID   1 2 3 4 5 6 7 8 910111213141516171819 20 21 22 23 24

                NAME      P S A S C J J J J J J J S S S S S S J  J  J  S  S
                          R E G E I A A A A S S S M A A A S S M N  R  M  R  M
                          I C E X A S P P C C C O S P N C C C O V  E  A  E  A
                          M Y     S S S H S P A T S S X S P A T R  D  T  D  T

CASE 251   INDEX .289    5 236 2 019 8 1 511 91726 52310 9 814 86  19 80 26 78
CASE 252   INDEX .292    5 235 2 0 6 8 7 511 41030 916 5 9 615106 27 97 69 94
CASE 253   INDEX .295    5 240 2 0 9 612 2 9 51525 526 6 7 613 80  18 83 26 85
CASE 254   INDEX .300    5 236 2 010 9 41013 71929 1122 7 9 517101 33 98 86112
CASE 255   INDEX .311    5 230 2 0 511 71214 81328 1328 710 7 7111 24 98 80112
CASE 256   INDEX .323    5 237 2 0 610 7 410 61723 18281111 715 95 19 90 65 92
CASE 257   INDEX .330    5 238 2 0 7 7 9 8 4 61336 835 9 2 6 9 88  23 85 52 70
CASE 258   INDEX .333    5 238 2 019 9 310141116 3314271011 717104 22 85 46 96
CASE 259   INDEX .337    5 232 2 0 811 5 5 8 611261322 813 9 9 89  14 84 26 89
CASE 260   INDEX .338    5 233 2 0 310 4 711 514191428 810 6 8 86  17 81 49 88
CASE 261   INDEX .342    5 240 1 0 9 8 7 8 3 41531 929 0 8 718 83   3 85 40 70
CASE 262   INDEX .343    5 239 1 01011 4 6 7 616271225 610 816118 32109 79123
CASE 263   INDEX .348    5 228 1 011 3 7 714 513291124 710 510 74  24 90 45 70
CASE 264   INDEX .352    5 236 1 01011 9 910 7162213221110 713 67   6 81 36 87
CASE 265   INDEX .356    5 240 1 0 911 7 911 515351021 810 814102 30 94 85120
CASE 266   INDEX .361    5 237 1 010 7 710 6 51132 819 9 9 816 78  14 84 13 86
CASE 267   INDEX .362    5 231 1 0 7 4 7 8141015 271310 8 7 8 9 85  18 82 33 75
CASE 268   INDEX .365    5 230 1 0 7 9 510101118 331523 9 81014105 21 93 46 85
CASE 269   INDEX .367    5 239 1 011 8 61210 9143151261112 714 88  26 91 65104
CASE 270   INDEX .372    5 231 1 0 3 9111010 4112712221110 413 77   9 74 23 70
CASE 271   INDEX .377    5 235 1 0 9 9 9 6 7 411321222 8 8 513 88   8 85 59 70
CASE 272   INDEX .586    9 135 1 0111012 5 5 811201530 0 3 811 78  18 86 50 92
CASE 273   INDEX .594    9 141 2 010 6 7 510 6 935 611 4 51022100 24 98 77107
CASE 274   INDEX .619    9 133 2 0 8 8 3 6 9 81635 830 7 8 713 94  24 84 52 95
CASE 275   INDEX .622   10 336 1 0 810 5 914112124151811 9 822107 31 97 82102
CASE 276   INDEX .624   10 333 1 0 4 5 5 611 81334 613 4121119103 27112 77114
CASE 277   INDEX .625   10 338 1 01110 21014 8153312171114 811109 30 90 80105
CASE 278   INDEX .629   10 339 1 0 8 9 5 814 915231728 912 513 73  27 76 66 84
CASE 279   INDEX .631   10 341 1 010 6 5 712 615281323 811 815 77  22 79 52 77
CASE 280   INDEX .632   10 341 1 01011 4 712 618261119 6 7 314 70  18 85 49 77
CASE 281   INDEX .633   10 330 1 011 3 5 812 921321218 8121022102 22 82 57 96
CASE 282   INDEX .634   10 335 1 011 8 81114 91534111512 8 820 83  30 93 83100
CASE 283   INDEX .635   10 332 1 01010 6 912 615291317 8 8 414 83  25 83 69 90
CASE 284   INDEX .637   10 333 1 011 6 81110 817301824 7 7 616 86   7 75 69 93
CASE 285   INDEX .641   10 337 2 01111 31013 918281122 3 5 919 93  23 90 72105
CASE 286   INDEX .642   10 332 2 0 3 912 1 6 314201632 2 5 112 85  21 71 69 81
CASE 287   INDEX .645   10 339 2 01111 8 510 919291423 714 812102 23 86 60 96
CASE 288   INDEX .646   10 335 2 01111 9 9111021301823 714 813103 29 93 63100
CASE 289   INDEX .648   10 335 2 01011 4 8111019331321 610 620 96  30 95 87101
CASE 290   INDEX .650   10 332 2 01011 3 914 820311522 712 620105 30 93 70107
CASE 291   INDEX .651   10 335 2 01111 21214102137 818 6 41021106 28108 73101
CASE 292   INDEX .652   10 331 1 011 3 611 8 510261721 8 9 815 80  11 85 61 94
CASE 293   INDEX .653   10 339 1 010 7 81111 6142715211011 515 66   8 72 42 80
CASE 294   INDEX .654   10 336 1 010 8 61010 616261419 6 7 416 82  16 77 53 98
CASE 295   INDEX .655   10 331 1 0 71111 610 115261930 813 214 89  18 82 62 88
CASE 296   INDEX .656   10 331 1 011 8 2121411213013191114 818121 27 89 73109
CASE 297   INDEX .657   10 333 1 011 5 5 810 31134 910 6 5 812 80  23 76 53 85
CASE 298   INDEX .658   10 335 1 010 5 9 8 2 41129131410 6 616 80  20 82 53 86
CASE 299   INDEX .659   10 341 1 0 9 6 7 7 9 516231620 7 7 715 75  20 81 45 80
CASE 300   INDEX .660   10 340 1 0 811 610141021331117 610 921110 34116 88117
```

```
          CARD            111111111122222222223333333333444444444455555555
          COLUMN   1234567890123456789012345678901234567890123456789012345 67

      VARIABLE  ID    1  2  3  4  5  6  7  8  9101112131415161718190  20  21  22  23  24

          NAME        P  S  A  S  C  J  J  J  J  J  J  J  S  S  S  S  S  S  J   J   J   S   S
                      P  E  G  E  L  A  A  A  S  S  S  M  A  A  A  S  S  S  M   N   R   M   R   M
                      I  C  E  X  A  S  P  P  C  C  C  O  S  P  N  C  C  C  O   V   E   A   E   A
                      M  Y        S  S  S  H  S  P  A  T  S  S  X  S  P  A  T   R   D   T   D   T

CASE  301   INDEX  .661  10  341  1  0  7  91110  9  617291627  9  9  719  72  21  78  49  77
CASE  302   INDEX  .663  10  334  1  0 911  5  714  819272023  611  615  88  20  85  57  95
CASE  303   INDEX  .664  10  341  1  0  7  9  9  813  322261228  612  920100  34105  81  98
CASE  304   INDEX  .665  10  339  1  011  4  410  7  411221720  811  412  88  14  84  45  92
CASE  305   INDEX  .667  10  333  1  0101011  811  518251523  5  8  515  80  11  85  49  80
CASE  306   INDEX  .669  10  340  1  011  3  31112  6152818131210  618  86  19  82  43  88
CASE  307   INDEX  .672  10  332  2  0  9  9  9  412  819261420  3  9  617  92  24  91  58  92
CASE  308   INDEX  .673  10  334  2  01110  91114  8183410121010  615  78  22  85  50  79
CASE  309   INDEX  .674  10  339  2  01110  9  710  816301028  2  4  313  73  27  76  57  92
CASE  310   INDEX  .675  10  332  2  0  9  8  61012  61325132210  4  410  78  26  92  73  96
CASE  311   INDEX  .677  10  335  2  010  3  7  9  8  517251221  7  5  719  87  14  74  54  83
CASE  312   INDEX  .679  10  332  2  011  9  4  413  715261423  9  9  616  82  18  71  51  83
CASE  313   INDEX  .680  10  337  2  0101110  811  9183211171010  715  70  28  75  56  83
CASE  314   INDEX  .682  10  336  1  010  8  6  7  4  815241424  7  5  615  86  17  80  48  82
CASE  315   INDEX  .683  10  333  1  011  4  5  2  9  414281217  2  7  313  96  13  82  41  93
CASE  316   INDEX  .684  10  335  1  010  1  5  210  411261119  9  9  416  89  21  86  57  80
CASE  317   INDEX  .687  10  333  1  010  8  3  6  8  710251516  6  9  811120  26111  83117
CASE  318   INDEX  .688  10  330  1  011  2  8  8  6  814291919  6  9  714  83  22  72  48  80
CASE  319   INDEX  .689  10  335  1  01010  2  811  8142916161012  515  80  25  82  54103
CASE  320   INDEX  .691  10  334  1  01010  2  711  715281321  710  514  98  22  98  84100
CASE  321   INDEX  .692  10  335  1  0  7  9  41113  514291417  912  617  81  22  84  77  85
CASE  322   INDEX  .694  10  341  1  01110  2  711  915281419  910  721  96  30  93  70  99
CASE  323   INDEX  .697  10  336  2  01110  3  714  71738  612  7101122  88  25  89  83  96
CASE  324   INDEX  .698  10  332  2  0  9  7  9  612  517341019  611  821  93  32  88  66  99
CASE  325   INDEX  .699  10  337  2  01011  3  7  8  714351426  7  9  617  74  19  78  52  86
CASE  326   INDEX  .703  10  330  2  010  4  9  4  9  518361216  8  9  619  80  15  74  51  84
CASE  327   INDEX  .704  10  334  2  011  3  1  412  815291418  410  617  88  29  83  58  95
CASE  328   INDEX  .705  10  341  2  011  810  910  414291125  9  8  618  89  25  91  72  90
CASE  329   INDEX  .706  10  330  2  010  3  9  5  7  612241320  9  9  612  83  30  86  67  96
CASE  330   INDEX  .708  10  341  2  010  4  5  310102136  817  1  91124114  37109  91102
CASE  331   INDEX  .710  10  341  2  01010  6  914  519321628  911  414  79  22  75  80  91
CASE  332   INDEX  .711  10  339  1  011  7  71214  813261621  9  8  611112  31  99  79  90
CASE  333   INDEX  .756  11  141  2  010  4  4  911  613331424  9  9  616  72  16  85  32  80
CASE  334   INDEX  .764  12  339  1  01111  51214111932131181011  714  95  13  95  73  92
CASE  335   INDEX  .77    2  332  1  31010  2  9  7  71835  61810121016  84  12  81  27  88
CASE  336   INDEX  .366   5  232  1  3  8  9  2  614  6203214251011  619  95  25105  89  98
CASE  337   INDEX  .368   5  237  1  3  8  5  31013  811321223  811  413  87  20  87  61  91
CASE  338   INDEX  .452   7  335  1  2  811  510  9  812251825  711  713116  31106  83111
CASE  339   INDEX  .829  13  135  2  4  7  6  9  2  5  41727  823  6  8  518  87  20  79  63  84
CASE  340   INDEX  .164   3  238  1  01110  5  4  6  410261421  3  4  511109  30  96  61  96
CASE  341   INDEX  .221   3  231  2  01011  5  714  518351325  810  718110  32102  98115
CASE  342   INDEX  .273   5  239  2  0  811  7  612  415291126  611  610  86  28  90   8  92
CASE  343   INDEX  .296   5  239  2  0  71010  812  414251526  5  8  516  98  35111  83114
CASE  344   INDEX  .306   5  241  2  0  7  9  6  410  616301126  6  8  313  89  36  91  78  97
CASE  345   INDEX  .627  10  333  1  0  911  7  413  515281717  7  9  817  93  31  92  86  95
CASE  346   INDEX  .636  10  333  1  011  9  81013  916261820  9  8  611116  32108  80114
CASE  347   INDEX  .071  10  330  2  010  9  9  512  519241624  612  417100  26  99  67112
CASE  348   INDEX  .676  10  334  2  010  9  71012  615311724  4  2  715  83  27  88  81  91
CASE  349   INDEX  .379   5  237  1  31010  811  8  616311118  9  9  618  86  15  73  29  89
CASE  350   INDEX  .389   5  235  1  41011  5  3  8  511261121  7  9  511  89  28  98  69  92
```

217

```
          CARD              111111111122222222223333333333444444444455555555
          COLUMN   123456789012345678901234567890123456789012345678901234567

VARIABLE      ID   1 2 3 4 5 6 7 8 910111213141516171819 20 21 22 23 24

          NAME     P S A S C J J J J J J J S S S S S S J  J  J  S  S
                   R F G E I A A A S S M A A A S S M N  R  M  R  M
                   I C E X A S P P C C O S P N C C O V  E  A  E  A
                   M Y     S S H S P A T S S X S P A T  R  T  D  T

CASE 351  INDEX .459   7 336 1 3 710 6 713 913291419 812 516103 24 99 65 99
CASE 352  INDEX .601   9 137 2 3 911 2 711 818311517 812 819 89 35 98 85115
CASE 353  INDEX .607   9 134 2 4 810 9 9 9 91131 928 6 6 718 85 20 84 60 93
CASE 354  INDEX .144   3 239 1 010 7 5 713 81432 924 713 921 82  2 70 15 78
CASE 355  INDEX .272   5 233 2 0 7 9 7 5 6 8 9301126 7 7 615 88  9 71 31 70
CASE 356  INDEX .559   5 237 1 010 9 2 9121117291417 910 715115 35130 71133
CASE 357  INDEX .397   5 231 1 0 5 8101010 41132 820 6 9 3 9 88 21 79 56 92
CASE 358  INDEX .250   3 337 2 011 8 7 5 9 4 7251623 8 9 511 90 27 91 71 90
CASE 359  INDEX .662  10 335 1 0 5 9121110 713311021 9 7 415 70  7 70 32 79
CASE 360  INDEX . 27   1 138 2 3 61011 512 81428121912 8 415 79 20 74  0 78
CASE 361  INDEX .566   9 131 1 3 9 210 9 6 1 916173310 4 311 83 23 76  0 70
CASE 362  INDEX .734  11 131 2 311 811 8 7 513291326 611 414 74 24 84  0 80
CASE 363  INDEX .758  12 359 1 311 7 71214 71718 8201111 615 85  4 79  0 78
CASE 364  INDEX .762  12 336 1 3111010 5 9 714241222 612 521 79  3 72  0 89
CASE 365  INDEX .774  12 339 1 3 4 911 2 1 5 8241626 3 7 210 80  3 76  0 81
CASE 366  INDEX .803  13 138 1 319 4 4 810 81633 8181211 917 83 19 91  0 86
CASE 367  INDEX .169   3 336 1 011 4 11111 512321221 5 4 517 98 21 87  0 77
CASE 368  INDEX .251   3 233 2 0101111 912 8112612231012 510 73 13 84  0 80
CASE 369  INDEX .690  10 338 1 0 6 3 8 8 6 5 9261626 8 3 514 79 15 85  0 78
CASE 370  INDEX .  2   1 136 1 3 7 911 7 8 818291526 710 718 90 16 83 67  0
CASE 371  INDEX . 12   1 134 1 31010 9 9 8 419261633 5 3 512 74 19 85 23  0
CASE 372  INDEX . 16   1 139 1 311 7 2 914 8193410201112 818 98 29 99  0  0
CASE 373  INDEX . 64   1 132 2 3 91010 2 3 61232 524 8 9 817 74 29 80  0  0
CASE 374  INDEX . 94   2 130 1 311 3 8 7 9 612271323 811 614 85 27 92  0  0
CASE 375  INDEX .107   2 133 1 3 6 410 7 7 310311325 8 4 312 88 10 78  0  0
CASE 376  INDEX .112   2 136 2 3 7 911 712 413291319 913 615 84 22 87  0  0
CASE 377  INDEX .132   2 133 2 2 9 510 612 41335 717 9 9 517 94 23 92  0  0
CASE 378  INDEX .310   5 231 2 3 810 71110 5142417261110 710102 27 91  0  0
CASE 379  INDEX .321   5 232 2 3 71110 4 4 112301225 410 418 88  4 73  0  0
CASE 380  INDEX .335   5 241 2 211 4 9 2 7 712281122 7 9 720100 32 92  0  0
CASE 381  INDEX .336   5 241 2 411 4 81113 815191523113 819 86 23 75  0  0
CASE 382  INDEX .341   5 234 1 2 810 61210 816351122 9 8 720110 33110  0  0
CASE 383  INDEX .363   5 240 1 310 2 0 7 9 71419 920 913 812 88 23 85  0  0
CASE 384  INDEX .374   5 231 1 310 712111310 5291426 610 411112 33 89  0  0
CASE 385  INDEX .387   5 237 1 3 611 6 810 614301123 711 718103 29106  0  0
CASE 386  INDEX .388   2 238 1 4 810 8 4 9 614171633 2 5 613 88  5 71 22  0
CASE 387  INDEX .396   5 234 1 4 81010 5 8 512291027 6 8 716 95 23 93  0  0
CASE 388  INDEX .413   7 330 1 311 4 4 511 914291320 910 512 97 18 93  0  0
CASE 389  INDEX .424   7 341 1 2 8 3 8 2 7 0 5211618 9 8 614 92 27 97  0  0
CASE 390  INDEX .440   7 335 2 311 8 9 8 9 61226162910 8 513 88  3 85  0  0
CASE 391  INDEX .442   7 334 1 3 21111 7 2 516281419 7 8 920137 10 85  0  0
CASE 392  INDEX .460   7 333 1 1 911 5 611 720251821 7 6 818109 35101  0  0
CASE 393  INDEX .469   7 339 2 3 811 7 512 921301122 7 81021 96 33 96  0  0
CASE 394  INDEX .577   9 135 1 3 211 4 214 618351123 9 7 921113 38101 85  0
CASE 395  INDEX .579   9 135 1 3 9 912 813 3 7261534 6 7 510 88 18 79  0  0
CASE 396  INDEX .580   9 139 1 110 3 41110 51227 818 511 510 88 25 91  0  0
CASE 397  INDEX .592   9 137 2 41011 9 7 9 615281323 6 7 518 67  4 85 54  0
CASE 398  INDEX .595   9 131 2 3 9 8 81111 416341126 8 9 716 94 10 91  0  0
CASE 399  INDEX .600   9 133 2 411 9 8 4 4 3 926 923 8 3 1 5 77 27 84 62  0
CASE 400  INDEX .604   9 137 2 31011 210131119351015 911 719103 24 94  0  0
```

218

```
           CARD              1111111111222222222233333333334444444444555555555
         COLUMN   123456789012345678901234567890123456789012345678901234567

     VARIABLE   ID   1  2  3  4  5  6  7  8  910111213141516171819 20 21 22 23 24

           NAME       P  S  A  S  C  J  J  J  J  J  J  S  S  S  S  S  S  J   J   J   S   S
                      P  E  G  E  L  A  A  A  S  S  M  A  A  A  S  S  M  N   R   M   R   M
                      I  C  E  X  A  S  P  P  C  C  O  S  P  N  C  C  O  V   E   A   E   A
                      M  Y        S  S  S  H  S  P  A  T  S  S  X  S  P  A   T   D   T   D   T

CASE 401  INDEX .620  0 132 2 31010 512 7 71734 91911 9 810 79 23 79  0  0
CASE 402  INDEX .728 11 139 1  3 910 6 913 81534 926 5 8 819 97 32 88  0  0
CASE 403  INDEX .731 11 132 2 311 9 3 8 7 910321321 910 616 83 15 81  0  0
CASE 404  INDEX .736 11 138 2  3 8 8 51014 61536 814 914 819 99 28 96  0  0
CASE 405  INDEX .742 11 137 2 21011 4 812 7113313181112 914 86 27 93  0  0
CASE 406  INDEX .775 12 331 2 31011 9 912 617281124 810 615 82 24 74 51
CASE 407  INDEX .778 12 332 2 21011 5 9 8 619311225 810 713 85 26 89  0  0
CASE 408  INDEX .783 12 333 2  3 9 7 3 611 811271422 7 9 512 99 33 96  0  0
CASE 409  INDEX .785 12 333 2 1 6 7 7 4 7 1 8331017 812 619 99 32 95  0  0
CASE 410  INDEX .787 13 137 1 4 9 8 6 7 9 41224 815 811 411 95 22 91  0  0
CASE 411  INDEX .789 13 137 1 311 6 5 613 81632 925 710 716121 32109  0  0
CASE 412  INDEX .798 13 139 1 311 0 9 811 51521 6121110 7 9103 18 79 55  0
CASE 413  INDEX .801 13 136 1 2 711 61113 9212018151214 920 88 28 89  0  0
CASE 414  INDEX .809 13 131 1 311 7 5 711 81634 92710 8 717121 34 97  0  0
CASE 415  INDEX .811 13 131 2  3 31010 910 822251424 9 6 718108 29 97  0  0
CASE 416  INDEX .814 13 131 2 3 510 8 6 8 719301430 610 613103 30 90  0  0
CASE 417  INDEX .820 13 137 2 2 7 9 9 812122131131812131122123 32122  0  0
CASE 418  INDEX .822 13 138 2 4 6 9111011 613321025 612 517 88 11 80  0  0
CASE 419  INDEX .826 13 137 2 4 21012 913 717311121 9 7 616 82  9 81 38
CASE 420  INDEX . 58  1 134 2 011 6 6 7 5 31835 918 713 519 93 26 92  0  0
CASE 421  INDEX .157  3 233 1 011 8 6 911 819181322 6 6 817 88  8 94  0  0
CASE 422  INDEX .167  3 228 1 010 7 2 513 917351522 811 616117 25100  0  0
CASE 423  INDEX .168  3 239 1 010 9 6111410173213171113 817112 32 94  0  0
CASE 424  INDEX .173  3 241 1 010 9 7 914 91037 818 812 819 87  6 89  0  0
CASE 425  INDEX .179  3 234 1 010 6 4 914 0 9251219 911 612 76 26 90  0  0
CASE 426  INDEX .183  3 235 1 011 7 3 812 5123410141012 818 76 10 84 14  0
CASE 427  INDEX .197  3 240 2 01111 5 813 714311222 812 516 78 23 87  0  0
CASE 428  INDEX .211  3 240 2 0 9 910 8141015371233 8 9 714 82 23 91  0  0
CASE 429  INDEX .213  3 237 2 0 9 9 911131020321225 911 719 77 24 84  0  0
CASE 430  INDEX .226  3 233 2 0 7 911 814 916341624 911 715106 23 98  0  0
CASE 431  INDEX .240  3 330 2 01011 6 411 915321624 7 6 413 80 23 90 47  0
CASE 432  INDEX .249  3 236 2 0 811 7 911 314291221 6 9 717 70 27 90  0  0
CASE 433  INDEX .270  5 233 2 0 7 6 5 411 515261128 612 417 82 27 81  0  0
CASE 434  INDEX .308  5 239 2 0 410 9 7 7 211311123 9 6 5 6 93 27 76  0  0
CASE 435  INDEX .315  5 234 2 0 3 3 3 8 3 416181328 9 5 613 88  4 85  0  0
CASE 436  INDEX .326  5 233 2 0 811 7 510 816241124 3 5 8 8105 34 96  0  0
CASE 437  INDEX .334  5 231 2 0 6 9 8 6 7 11328152711 8 413 82 22 87  0  0
CASE 438  INDEX .344  5 232 1 0 9 4 3 911 711331222 912 811 84 16 89  0  0
CASE 439  INDEX .360  5 233 1 01110 8 910 81428 72610 9 713 86  7 75  0  0
CASE 440  INDEX .386  5 236 1 0 6101110 9 414251826 8 9 612 70 24 74  0  0
CASE 441  INDEX .563  9 137 1 010 5 4 8 9 513291625 7 7 613 97 16 79  0  0
CASE 442  INDEX .615  0 137 2 0 510 9 5 9 212231225 6 4 613 78 11 76  0  0
CASE 443  INDEX .623 10 338 1 0 811 9 812 719271418 912 915 83 23 76  0  0
CASE 444  INDEX .628 10 333 1 010 8 3 913 9182914191114 821 77 32 85  0  0
CASE 445  INDEX .630 10 335 1 01010 6 5 9 417271420 611 616 76 19 77  0  0
CASE 446  INDEX .639 10 335 1 010 711 814 9212513211011 714 91 25 79 66  0
CASE 447  INDEX .666 10 335 1 010 4 310 8 613251021 7 9 317 74  6 85 24  0
CASE 448  INDEX .685 10 341 1 010 9 81114 920311419 6 9 818104 31 99 66  0
CASE 449  INDEX .686 10 336 1 0 4 5 5 511 615291412 710 916 95 23 82  0  0
CASE 450  INDEX .696 10 239 1 011 5 5 5 9 31433 8211012 516 70 12 85  0  0
```

```
          CARD           1111111111222222222233333333334444444444455555555
        COLUMN 12345678901234567890123456789012345678901234567890123456 7

VARIABLE  ID    1 2 3 4 5 6 7 8 910111213141516171819 20 21 22 23 24

        NAME    P S A S C J J J J J J J S S S S S S S J  J  J  S  S
                R E G E L A A A S S S M A A A S S S M N  R  M  R  M
                T C E X A S P P C C C O S P N C C C O V  E  A  E  A
                M Y     S S S H S P A T S S X S P A T R  D  T  D  T

CASE 451  INDEX .700 10 230 2 010 611 813 518241123 7 8 716 85 14 82   0   0
CASE 452  INDEX .701 10 332 2 0 9 310 7 9 51522122410 4 710 72 23 80   0   0
CASE 453  INDEX .707 10 235 2 0 910 7 614 717351721 811 719124 25102   0   0
CASE 454  INDEX .709 10 339 2 0 8 911 8 2 51727 627 1 6 411 67 16 72 33   0
```

↑***

220

Appendix 3. Two Classification Techniques

With so many different procedures available it is only possible here to describe the basics of two commonly used methods. This approach is not as restricted as it might first appear since most methods operate in a similar way to one or other of these two. *Ward's method* (Ward 1963) is an hierarchical agglomerative grouping method. Starting with N individuals measured on M variables the procedure progressively combines individuals and groups until eventually one group comprising all N cases results. A solution to the classification problem will be offered by one or more of the intermediate classifications produced during this process. The *centroid relocation method* (Wishart, 1969, 1972; Anderberg, 1973) starts with a partitioning of the N individuals into K groups. Individuals are relocated into the group with which they show greatest similarity and then the two most similar groups are fused. This joint process of relocation and fusion is repeated until a single group of N cases remains, as in Ward's method. There are two fundamental differences between these methods. Firstly, by starting with a relatively small number of groups (typically between 10 and 20) the centroid method is considerably quicker than Ward's and can accordingly cope with larger samples. Secondly, group fusions are determined by similarity and the mathematical definition of similarity differs for the two methods.

Table A3.1   Behaviour data for clustering demonstrations

(A) *Questions and responses*

	Cases							
	1	2	3	4	5	6	7	8
1. Do you often look out of the classroom window?	YES	YES	NO	YES	YES	YES	NO	NO
2. Have you had things taken from you by the teacher?	YES	YES	YES	YES	YES	NO	NO	NO
3. Is your work usually neat?	YES	NO	NO	NO	NO	NO	YES	NO
4. Do you nearly always answer if teacher asks you a question?	YES	YES	YES	YES	NO	NO	YES	YES
5. Do you often talk to the person next to you in class?	YES	YES	YES	YES	YES	YES	NO	NO

(B) *Coding*
1 11111
2 11011
3 01011
4 11011
5 11001
6 10001
7 00110
8 00010

As with any multivariate method in addition to the choice of method there are a number of further considerations to make before an analysis can be fully specified. These include the selection of variables and variable transformations as well as other details specific to particular methods. Some of these points are dealt with more fully in Chapter 9, Section 9.1. The rest of this section comprises a detailed description of the two methods selected. So much computation is involved that it would be impossible to show these details using the complete transfer sample. Instead, a token sample of eight cases will be used. To simplify the calculations even further answers to five questions taken from a Behaviour in School Inventory (Bennett and Youngman, 1973) will be used rather than the transfer measures. Table A3.1 lists these responses; they are coded 1 = YES/0 = NO in the following computations. By applying cluster analysis to these responses it becomes possible to identify groups of children showing similar behaviour. Part of the outcome is immediately obvious since cases 2 and 4 have identical response patterns. For the rest the problem is not trivial because there are varying degrees of overlap in the responses.

1. Ward's method

STEP 1: Compare each individual with every other by means of the distance measure
In Ward's method similarity is defined in terms of *distance*, low distance implying high similarity. For two cases A and B the distance between them is:

$$D(A, B) = \frac{1}{2} \sum_{i=1}^{M} (X_{Ai} - X_{Bi})^2 \qquad (A3.1)$$

where: M is the number of measures used
         X_{Ai} is the score of case A on measure i
For N cases there are $N \times (N-1)/2$ such computations which explains the need to limit the method's application to relatively small samples, usually of no more than 100 cases. Figure A3.1 gives the distances for all pairs of the eight sample cases. The slight reordering is needed so that the successive fusions can eventually be plotted. These distances are effectively the error potentials associated with fusing the corresponding pair of cases, $E(A,B)$.

STEP 2: Combine the two cases with the smallest associated distance
Cases 2 and 4 have identical responses and therefore their distance is 0.0. Since this is smaller than for any other pair, cases 2 and 4 are combined to form a cluster of size two, labelled 24.

STEP 3: Compute the error potential increases associated with combining the new cluster with each of the others
Ward's method is concerned with minimizing within-group variance. As a result the original distance formula for individuals has to be modified when clusters are involved.

222

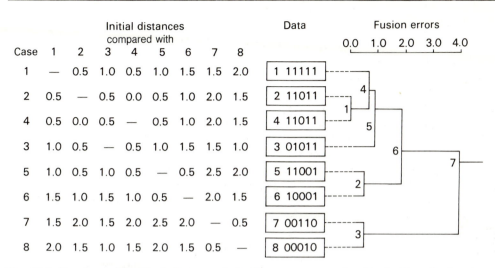

	Initial distances compared with								Data	Fusion errors
Case	1	2	3	4	5	6	7	8		0.0 1.0 2.0 3.0 4.0
1	—	0.5	1.0	0.5	1.0	1.5	1.5	2.0	1 11111	
2	0.5	—	0.5	0.0	0.5	1.0	2.0	1.5	2 11011	
4	0.5	0.0	0.5	—	0.5	1.0	2.0	1.5	4 11011	
3	1.0	0.5	—	0.5	1.0	1.5	1.5	1.0	3 01011	
5	1.0	0.5	1.0	0.5	—	0.5	2.5	2.0	5 11001	
6	1.5	1.0	1.5	1.0	0.5	—	2.0	1.5	6 10001	
7	1.5	2.0	1.5	2.0	2.5	2.0	—	0.5	7 00110	
8	2.0	1.5	1.0	1.5	2.0	1.5	0.5	—	8 00010	

Fig. A3.1 *Structure of the Ward cluster analysis. The rows are reordered to facilitate the drawing of successive fusions on the right of the figure. The numbers 1 to 7 show the order in which these fusions occur.*

The increase in the error potential resulting from fusing the new cluster AB with any other cluster C is given by:

$$E(AB, C) = \frac{a+c}{a+b+c} E(A, C) + \frac{b+c}{a+b+c} E(B, C) - \frac{c}{a+b+c} E(A, B) \qquad (A3.2)$$

where: $E(A,C)$ etc. are the original distances or errors for individuals.

a, b, c are the sizes of clusters A, B, C respectively.

Thus $E(24,1)$, the error associated with fusing the new cluster 24 with case 1 becomes:

$$E(24, 1) = \tfrac{2}{3} \times 0.5 + \tfrac{2}{3} \times 0.5 - \tfrac{1}{3} \times 0.0 = 0.67$$

For the remaining individuals the errors are:

$E(24,3) = 0.67$
$E(24,5) = 0.67$
$E(24,6) = 1.33$
$E(24,7) = 2.67$
$E(24,8) = 2.00$

Inserting these new values in the original distance matrix of Fig. A3.1 produces the error potential matrix shown in Table A3.2.

STEP 4: Combine the two clusters for whom the error increase is smallest

The smallest error potential is the 0.5 resulting from fusing clusters 5 and 6, or 7 and 8. Where errors are the same the lowest numbered choice is usually taken and therefore cases 5 and 6 are fused.

223

Table A3.2 Ward error potentials after the first fusion

	1	24	3	5	6	7	8
1	-						
24	0.67	-					
3	1.00	0.67	-				
5	1.00	0.67	1.00	-			
6	1.50	1.33	1.50	0.50	-		
7	1.50	2.67	1.50	2.50	2.00	-	
8	2.00	2.00	1.00	2.00	1.50	0.50	-

The fusion of cases 2 and 4 requires the error potential associated with fusing this new group with each of the rest to be computed. For the remaining single cases the error potential is simply the distance.

STEP 5: Recycle with STEP 3 followed by STEP 4

The error potential matrix is now updated by computing the error increases associated with the new cluster 56 using Eq.(A3.2). As the fusion summary to the right of Fig. A3.1 shows, the next fusion combines cases 7 and 8. Subsequent fusions are as shown, the length of the branch indicating the error increase at each fusion. The process terminates by combining the cluster comprising cases 1, 2, 3, 4, and 5, and 6 with cases 7 and 8.

STEP 6: Choice of a solution

This is by no means a trivial or automatic step and Chapter 9, Section 9.1 discusses it in detail. One of the many available criteria derives from the basic objective of cluster analysis, namely to generate groups with minimal internal variation, but maximum separation. Since the error measure indicates the degree to which this objective is violated, it follows that sudden jumps in error represent the fusion of relatively dissimilar groups. In Fig. A3.2 the error increase for each fusion is plotted. It is clear that while the error increases slowly initially, a large increase occurs in moving from three to two clusters. This suggests that the three-cluster classification is a possible solution as it is parsimonious in having a small number of groups, yet it also maintains homogeneity.

STEP 7. Diagnosis of clusters

Again this aspect of clustering is dealt with more fully in Chapter 9. Here it is sufficient to acquire a pen-picture of the three clusters. The easiest approach is to compute the average scores of each cluster on the M measures:

	cases	scores				
		1	2	3	4	5
CLUSTER 1	1	1	1	1	1	1
	2	1	1	0	1	1
	3	0	1	0	1	1
	4	1	1	0	1	1
profile of means		$\frac{3}{4}$	1	$\frac{1}{4}$	1	1

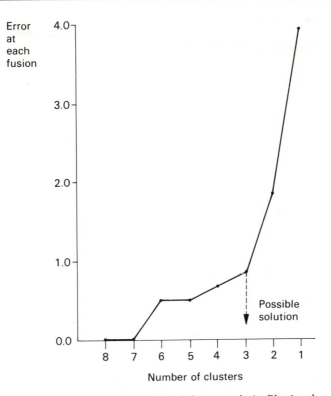

Error at each fusion

Number of clusters

Fig. A3.2 *Error plot for the Ward cluster analysis. Plotting the error associated with each fusion shows a gradual increase initially, followed by a sharp increase in moving from three clusters to two. This suggests that the three-cluster classification might present an acceptable solution.*

	cases	scores				
CLUSTER 2	5	1	1	0	0	1
	6	1	0	0	0	1
profile of means		1	$\frac{1}{2}$	0	0	1

	cases	scores				
CLUSTER 3	7	0	0	1	1	0
	8	0	0	0	1	0
profile of means		0	0	$\frac{1}{2}$	1	0

So cluster 1 comprises those children who tend to agree with all statements except the one about neatness. Cluster 2 shows less agreement, while cluster 3 has the most positive attitude to school.

2. Summary of Ward's method

STEP 1   *Compare each individual with every other using the distance formula.*
STEP 2   *Combine the two cases with the smallest distance.*
STEP 3   *Compare the error potential increases associated with combining the new cluster with each of the rest.*
STEP 4   *Combine the two clusters with the smallest error increase.*
STEP 5   *Repeat STEPS 3 and 4 until all clusters have fused.*
STEP 6   *Select one or more classifications from the complete set.*
STEP 7   *Obtain the characteristics of the clusters comprising the selected classification(s).*

3. Relocation method

The relocation centroid method differs from Ward's method in that it is normal to start with a partitioning of the cases into a small number, K, of groups. This initial grouping can be random or it may be based on some known classification. Either way it is important that K should be larger than the anticipated number of clusters since the early stages of a relocation analysis may not be particularly reliable. Anderberg (1973) discusses starting configurations in detail.

STEP 1: Allocate the N cases to K initial clusters

Two common methods for generating starting groups are to allocate cases sequentially to K groups (Youngman, 1976) or according to some supplied classification array (Wishart, 1969). For the eight sample cases a six-cluster sequential start implies that the cases are grouped as shown in Fig. A3.3. There is no reason to believe that this random grouping has any value and therefore it is necessary to optimize it by relocating each individual into the group with which it shows greatest affinity.

STEP 2: Compute the centroid of each cluster

Before similarity with clusters can be assessed the character of each cluster must be quantified by computing its *centroid*. This is simply the list of average scores for all the cluster members on each variable:

$$\text{Centroid } U_A \text{ is } \frac{1}{a} \Sigma X_{A1}, \frac{1}{a} \Sigma X_{A2}, \ldots, \frac{1}{a} \Sigma X_{Ai}, \ldots, \frac{1}{a} \Sigma X_{AM} \qquad \text{(A3.3)}$$

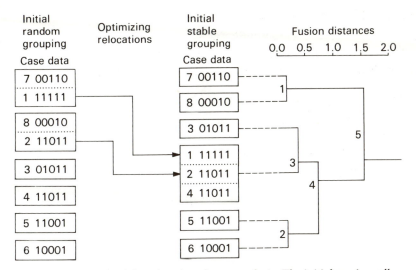

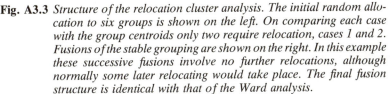

Fig. A3.3 *Structure of the relocation cluster analysis. The initial random allocation to six groups is shown on the left. On comparing each case with the group centroids only two require relocation, cases 1 and 2. Fusions of the stable grouping are shown on the right. In this example these successive fusions involve no further relocations, although normally some later relocating would take place. The final fusion structure is identical with that of the Ward analysis.*

where: M is the number of measures

a is the size of cluster A

X_{Ai} represents the score of a member of A on variable i

For cluster 1 containing the two cases 1 and 7 the centroid becomes:

$\frac{1}{2}\frac{1}{2}$ 1 1 $\frac{1}{2}$

One slight modification to Eq.(A3.3) is needed when an individual is being compared with its parent group as opposed to one of the other groups. In order to ensure that the comparison is unbiased, the *reduced centroid* is computed by omitting the scores of the individual under consideration.

STEP 3: Compute the similarity between each case and the K clusters
Computing the similarity between an individual and a group is only the special case of computing the similarity between two groups. For the latter an error sum of squares distance measure is used:

$$D(A, B) = \frac{2ab}{M(a + b)} \sum_{i=1}^{M} (U_{Ai} - U_{Bi})^2 \qquad (A3.4)$$

where: A and B are the two clusters being compared

227

a and b are the respective cluster sizes

M is the number of measures

U_{Ai} represents the centroid value for cluster A on variable i

In comparing an individual A with cluster, B, then $a = 1$ and U_{Ai} becomes the actual scores X_i for the individual. For Fig. A3.3 the comparison between case 1 and cluster 1 can be expressed as $D(S1,C1)$, the letters S representing a single case, C a cluster. Since this is a parent comparison (case 1 is in cluster 1) then case 1 must be removed from the group before the centroid is computed. The comparison effectively becomes $D(S1,S7)$.

$$D(S1,C1) = D(S1,S7) = \frac{2 \times 1 \times 1}{5 \times 2} [(1 - 0)^2 + (1 - 0)^2 + (1 - 1)^2 + (1 - 1)^2 + (1 - 0)^2]$$

$$D(S1,C1) = \frac{2 \times 1 \times 1}{5 \times 2} \times 3 = 0.6$$

Similarly: $D(S1,C2) = \frac{2 \times 1 \times 2}{5 \times 3} [(1 - \tfrac{1}{2})^2 + (1 - \tfrac{1}{2})^2 + (1 - 0)^2 + (1 - 1)^2 + (1 - \tfrac{1}{2})^2]$

$$D(S1,C2) = \frac{2 \times 1 \times 2}{5 \times 3} \times \frac{7}{4} = 0.4667$$

$$D(S1,C3) = D(S1,S3) = 0.4$$

$$D(S1,C4) = D(S1,S4) = 0.2$$

$$D(S1,C5) = D(S1,S5) = 0.4$$

$$D(S1,C6) = D(S1,S6) = 0.6$$

STEP 4: Allocate each case to its closest group
Since case 1 has greatest similarity (least distance) with cluster 4 with the value of 0.2 it is moved from cluster 1 to cluster 4. This is done for all N individuals and it comprises one complete relocation iteration cycle. Figure A3.3 shows that case 2 also switches into cluster 4.

STEP 5: Recompute cluster centroids
The switching of individuals between clusters necessitates recomputation of the cluster centroids at the end of the cycle to take into account the new membership.

STEP 6: Repeat STEPS 3, 4, and 5 until no individual changes clusters throughout a complete relocation cycle
Normally several relocation cycles are needed before no individual switches during a complete iteration. When this is achieved the classification is deemed to be *stable*.

STEP 7: Compute similarities between all pairs of clusters and fuse the closest
Distances between all pairs of clusters are computed using formula Eq.(A3.4). In the

example the two closest are clusters 1 and 2 at a distance of 0.2. These two are then fused, reducing the number of clusters by one.

STEP 8: Repeat the whole relocation and fusion process

It is now necessary to repeat the relocation scans since the formation of the new cluster may have disturbed the original stability. The whole process of relocation and fusion reiterates until a single cluster comprising the complete sample is reached. From this point the analysis matches Ward's method.

STEP 9: Choice of a solution

The distance plot in Fig. A3.4 is less helpful than the Ward error plot because the relocation process tends to remove the discontinuities associated with unsuitable fusions. Even so Fig. A3.4 does suggest that classifications after the three-cluster solution are unsatisfactory. In fact the relocation three-cluster grouping is identical with the Ward solution.

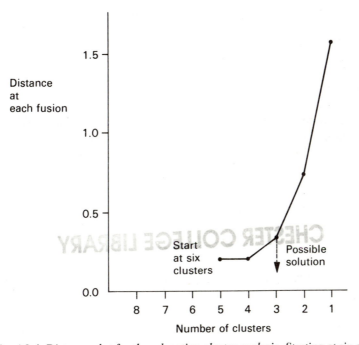

Fig. A3.4 *Distance plot for the relocation cluster analysis. Starting at six clusters means that only five fusion distances can be plotted. Although the rate of increase in distance is smoother than in the Ward analysis, again the large increases occur after three clusters.*

STEP 10: Diagnosis of clusters
Apart from the general comments given in STEP 7 of the Ward analysis outline, more detailed guidance on diagnosing clusters appears in Chapter 9.

4. Summary of the relocation method

STEP 1   *Allocate the N cases to K initial clusters.*
STEP 2   *Compute the centroid of each cluster.*
STEP 3   *Compute the similarity between each case and all K clusters.*
STEP 4   *Allocate each case to its closest cluster.*
STEP 5   *Recompute the cluster centroids.*
STEP 6   *Repeat STEPS 3, 4, and 5 until no individual switches during a complete relocation scan.*
STEP 7   *Compute similiarities between all pairs of clusters and fuse the closest.*
STEP 8   *Repeat the whole relocation and fusion process until one cluster remains.*
STEP 9   *Select one or more classifications.*
STEP 10   *Obtain characteristics of the clusters in each selected grouping.*

References
Anderberg, M. R. (1973) *Cluster Analysis for Applications*, New York, Academic Press.
Bennett, S. N. and M. B. Youngman (1973) 'Personality and behaviour in school', *Brit. J. Educ. Psychol.*, **43**, 228–233.
Ward, J. H. Jr. (1963) 'Hierarchical grouping to optimize an objective function', *American Statistical Association Journal*, 58, 236–244.
Wishart, D. (1969) *CLUSTAN IA: User Manual*, St. Andrews, Scotland. University of St. Andrews Computing Laboratory.
Wishart, D. (1972) 'A general tripartite clustering method and similarity generating function', London, Civil Service Statistics Division, Report R-31.
Youngman, M. B. (1976) *Programmed Methods for Multivariate Data*, Version 5, School of Education, University of Nottingham.

Index

A posteriori comparisons, 83–88
A priori comparisons, 83–88
Ability data, 21, 28, 44
Age coding, 20, 28
Alpha, 45, 161–163, 180, 184–187, 204
  maximization, 183–185, 187
Analysis specifications, 26–28, 33–39, 203
  strategies, 3, 4, 9–13, 96, 190
Applications, 138
Association measures, 69–77
Attitude data, 20, 28, 44 47
  scales, 7–8, 10, 46–47, 60–61, 102, 157–161, 172
Attributes, 163–168, 202, 205
Atypicality charts, 88–90
Atypicality tests, 11, 13, 83–88, 93, 134–135,
    203–204
Automatic Interaction Detection, 26
Average, 10, 57–58, 83–88
Axes for plotting, 62, 98, 100, 204

Bancroft's procedure, 80
Bartlett variance homogeneity test, 82–84, 88,
    203–204
Basic statistics, 14–15, 24, 56–61
Batch processing, 40
Beta weights, 116, 122
Between groups testing, 81–95, 203–205
Biased estimates, 59
Bimodality, 60–61
Binary data, 10, 20, 30, 129, 161–169, 202–203,
    205
Biographic data, 19, 20, 28, 44
BMD programs, 26–27, 186
BMDP programs, 27, 33–36, 41, 61, 76, 93, 122,
    149, 169, 187, 197

Calculations, 13–14, 95, 104
Calculators, 41
Categoric data, 7, 9, 30, 113, 203
Categories, for data, 56, 65–67
Causal path analysis, 10, 122–123
Cells, in tables 65–67, 71, 91, 154–156, 204
Centroid clustering, 128, 130, 149, 221, 226–230
Change measurement, 10, 43, 70, 189–197
Characterizations of data, 7–9
Checking, 13, 22, 23–25, 32–33, 39–40, 207
Checklists, 22, 138
Chi-square analysis, 10, 11, 62, 68–73, 76, 80, 83,
    84–88, 95, 142, 156–159, 202
Cicchetti's estimate, 91–92

Classification, 10–14, 26, 93, 125–139, 146–147,
    221–230
Cluster analysis 10–14, 22, 125–139, 146, 165–169,
    183–184, 187, 202–203, 205, 221–230
  centroid, 128–129, 224, 226
  comparison, 126–127, 147–148, 149
  diagnosis, 132–135, 139–146, 149, 165–168, 224,
    230
  fusion, 224–225, 228–229
  level, 130–132, 224–225, 229
  methods, 128, 149, 221–230
  refinement, 135–137
  starting points, 126, 130, 226
  validation, 137–139
CLUSTAN, 26, 205
Cochran's Q-test, 10, 73, 76, 93
Codebook, 27, 28, 173–174
Coding forms, 17–18, 20–21
Coefficient:
  of concordance, W, 121–122, 202, 206
  of equivalence, alpha, 45, 161–163, 180,
    184–187, 204
Columns on cards, 32, 39–40
Combining categories, 65–67
Communality, 104–105
Comparing cases, 9–14
Comparing measures, 9–14
Computer cards, 17, 22–25, 27–28
  coding, 10, 16–25, 27–28, 154, 173–174
  errors, 15, 22–25, 39–40
  files, 29, 207
  output, 29, 34, 62–65, 85–86
  programs, 4, 26–27, 33, 40, 74, 147, 201–209
  usage, 4, 13, 26–42, 62
Concurrent validity, 181
Confounded comparisons, 91–93, 204
Construct validity, 181
Content validity, 181
Contingency coefficient, 10, 70, 71, 76, 157–159,
    202
  tables, 65–69, 156–157
Continuous data, 9–11, 20, 30, 56, 70, 74–77, 113,
    119
Controlling measures, 10, 189–197
Cooley, W. W. and Lohnes, P. R. 41, 61, 76, 122,
    149, 169, 187, 197
Correlated groups, 10–14, 146, 190
Correlation, 10–12, 22, 62, 68–77, 102, 110,
    179–182, 190–197, 202
  plots, 98–100

Correlation (*continued*)
    product moment 10, 12, 22, 33–35, 64, 70,
        73–77, 95, 98–100, 102, 110, 112, 128–129,
        202, 204–205
    rank order, 10, 70, 73, 76, 202, 206
Covariance, analysis of, 10, 119–120, 122,
    193–197, 202, 206
Covariates, 193–197
Cramer's *V*, 70–71, 76
Criterion correlation, 116–118, 120
Cronbach's alpha, 45, 161–163, 180, 184–187, 204
Cross-tabulation, 10, 57, 62, 65–69, 71–74, 76,
    156–157, 169, 204
Cross-validation, 116–118, 122, 137–139, 203, 206
Curtailment, 53

Data, 3, 7–9, 10–12, 43–49, 53, 210–220
    checking 10, 23–25, 39–40, 53, 110, 207
    coding 10–12, 16–22, 27, 33, 53, 79, 153–154,
        173–174, 207
    description, 10–11, 53
    format, 29–33, 201, 203
    listing, 23–24, 210–220
    modification, 10–11, 21–22, 34, 59
    order, 19, 28
    preparation, 16–25, 79, 207
    recoding, 10–11, 21–22, 40, 56, 65–69, 76
        155–165, 169, 202, 204, 207
    reduction, 22, 109–111, 122, 202, 206
    spacing, 19–21
    transfers, 16
    see also:
        Binary data; Categoric data; Continuous data;
        Dichotomous data; Interval data; Nominal data;
        Ordinal data; Ratio data; Transformation of data
Decimals, 19–20, 30–31, 58
Degrees of freedom, 71, 82, 83, 115
Dendrograms, 131, 149
Dependence, 70, 83, 93
Dependent groups, 10–14, 70
Dependent variables, 111, 204
Descriptors, format, 29–33
Deviations, 58–59
Dichotomous data, 9, 10, 20, 74, 85, 113, 119–122
Difference scores, 11, 190–193, 197
Differentiating groups, 9–14, 70, 80–96, 132–135,
    137–146, 149, 204–206
Differentiating measures, 76, 95–124
Direct coding, 16–17
Directionality, 7
Discriminant function, 10, 135, 139–146, 149, 202,
    205–206
    scores, 141, 143–146, 147, 149, 202, 205
    structure, 143, 146, 149
    weights, 141, 146, 149
Distance measures, 128–130, 137, 146, 147, 222
    simplicity, 122
Distributions, 6, 40, 53, 57–61, 74, 154–155, 202,
    204

Documentation, 28, 201
Dummy variables, 119–122, 203
Duncan test, 84

Editing data, 207
Eigen-values, 105–107
Engineering Training Survey, 154–174
Error, 80–81, 83–88, 223
    type I, 80, 83, 84, 88
    type II, 84
Error sum of squares, 129
Errors in data, 10, 16, 23–25, 39–40, 53, 201, 207
Estimates, 59, 81
Expected frequencies, 71, 127, 157
Experiments, 80, 83, 91–93
Experimentwise error, 80–81, 88
Explained variation, 74–75
Extended residuals, 11, 191–195, 197
Extreme groups, 80
    item analysis, 176–179, 182, 187

F-descriptors, 30–31
F-ratio, 81–82, 85, 114
Factor analysis, 3, 10, 12, 14, 22, 95, 97–111, 141,
    159–161, 183–184, 187, 202, 206
    communality, 104–107
    comparison, 110–111, 122
    intercorrelation, 102, 108–109, 111, 122
    interpretation, 107–109, 111, 122
    loadings, 100, 102, 106–111, 160
    oblique, 102–104, 109, 161, 202, 206
    orthogonal, 100–104, 202, 206
    pattern, 102, 108, 111, 160
    reflection, 108, 111, 160
    rotation, 102, 111, 122, 202, 206
    scores 109–111, 122, 202, 206
    significance, 106–107, 109, 122
    simplicity, 122
    structure, 102–111, 141
    variance, 100, 105–107, 111, 122
    varimax 102–111, 122
Ferguson, G. A., 80, 82, 83
Field, 29
Field descriptors, 29–31
Fisher exact probability test, 10, 68, 70, 72–73, 76,
    84, 203–204
Fixed-format coding, 17–33
FORTRAN, 26, 29–33, 38–39, 201
Frequencies, 10, 53, 57, 61, 69, 71, 154–155, 202,
    204

Group allocation, 141, 146–147, 149
    differentiation, 9–14, 78, 80–94, 133–135,
        137–146, 149, 204–206
    identification, 9–14, 78–80, 202, 204–206
Groups, 9–14, 78–94, 125–150
Guttman scalogram analysis, 11, 183–184, 187

Histograms, 10, 56
Homogeneity of variance, 82, 88, 93, 203–204
Hypotheses, 3–9, 96

I-descriptors, 30
IBM, 28, 208
ICL, 28, 208–209
Identification numbers, 17, 28, 30, 79, 203
Identifying groups, 10–14, 78–79, 125–150
Identifying patterns, 10–14, 95–124
Independence, 70, 83, 93
Independent groups, 10–14, 83
Independent variables, 13
Integer values, 19, 30–31
Intellectual data, 20, 28, 44
Interaction effects, 91, 95
Interactive computing, 40–41, 154
Intermediate categories, 8, 60–61, 159
Internal consistency, 179–180, 187
Interpretation, 40, 53, 88–90, 95, 195–196
Interval data, 8, 57–58
Item analysis, 11, 111, 161–163, 175–186, 203–204
   discrimination, 177–178
   facility, 176
   response-level, 176–178
   -total correlation 177–178, 182, 204

Joint effects, 65, 90–93, 95

Kaiser, H. F., 102, 161, 206
Kappa, 10, 126–127
Kendall's coefficient of concordance, W. 10, 121–123, 202, 206
   rank order correlation, tau, 10, 70, 73, 76, 202, 206
   S–method, 10, 68, 70, 73–74, 76
Keslinger, F. N., 83, 112, 119–121
Kirk, R. E., 78, 82, 84
Kudar–Richardson formula, 180
Kurtosis, 10, 60

Labels, 27, 63, 134–135, 203–204
Level of measurement, 7–9, 70
Line charts, 88–90, 133
Linear dependence, 96, 104, 120
Linear trend test, 10, 80–82, 93, 203–204
Listing data, 23–24, 210–220
Lord's paradox, 195–196

McCall, R. B., 62–65
McNemar test, 10, 70, 73, 76, 190
Mann–Whitney U-test, 10, 93, 203, 206
Marginal totals, 72
Mean, 6, 24, 33–35, 57–58, 61, 83–88, 120, 202, 204–205
Mean deviation, 58
Measurement, 3, 7–9
Measures:
   of shape, 58–60
   of spread, 58–61
   of tendency, 57–58
Median, 10, 57–58, 61
MIDAS programs, 41, 154
Minus signs, 20

Missing data, 21, 53, 58, 65–67, 91–92, 96, 113, 129, 146–147, 153, 159, 202, 204–205, 207, 210
Mode, 10, 57–58, 60–61
Multi-way analysis of variance, 10, 13, 90–93, 203
Multidimensional scales, 175, 185–186
Multidimensional scaling, 10, 26, 139, 147–149
Multiple cards per case, 30
Multiple classification analysis, 26
Multiple classifications, 90–93, 120
Multiple comparisons, 10, 78, 81–88
Multiple correlation, 10, 11, 104, 112–122
Multiple datasets, 34, 203–205
Multiple discrimination, 139–146, 149
Multiple regression, 10–12, 14, 22, 40, 61, 95–98, 111–112, 147, 168, 183, 187, 202–203, 206
   equation, 112–116, 122
   models, 111–122, 183, 187
   significance, 113–115, 118, 122
   structure correlation, 116–118, 120, 122
Multiple responses, 17
Multivariate analysis of variance, 10, 139, 147, 149
Multivariate statistics, 10–15, 41, 62, 95–150

Negative scores, 20
Neuman–Keuls test, 84
Nominal data, 7, 10, 56–57, 62, 70–73, 78, 80, 129, 202–203
Non-parametric tests, 65–74, 93, 121–123
Non-response, 153
Normal distribution, 6, 53–56, 59–61, 74
Numerical taxonomy, 125–139

Oblique factors, 102–111, 122, 202
Observed frequencies, 71
One-tailed test, 7
One-way analysis of variance, 10, 11, 70, 80–81, 203–204
Operating system commands, 23, 27–29
Ordered groups, 11–13
Ordinal data, 7–8, 10, 57–58, 67, 69, 70, 73–74, 80
Orthogonal factors, 100–111, 122, 202
OSIRIS package, 26, 41, 61, 76, 93, 122, 149, 169, 187, 197
Outliers, 74, 136–137

Pairwise comparisons, 12, 80–81, 84
Parameters, 34–35, 39–40, 74
Parametric tests, 80
Partial correlation, 10, 122
Partitioning data, 11, 59, 69
Path analysis, 10, 122–123
Patterns, 10, 12, 62, 97, 98, 161–168
Pearson's $\bar{r}$, 70, 74–77, 202
Percentages, 10, 57, 66, 157, 202, 204
Personality data, 20, 28, 45, 48
Piloting, 4
Phi coefficient, 10, 70, 74, 76
Planned comparisons, 83–85

Plotting, 10, 53, 61–62, 98, 132–135, 143–146, 148, 202, 204
PMMD programs, 25, 27, 33–34, 41, 61, 76, 79, 93, 122, 149, 169, 187, 197, 201–209
Point biserial item analysis, 177–178, 182, 204
Population estimates, 59, 74
Positive scores, 20
Post mortem test, 83–88
Predicted scores, 112, 116, 122
Prediction, 10–14, 76, 111–121
    models, 40, 112
Predictive validity, 181
Presentation of results, 40, 88–90, 98
Principal components analysis, 100–111, 112, 122, 202, 206
Probability, 5, 72, 203
Product moment correlation coefficient, 70, 74–77, 202
Profiles, 88–90, 132–135
Program availability, 41, 61, 93, 122, 149, 169, 186–187, 196–197, 208
Proportionate agreement, 126–127

Q correlation coefficient, 128–129
Questionnaires, 11, 16, 65, 102, 153–174, 203

Range, 58, 202, 204
Ranking, 10–11, 70, 73, 76, 121–123, 202, 206
Rasch item analysis, 177–179, 182, 187
Rating scales, 58, 157–161
Ratio data, 8–9
Recoding data, 10–11, 21–22, 40, 56, 65–69, 76, 155–165, 169, 202, 204, 207
Records, 16, 29
Reduction of data, 97
Regression, 10–11, 61, 81–82, 98, 111–121
Regression constant, 112, 114, 116, 120
Reliability, 11, 45, 105, 137, 175, 179–180, 190
Relocation cluster analysis, 10, 126, 128, 130, 149, 165–168, 205, 221, 226–230
Repeater, 29–30
Research design, 3–5, 9–13, 43–49, 83, 153, 189–190
Residual change measure, 11, 121–122, 190–197, 202, 206
Rho, 10, 70, 73, 76
Row variables in tables, 66, 71
Rummel, R. J., 97, 107, 110

Sample, 3, 29, 43–44, 59, 71, 74, 79, 109, 112, 117, 128, 202–209
Scale construction, 11, 159–161, 175–188
Scales, 7–8, 11, 16, 46–48, 53–55, 58, 97, 102, 157–161, 202, 204
Scatter plots, 10, 62–65, 74, 76, 202, 204–205
Scheffé test, 10, 11, 81, 83–88, 90, 93, 167, 203–204
School coding, 20, 28
School transfer, 5, 43–49, 210–220
SCSS programs, 41, 154

Semantic differentials, 60–61, 157–161, 172
Semi-interquartile range, 58
Separators, 29
Sex coding, 20, 28
Shrunken multiple correlation, 115–116, 122
Siegel, S. S., 70, 71, 73, 93, 123
Sigma, 59
Sign test, 10, 93
Significance, 5, 10–11, 71, 74, 80, 203
    of rows in tables, 71
    testing, 65, 68, 74, 113–115, 118, 122–123, 134, 141
Similarity, 126–129, 137–138, 222, 227–228
Skewness, 10, 53–56, 57, 59–61
Social class coding, 20, 28, 44
Solidus, 29, 31–32
Spearman–Brown formula, 179–180
Spearman's rank order correlation, rho, 10, 70, 73, 76
Specific comparisons, 82–88
Specific residuals, 11, 191–195, 197
Split-half reliability, 179–180, 187
SPSS programs, 26–27, 33, 35, 38–39, 41, 61, 76, 79, 93, 122, 149, 169, 186–187, 197
Squared multiple correlation, 105, 108, 122
Standard deviation, 6, 10, 24, 33–35, 58–59, 61, 202, 204–205
Standard error, 74, 107, 179
Standardized data, 21–22, 53, 129–130, 202, 207
Statistical tests, 5, 7, 10–11, 65, 68, 83, 203
Statistical texts, 14–15, 57, 95, 111–112, 123, 125, 141, 176, 189
Stepwise regression, 112, 122
Structuring, 98, 139
Subdomains, 185–187
Subgroups, 10–14, 75–95, 202, 204
Suppressor variables, 115–117

T-test, 10, 11, 78, 83–88, 93, 190, 203–204
Tabulation, 10, 24, 53, 65–69, 154–157, 169, 204
Tau, 10, 70, 73, 202, 206
Tautology, 96
Terminal variance, 116–117
Test collections, 186
Test construction, 111, 175–188
Test–retest, 70, 179, 189–197
Three-way tables, 10, 12, 65, 67–68, 157–159, 169, 202, 204
Thresholds, 126, 135–136
Time, 3, 27, 29
Total group item analysis, 177–179, 187
Transformation of data, 21–22, 34, 59, 113, 129–130, 203, 206–207
Treatments, 13
Trend analysis, 10, 13, 80, 81, 85–88, 93, 203–205
Tukey test, 10, 79, 81, 84–88, 92, 203–204
Two-group comparisons, 10–12, 78, 83–88
Two-tailed test, 7
Two-way analysis of variance, 91–93, 203–204
Two-way tables, 10, 65–74, 157–158, 202, 204

Type I error, 80, 83, 84, 88
Type II error, 84

Unconfounded comparisons, 91–93, 204
Uncorrelated groups, 10–14
Understanding data, 97
Unequal-sized groups, 80, 91–92
Unidimensional scales, 175, 185–186
Univariate statistics, 10, 63–71, 95
Unrelated groups, 10–14

Validity, 11, 45, 175, 179, 181–182
Variable, 30, 32, 66, 79, 96–97, 104, 110, 112, 126, 205
  criterion, 111–113
  dependent, 111
  independent, 113
  labels, 27
  lists, 27
  predictor, 111–113

selection, 104–105, 112–113, 129
suppressor, 115–117
Variance, 58, 74–75, 81, 84, 100, 113, 116–117, 129, 142, 179, 192
  analysis of, 10, 70, 80–94, 95, 119–120, 139, 190, 203–205
Varimax factors, 102–111, 122
Veldman, D. J., 26, 41, 61, 76, 113, 119, 122, 141, 149, 169, 187, 197, 205
Visual analysis, 10

Ward's clustering method, 10, 126, 128, 130, 137, 149, 221–226
Width of values, 19–20, 29–31
Wilk's lambda, 142, 149

X-descriptors, 30–31

Yates' correction, 72

Zero codes, 20, 21, 53, 67, 204

Printed in Great Britain by Spottiswoode Ballantyne Ltd., Colchester and London